THE UNITED STATES IN CENTRAL AMERICA

An Analysis of the Kissinger Commission Report

Second Edition

Larry Hufford

Foreword by Maury Maverick, Jr.

The Edwin Mellen Press
Lewiston/Queenston/Lampeter

Library of Congress Cataloging-in-Publication Data

Hufford, Larry.
  The United States in Central America

  Bibliography: p.
  Includes index
  1. United States. National Bipartisan Commission on Central America.
Report. 2. Central America--Foreign relations--United States. 3. United
States--Foreign relations--Central America. 4. Central America--Politics
and government--1951-1979. 5. Central America--Politics and
government--1979- . 6. Central America--Social conditions--1979- .
7. Central America--Social conditions--1979- . 8. Central America--National
Security. I. Title.

F1436.8.U6U54 1984 Suppl. 327.730728   87-25704
ISBN 0-88946-006-X
Revised Second Edition

A CIP catalog record for this book
is available from the British Library.

        The Edwin Mellen Press   The Edwin Mellen Press
             Box 450   Box 67
           Lewiston, NY   Queenston, Ontario
           USA 14092   CANADA L0S 1L0

                    The Edwin Mellen Press, Ltd.
                    Lampeter, Dyfed, Wales,
                 UNITED KINGDOM SA48 7DY

            Printed in the United States of America

This work is dedicated to
Peter Wallensteen,
Bob Mullen
and
the memory of Olof Palme,
friend of the oppressed
in Central America

TABLE OF CONTENTS

FOREWORD

When a college or university professor writes a book concerning a critical subject intended for the general public and it is difficult to understand because it is filled with gobbledygook (a word my father, Maury Maverick, coined) then I am tempted to abandon my 30 years as an ACLU lawyer and let the professor be taken out and shot without trial by jury. Well, not really, but the thought has entered my mind.

Don't get me wrong, I take to university teachers like a duck takes to water since I have been one myself. What's more, I even had one for a stepfather; Dr. Walter P. Webb, who Arnold Toynbee described as the greatest authority in the world on the American West. Dr. Webb could write. The point is I like nearly all teachers but I am wild about the ones you can understand.

I am not saying that a professor should write a book using such language as "Baby Ray ran up the hill; watch baby Ray run down the hill." Rather, what I am saying is that in writing about a life and death issue intended for general readership, a writer ought to make himself immediately understood.

Some two years ago as a journalist I went to Honduras and Nicaragua. In trying to prepare myself for the trip, I desperately needed, but could not easily find, a book that would make it possible for me to quickly become familiar with the historical and contemporary events of Central America. Now I have found that book. It is this one for which I am writing the Foreword.

Dr. Hufford has given us much to be proud about. For example, as to Guatemala he writes, "Between 1954 and 1983, 80,000 Guatemalans died violently, almost all at the hands of government forces. At the height of one bloody repression in 1971, twenty-five U.S. officers and seven former U.S. policemen worked with the Guatemalan political/military forces." (That's only one of many such examples given by Dr. Hufford.)

Pray tell, who are the real terrorists in Central America?

In 1942, fresh out of the University of Texas, and while stationed at Marine Barracks, Quantico, Virginia, I remember being given training in the Smedley Butler Memorial stadium. Butler was a famous Marine General who died in 1940.

At the time I did not know about his comments on Central America, but now these many years later, I have had the oppportunity to reflect on these words of General Butler: "I spent 33 years [in the Marines] and most of my time being a high class muscle man for Big Business... I helped in the rape of a dozen Central American republics for the benefit of Wall Street..."

Well, the Wall Street chickens have come home to roost and they are raising a ruckus.

This book is for civilized Americans, conservative and liberal, who want to deal with those chickens in an intelligent manner. My father used to say that the answer is "liberty and groceries." In a way this book is about liberty and groceries.

In reading this book, you will have an exciting adventure. More importantly, you will come out of it better equipped to help our country prosper and survive in the face of third World revolutions engulfing this planet.

Get on with it, gentle reader. The roosting chickens are waiting and watching and so is the ghost of Thomas Jefferson.

Maury Maverick, Jr.

1987

PREFACE

In the middle of the long dark winter in Sweden, Professor Peter Wallensteen, who holds the Dag Hammarskjold Chair in Peace Research at Uppsala University, entered my office and requested that I prepare a lecture on U.S. foreign policy in Central America. I was, during the academic year 1984/1985, a visiting researcher at the Department of Peace and Conflict Research, Uppsala University. Dr. Wallensteen chairs the Department.

I was in the middle of another manuscript which has since remained untouched. I have become "absorbed" both as a researcher and as an activist with Central America. I have journeyed to Central America on two occasions for exhaustive study tours which, while emotionally draining at the time, ultimately energized me. I firmly believe that the major problem in Central America has been, and continues to be, U.S. foreign policy. As a citizen of the United States that is an empowering realization. Realizing this fact, one leaves Central America with hope -- a hope that our country, the United States, can become part of the solution by recognizing that our greatest contribution to civilization has been the Declaration of Independence. This document should be our chief export to the people of Central America.

The prerequisite for exporting the Declaration of Independence is the development of an equality of respect doctrine between the people and the decision-makers in the United States and Central America. Thus, while this book argues that present U.S. foreign policy in Central America is predestined to failure, it is also meant to be a book of hope.

x

I would like to thank Peter Wallensteen for motivating me to write on this topic; Bob Mullen a friend of twenty years for his support of my study tours to Central America, and my spouse Linda and daughter Ewa Kristina. Linda showed infinite patience and tolerance as our living room became a "research center," with newspaper clippings and journals covering the floor and every piece of furniture during the month of May. I would also like to express my gratitude to two Incarnate Word College colleagues, Vasilios Aivaliotis and Bonnie Chew for their technical assistance. As always, I alone am responsible for the contents.

L.G.H.

Regarding the second edition I would again like to thank Linda and Ewa Kristina for their patience. Vasilios Aivaliotis deserves thanks for his work on updating the index; IWC student Guillermina Rivera deserves thanks for her efforts in typing the first draft of the update; and, most of all, Paul Fayfich deserves a thousand thanks for his technical skills. I remain responsible for the contents.

L.G.H.
San Antonio, Texas
June 1, 1989

INTRODUCTION

"Read the Eight Beautitude of Matthew 5"
- Col. Oliver North to a reporter
the day after the Tower Commission
issued its report.

"Quis custodiest ipsos custodes"
- Quote from the Roman satirist
Juvenal. An epigraph chosen by the
Tower Commission.

"Blessed are they which are persecuted
for righteousness' sake."
- The Eight Beatitude of Matthew 5

"Who shall guard the guardians?"
(Quis custodiet impos custodes)

The setting in Central America can be viewed as a classic Greek tragedy, with the actors on all sides functioning single-mindedly, in terms of their own beliefs, premises, conceptions and perceptions -- "fulfilling their nature."

The greatest tragedy of the Reagan administration has been the unilateral decision to place the crisis in Central America squarely within the East/West geostrategic struggle. Why is this a tragedy? Because the Central American conflicts are rooted in the historical reality of the region.

From the outset, the Regan administration conceptualized the Central American situation as essentially a Cold War ("us versus them", "good versus evil") problem. Among the reasons for this categorization are:

xii

1. The Reagan administration's conviction that
   Carter's "liberal" human rights policies had
   destabilized the region;
2. the Central American crisis reflects a loss
   of control in the United States' "backyard,"
   plus a deterioration of U.S. power which could
   be reversed by the exercise of will;
3. the region's violence is essentially fueled by
   the USSR through Cuba and Nicaragua; and,
4. Soviet/Cuban influence would expand on "the
   ground" from Nicaragua to the remaining Central
   American nations and, ultimately, Mexico.

This illustrates why the two quotations cited at the
beginning of this chapter are pure poetry, for the texts point to
the two opposing views of human nature.

In the United States the secular, Roman tradition is embodied
in the Constitution with its checks and balances, and in the
public architecture of Washington, D.C., notably in the Capitol
building.   In this tradition, secular rationalism is the
foundation of the state and the law of the land. (Fitzgerald,
1987).

The Judeo-Christian tradition plays no parallel role in
government, yet one particular strain of it, evangelical
Prostestantism, has profoundly colored American civic culture.
It underlies the notion of American exceptionalism: The idea of
America as a redeemer nation, a people charged with a divine
mission in the world.   (Fitzgerald, 1987).   In a sense, the
secular and religious traditions cluster about the two names for
the country: "the United States" being the secular, constituted
Republic, "America" being the organic mythic or moral land.
(Fitzgerald, 1987).   In the Reagan administration, this latter
tradition has been visibly strong.

Theologically, and as a habit of thought, evangelicals put
the emphasis on direct experience rather than knowlegde of
doctrine or ritual practice: the individual, once born again,

becomes a regenerate being, free of the past. Evangelicism is thus by its nature anti-intellectual and ahistorical. It is also highly individualistic and disposed against institutions. It focuses on the future and the quality of will or intention rather than on the record of past deeds, good or bad. (Fitzgerald, 1987). The political evangelicals brought to Washington by President Reagan were thus temporarily impatient, and, as pessimists of the right, they looked forward to impending national destruction if they did not succeed.

In the international arena, right-wing evangelicals see politics not as the collision of differing self-interest but as the expression of a transcedent power struggle betwen good and evil. For the, the enemy is a free agent, not one caught up in history or confined by geography and local politics. Thus, on the global battlefield there can be no stable balance of power and no agreement to disagree: "the threat to national security is everywhere at once." (Fitzgerald, 1987).

Such thinking by Reagan administration policy makers, allowed the President and his appointees to become actors in a play in which the theme is that of a self-fulfilling prophecy. This is a tragedy. But, as the eminent humanist, Noramn Cousins, says, "when it is darkest, the stars shine brightest." The evangelical tradition has led "America" to become a significant part of the problem. That can be changed. As citizens of the "United States" we can work to change the approach of policy makers and Presidents, so that the "United States" becomes part of the solution. If, by analyzing the failure of the evangelicals in U.S. foreign policy decision-making, this book contributes to individuals, groups and decision makers in this country, becoming part of the solution to the conflicts in Central America, then the effort will have been justified.

Larry Hufford
San Antonio, Texas
July, 1987

CHAPTER 1

REAGAN DOCTRINE: AN OVERVIEW

Under President Reagan's Central America policy the United States' moral authority has been, once again, suffering self-inflicted wounds. The Reagan administration has demonstrated a failure of social imagination and moral responsibility.

The real sources of the Administration's actions in Central America are concealed in President Reagan's anticommunism--an evangelical belief. Alan Riding, as the Mexico City bureau chief of the New York TIMES, wrote that "The Reagan administration's unwavering objective, in fact, would seem to be the cleansing of leftists from Central América." (Dugger, 1983) The problem is that Reagan makes no distinctions between liberal reformers, social democrats and Marxist-Leninists. The same animus in him toward Americans who support a nuclear freeze and oppose nuclear power (they are manipulated by Moscow, giving the Kremlin joy) finds targets abroad. And abroad he can deploy guns, helicopters, and bombs, and send destroyers offshore to gather intelligence. Reagan's foreign policy is not only military anticommunism, it is also military Mc Carthyism." (Dugger, 1983)

President Reagan and his political evangelicals truly believe Nicaragua is the first domino in a Soviet-Cuban move to establish a land based satellite in Central America. Ultimately, according to the Administration this land base would be used to extend Soviet influence into Mexico to the North and Panama (the Panama Canal) to the South. Thus, Reagan's logical conclusion is that if the United States does not take drastic action to prevent this from occurring, commercial shipping will be threatened by Soviet influence in the Canal Zone; and, increased Soviet influence in Mexico would pose a direct threat to the United States. If the U.S. does not act now to stop this Soviet move, the Administration argues, we would have to expend so much military personnel and hardware in Central America (in the future) that America would be seriously weakened in its ability to respond in areas further away (especially the Middle East). Therefore, Reagan and his evangelicals believe that Nicaragua represents a major Soviet effort to permanently disrupt the current balance of power between East and West.

NURTURING A DOCTRINE

The nurturing of an anticommunist doctrine has deep roots in the Reagan administration. To illustrate this, I will cite but two of numerous examples.

The Republican party embraced and developed this doctrine prior to Reagan assuming the office of president. Jeane Kirkpatrick, a Georgetown University professor (later Reagan's U.S. Ambassador to the United Nations), had written two articles stating that President Carter's policy had "positively contributed... to the alienation of major nations, the growth of neutralism, the destabilization of friendly governments, the spread of Cuban influence, and the decline of U.S. power in the region." (Pastor, 1987)

Kirkpatrick criticized Carter's alleged destabilization of Nicaraguan dictator Anastasio Somoza and other military governments, and made a distinction between friendly authoritarian and unfriendly totalitarian governments, implying that the only valid criteria for making United States policy should be if the regime is friendly with the U.S. No matter how tenuous its legitimacy or how repressive its actions, a friendly regime should receive American support, since the alternative is, at best, uncertain and, generally, worse.

Following the November, 1980 election, several prominent conservatives formed a group called the Committee of Santa Fe to recommend a new foreign policy for the incoming Reagan administration.

The Committee of Santa Fe offered several clear recommendations for United States policy. Regarding Latin America, it called for the revitalization of the Monroe Doctrine and urged strengthening security agreements in the region and renewing military assistance agreements with military governments. The Committee of Santa Fe directly confronted the trade-off between human rights and security, and concluded that the human rights policy:

> ... must be abandoned and replaced by a non-interventionist policy of political and ethical realism.... [The human rights policy] has cost the United States friends and allies and lost us influence.... The

reality of the situations confronted by Latin American governments that are under attack.... must be understood not just as a threat to some alleged oligarchy, but as a threat to the security interests of the United States (Committee of Santa Fe, 1980)

The 1980 Republican party platform adopted similar positions. It deplored "the Marxist Sandinista takeover of Nicaragua"; recommended the end of the aid program to Nicaragua; and called for closer cooperation with Mexico. But, once again, the principal theme of the platform and of Reagan's campaign for the presidency was that Soviet-Cuban power was advancing in the world and the United States must devote all its energies to stopping and then rolling back the communists. (Pastor, 1987)

DRAWING THE LINE IN CENTRAL AMERICA

Upon assuming office the Reagan administration chose to send the Soviet Union a signal by drawing a line in Central America. The signal was intended to warn the Soviets that their time of "unresisted adventuring in the Third World was over..." (Haig, 1984)

Secretary of State Alexander Haig defined the Central American problem by stating: "... it is our view that this is an externally managed and orchestrated interventionism, and we are going to deal with it AT THE SOURCE." (Pastor, 1987) Between August and October 1981, Assistant Secretary of State Thomas Enders visited Managua for the stated purpose of negotiating an agreement between the U.S. and Nicaragua. Enders offered a five-point plan that included an end to Nicaraguan support for the insurgency in El Salvador as well as an end to Nicaragua's internal affairs and enforcement of U.S. neutrality laws, renewal of economic aid to Nicaragua and an expansion of cultural relations. The proposal was phrased in such a way that Arturo Cruz, Nicaragua's Ambassador to the U.S. at the time and participant in the negotiations, stated it sounded "like the terms of a surrender." (Pastor, 1987) While the Nicaraguans were considering the proposal, the Reagan administration launched its first large military exercise off the Caribbean coast of Honduras.

The Sandinistas interpreted the Reagan administration's pledges to enforce its domestic laws and international obligations as disingenuous, since the United States should have been enforcing them in the first place.

Having "tried" negotiations, the Administration at a meeting of the National Security Council on November 16, 1981, formalized National Security Decisions Directive #17 signed the next day by President Reagan. The most important part of NSDD #17 was the decision to have the CIA fund and direct a secret anti-Sandinista guerrilla force. The groundwork for such a proposal had come earlier in 1981, when the Administration decided not to enforce the neutrality laws against Nicaraguan and Cuban exiles who were training in Florida and California to overthrow the Nicaraguan government. The Administration initially saw these camps as bargaining chips to be used in negotiations with Nicaragua in 1981, and subsequently admitted that it offered "to enforce laws pertaining to exile activities in the United States" if the Sandinistas were responsive to American concerns. (Pastor, 1987) On February 14, 1982, the Washington POST disclosed the $19 million covert action program and indicated that the money had been used to support about 1000 fighters and to help middle-class leaders in Managua.

RECONSTITUTING THE CIA

With NSDD #17 the Reagan administration set out at once to reconstitute the CIA as a potent foreign policy tool. Reagan's appointment of Wall Street millionaire William Casey as director in 1980 signaled its new prominence. Casey had entered public life in the Office of Strategic Services, the World War II forerunner of the CIA. Casey vowed to minimize restrictions and restore morale in his effort to revive an agency he believed to have been wounded by Congress.

Given the agency's record, it may be surprising that the 1947 law establishing the CIA deals solely with intelligence gathering. However in authorizing "other functions" at the request of the president, it set up a legal loophole for covert activities: over time these became defined as an "operation or activity designed to influence foreign governments, organizations, persons or events in support of U.S. foreign policy." (IN THESE TIMES, May 4-10, 1983) Such broad empowerment has made congressional restriction of the agency's covert activities difficult.

President Reagan assisted the CIA's comeback with lavish funding. From 1981-86 the CIA's budget was fattened by an estimated 25% a year. Casey, for his part, allocated a growing proportion of agency dollars to clandestine and paramilitary activities. According to former CIA official David MacMichael, "The operational tail is increasingly wagging the intelligence dog." (IN THESE TIMES, March 26-April 1, 1986) In 1985, for the first time, the CIA allotted more money to covert activities than to technical and secret intelligence gathering. The 1986 CIA budget for covert actions around the world (not including the contra war) stood at $500 million. (Matthews, 1986)

The Central America crisis provided both stimulus and rationale for the resurgence of the CIA. Overseas the agency mounted a campaign to overthrow the Sandinistas, built around recruitment and support of a proxy army widely known as 'contras'. At home, under a December 1981 executive order, the CIA was authorized for the first time to conduct covert operations INSIDE the United States, including surveillance of U.S. citizens and domestic organizations. (Matthews, 1986)

In its early years the Nicaragua operation was managed by a restricted interagency group or RIG, headed by the assistant secretary of state for inter-American affairs, first Thomas Enders and later Langhorne Motley. Other members included the head of the U.S. Southern Command, General Paul Gorman; deputy secretary of defense for inter-American affairs, Nestor Sanchez; White House liaison to the National Security Council and paramilitary expert

Marine Lt. Col. Oliver North; and the CIA's operations director for the covert war, Duane Clarridge, alias "Dewey Maroni." (Los Angeles TIMES, March 3, 1985)

The CIA runs its Central America project in cooperation with the National Security Council. Although President Reagan's executive order on the nation's intelligence agencies describes the NSC as "the highest government entity with responsibility for intelligence activities," between 1981 and 1984 the NSC functioned more as the junior partner in the project. In May 1984, congressional restrictions on the CIA's role in the contra war resulted in the NSC taking over virtually all related coordinating activities. (Matthews, 1986)

In mid-1981, Gen. Vernon Walters, special assistant to the secretary of state and former deputy director of the CIA, arranged the unification of the fragmented bands of ex-National Guardsmen raiding Nicaragua from Honduras into the 15th of September Legion. Since 1980 the CIA had been funding the Miami-based anti-Sandinista exile party, the Nicaraguan Democratic Union (UDN), through one of its leaders, Francisco Cardenal. (Matthews, 1986)

In 1981, Walters and CIA officials paid the UDN to merge with the newly constituted military front, preparing the documents and arranging a signing ceremony in Guatemala City. (Chamorro, 1985) The new organization, called the Nicaraguan Democratic Force (FDN), gave the military forces a much-needed facade of respectability.

Because CIA training of the contras was a sensitive issue with Congress, CIA director Casey began working with the Argentineans

Because CIA training of the contras was a sensitive issue with Congress, CIA director Casey began working with the Argentineans in 1981. The CIA directed Argentinean military personnel (who had been advising the ex-National Guardsmen since late 1979) to expand their effort to build a true rebel army. (Chamorro, 1985) When U.S.-Argentinean relations soured as a result of the Malvinas/Falklands war in the Spring of 1982, the CIA took over the job of advising and training the counterrevolutionaries. Top agency officials were also directly involved in strategic military planning and tactics. Aided by U.S. military construction in Honduras as part of U.S. military maneuvers, the CIA established logistical supply lines into Honduras, Costa Rica and Nicaragua itself. (Matthews, 1986)

The CIA also took charge of all major political decisions. After the media (led by a November, 1982 NEWSWEEK cover story) had made the contra war the biggest public secret of the time, the CIA moved to put a respectable face on its operations. A month later the CIA "repackaged" its Nicaraguans by reorganizing the FDN's directorate to lower the profile of the Somocistas (supporters of Somoza) and convey the illusion of a revolt led by former anti-Somocistas and disaffected Sandinistas. Then, in October 1983, the CIA decided that the FDN needed a "single spokesman in order to more effectively persuade Congress." Duane Clarridge, Casey's handpicked coordinator of the covert operation, chose Aldolfo Calero, the owner of the Coca-Cola franchise in Nicaragua during Somoza's rule. (Matthews, 1986)

THE ROLL-BACK DOCTRINE

The goal of the Reagan Doctrine from its inception, has been
to "roll-back" the Soviet empire by attacking it at its weaker
extremities in the Third World.   The means by which this goal is
to be realized is worldwide sponsorship of counterrevolutionaries,
specifically the use of proxy armies.   The rationale is the defense
of "freedom."   In his February 1985, State of the Union address,
President Reagan declared: "We must not break faith with those who
are risking their lives--on every continent....to defy Soviet-
sponsored aggression and secure rights which have been ours since
birth.   SUPPORT FOR FREEDOM FIGHTERS IS SELF-DEFENSE." (Emphasis
added)

Secretary of State George Shultz wrote in 1985 (specifically
referring to Central America) "Our policy is to promote democracy,
reform and human rights.... to help provide a security shield
against those who seek to spread tyranny by force.... Our nation's
vital interests and moral responsibility require us to stand by our
friends in their struggle for freedom."   The morality invoked for
the support of anti-communist insurgencies is the spread of freedom
and democracy.   Thus, in Reagan's words, the rebels trying to
overthrow the government of Nicaragua are "the moral equivalent of
our Founding Fathers.... The struggle here is not between Right
versus Left, but right versus wrong."   (New York TIMES, March 3,
1985)

The most enlightening rationale (in its lack of logic) for preserving the moral authority of the United States in Central America is found in the Report of the Presidents' National Bipartisan Commission on Central America:

> To preserve the moral authority of the United States. To be PERCEIVED by others as a nation that does what is right because it is right is one of this country's principal assets. (Report, p. 37)

In analyzing this goal, Timothy Garton Ash, in a November 22, 1984 article in the NEW YORK REVIEW was concerned about the dubious amalgamation of the notions of moral duty and national interest. Ash writes that the Commission does not say "we must DO what is right because it is right." The Commission says "we must be PERCEIVED as doing 'what is right because it is right' because it is in our national interest so to be seen." However, as Ash points out, "if you are doing what is right because you think it is in your own interest so to be seen, then you are NOT doing it because it is right. Rather, you are being self-interested, not disinterested; selfish, not selfless; political, not moral. If you pretend otherwise you are being hypocritical."

President Reagan has altered the rules of the game. At its radical core, the doctrine of rollback asserts that only by taking OFFENSIVE action can the Soviet Union be contained. As such, it goes beyond the postwar goal of containment, proposing to shape events by projecting U.S. interests in the world, not just react to Soviet behavior.

Such a policy is at once a logical extension and the obverse of counterinsurgency support for pro-Western governments threatened with revolution. In its reliance on proxies, the doctrine owes much to John Kennedy's counterinsurgency projects and the Nixon and Truman Doctrines, according to which the United States could intervene through surrogate forces of friendly governments to protect U.S. interests anywhere. Under the Reagan Doctrine, U.S. allies are to be insurgents fighting "unfriendly" governments. The concept envisions a groundswell of successes beginning at the margins of Soviet influence. Surrogate armies avoid direct confrontations with the Soviets or fatal quagmires such as Vietnam that could reverse the momentum. The strategy is seen as "maximally efficient." In the words of Arnaud de Borchgrave: "It is low-intensity warfare in which U.S. troops are not involved. It also involves a small amount of money.... It is low-risk warfare with a tremendously high political pay-off." (Matthews, 1986)

LOW-INTENSITY WARFARE (LIW)

Low-intensity warfare (LIW) is a modernization and adaptation of earlier counterinsurgency methods. Like LIW today, counterinsurgency stressed the coordination of the different foreign policy bureaucracies—AID, the CIA, the Pentagon and the United States Information Agency (USIA). The aim was to achieve an interlocking and synchronized approach to "political warfare."

Psychological operations, counterterror civic action, economic assistance, agrarian reform, military assistance programs to host country troops and special forces activity, all became prominent tactics in the offensive against Third World revolution. On January 18, 1962, President Kennedy signed National Security Action Memorandum No. 124, which called for "proper recognition throughout the U.S. government that subversive insurgency, i.e., wars of liberation, is a major form of politics-military conflict equal in importance to conventional warfare." (Kornbluh & Hackel, 1986)

Obviously the shift in domestic and international circumstances in the 1970s created a new and changing environment for U.S. policy makers. The new generation of revolutionary governments that emerged in the mid and late 1970s, and the advancing guerrilla wars in El Salvador, the Philippines and South Africa created a crisis of control for the incoming Reagan national security managers. According to Secretary of State Alexander Haig, "the so-called wars of national liberation, are putting in jeopardy our ability to influence world events." (Kornbluh & Hackel, 1986)

Consolidated revolutionary regimes such as Nicaragua's meant that traditional counterinsurgency had to be revamped. Earlier strategies, oriented toward containment and prevention, gave way to offensive programs that could roll back established governments. President Reagan told Congress in April 1983, when he first hinted at a policy of support for anti-communist insurgencies: "Communist subversion is not an irreversible tide. We have seen it rolled back.... All it takes is the will and resources to get the job done."

Domestic constraints also prompted the Reagan administration to revamp traditional counterinsurgency. The defeat in Vietnam and the resulting breakdown of the public consensus on U.S. intervention in the Third World has placed political restraints on the Reagan administration's ability to revive intervention in its baldest forms. Therefore, the evolution towards low-intensity warfare. As a military strategy, low-intensity warfare reflects that reality. The military component of LIW ranks in many cases, behind psychological, economic and political warfare.

LIW is not only a military strategy: it is a political strategy, which has emerged as a subtle vehicle for the Reagan administration to erode public and congressional resistance to escalating intervention abroad. In military terms, low-intensity warfare is a response to the Vietnam syndrome; politically, it is a low-intensity attack on the remaining constraints on U.S. foreign policy. (Kornbluh & Hackel, 1986)

The Army's publication in 1981 of its FIELD MANUAL ON LOW INTENSITY CONFLICT officially placed LIW strategy within military operations for the first time. That manual is now regarded as a bridge between the older counterinsurgency theory and the latest formulations of LIW theory. It presents LIW as an expression of the "Internal Defense and Development (IDAD) theory of counterinsurgency which evolved in the 1970s. IDAD theory, an extension of the counterinsurgency strategy of the 1960s, emphasized the organization of pacification and civic action campaigns.

The 1981 field manual outlines the need for national IDAD pacification campaigns that consolidate civilian and military institutions. These campaigns would be administered by national and local coordination committees that would deploy military, paramilitary, and economic resource to strengthen the nation. Psychological operations would "make population and resource control measures more acceptable to the population." (Barry & Preusch, 1986) Local self-defense patrols and other paramilitary forces should be organized to guarantee the security of pacified areas.

LIW IN CENTRAL AMERICA

Since 1983 signs of escalating low-intensity strategy have become increasingly visible in Central America, reflected in the steady increase of U.S. military presence, military and economic aid, and maneuvers in the region.

Developments such as increased coordination between the DOD, the State Department and AID, renewed training of Central American police forces, the creation of a Pentagon Office for Humanitarian Assistance, DOD and AID cooperation in El Salvador's pacification plan, AID support of the Guatemalan Army's civic action program (the military's Inter-Institutional Coordination Committees bear striking resemblance to the coordination and consolidation committees described in the U.S. Army manual), the training of Civil Guards in Costa Rica, coordination of U.S. military plans with private right-wing organizations and mercenary groups such as the World Anti-Communist League and Friends of the Americas; economic and military aid (covert and approved) for the contras; and an expanded role for psychological warfare through USIA, the CIA, the American Institute for Free Labor Development, the National Endowment for Democracy (charged with funding organizations such as LA PRENSA in Nicaragua, to organize and propagate for U.S. interests throughout the region), and the Pentagon's new level of consensus and commitment toward LIW.

Viewing Central America as a "laboratory" for LIW theory, U.S. strategists do not expect to win by outfighting the "enemy" in battle. Instead the U.S. aims to separate the enemy from the civilian population and neutralize enemy social structures--whether embryonic ones in FMLN zones of control in El Salvador, or the institutionalized ones in Nicaragua. In those countries where significant armed insurgencies exist, the essential counterpart would be to hold the insurgent forces at bay while the U.S. constructs "democratic" regimes and alternatives, counterrevolutionary political, economic and social institutions for the region.

Thus, LIW strategy in Central America combines both "active" (Guatemala, El Salvador, Nicaragua) as well as "preventive" (Honduras, Costa Rica) measures within each country, the choice of emphasis determined by whether an armed insurgency already exists.

The measures adopted in each country, whether active or preventive, are in turn designed to fit into an overall U.S. strategy at the regional level. At the same time, low-intensity strategists hope that the terms of their doctrine, which explicitly favors keeping U.S. troops out of combat, would preempt public opposition to war.

As part of the psychological component of low-intensity warfare, the Reagan administration pays lip service to regional peace efforts such as Contadora and Carballada. Negotiation proposals become just one more component of LIW. In fact, in LIW theory, a negotiated peace is seen as an intolerable accommodation --a "surrender"--to enemy forces. Sharing power with the FMLN in El Salvador or the Sandinistas in Nicaragua is simply unacceptable.

Keeping U.S. troops out of combat does not preclude their presence in the region. The almost non-stop military maneuvers in Honduras (within twelve miles of Nicaraguan border) are very much a part of LIW.

On December 30, 1986, about 3,000 United States troops began a joint four-month exercise with Honduras. In addition, the first of 4,500 National Guardsmen from eight states and Puerto Rico began arriving for a separate four month exercise. More than 15,000 United States troops have taken part in nearly continuous "joint" maneuvers with the Honduran armed forces since June, 1982, under a 1954 mutual assistance pact.

These maneuvers have allowed the Reagan administration to provide additional arms and training to the Salvadoran and Honduran armies, as well as to the Nicaraguan contras. Washington has supplied all three of its proxies with daily reconnaissance and intelligence support for their air and ground operations, strengthened regional intelligence and communications networks among the armies; and bolstered the contras' supply lines and civilian supporters in Honduras through large-scale civic action and "refugee assistance" programs administered by U.S. government agencies and private sector groups. Through the constant maneuvers, the United States has rapidly developed the infrastructure to wage unconventional war over an extended period. All this is what low-intensity doctrine calls the "total preparation of the conflict area." In the words of Majors Morelli and Ferguson of U.S. Army Training and Doctrine Command,

> Total preparation of the conflict area is the basis for the low-intensity campaign. This effort involves the employment of military assets, normally small teams orienting on intelligence, communications, logistics, engineer, medical and psychological operations support to indigenous efforts... and the employment of teams on a regional as well as a country-specific basis. The emphasis is on providing for indigenous tactical success, ensuring regional stability and developing an intelligence, logistical and psychological infrastructure that will replace U.S. forces. (Morelli & Ferguson, 1984)

Certainly, the Reagan administration deliberately misled Congress and the U.S. public about the nature and scope of the maneuvers and their role in LIW strategy. Indeed, it did not call this a war strategy at all, but a plan for promoting "peace and democracy." At the same time, it obscured the comprehensive nature of the new strategy by implementing it in stages, under different legal and bureaucratic authorities; it misled the public about the increasing role of the National Guard and other U.S. military service components.

But this pattern of official deception does not imply that the real plan is to invade Central America. The overall goal of U.S. military maneuvers on the Honduran coast has been to make the Sandinistas believe that the "worst-case scenario" of war with the United States was also the most probable, and plan their strategy accordingly. The threat is one the Sandinistas can ill-afford to ignore; yet reacting to it might only wear them down more rapidly by diverting limited resources to preparing for an invasion that did not happen. Gen. Vernon Walters summed up the Administration's intent of creating a double bind: "Let them worry. We have found that constructive ambiguity is a very powerful weapon in American foreign policy." (Miles, 1986)

The U.S. military maneuvers are part of a strategy aimed at realizing U.S. goals in three areas. In the economic sphere, they would force Nicaragua to devote over half its budget to defense; in the military they would compel the Sandinistas to engage in a conventional buildup of their armed forces; and in the political, they would lock Nicaragua into a regional diplomatic framework controlled by Washington. And the secondary effects of each set of attacks would feed on each other to create an environment of total war.

The Reagan administration may have learned from earlier U.S. mistakes, to the extent that it has, to date, avoided committing combat forces to Central America. However, the conflicts in

Central America cannot be reversed by theory alone. Especially if the theory fails to accurately comprehend the historical reality of the region, that is, the roots of rebellion in Central America. Policy makers need to understand the politics of confluence, that is, the manner in which East/West-North/South issues are converging. In Central America the historical reality of the region lies in the North/South frame of reference.

BIPARTISAN COMMISSION

On January 11, 1984, the President's National Bipartisan Commission on Central America released its report. The twelve member commission was chaired by former Secretary of State Henry Kissinger, a fact which caused great skepticism about the Commission's role throughout Latin America. In a June, 1969, meeting with the Foreign Minister of Chile, Gabriel Valdes, Secretary of State Kissinger remarked:

> You come here speaking of Latin America, but this is not important. Nothing important can come from the South. History has never been produced in the South. The axis of history starts in Moscow, goes to Bonn, crosses over to Washington, and then goes to Tokyo. What happens in the South is of no importance. (SOJOURNERS, 1984)

The Bipartisan Commission Report was a major success for the Reagan administration's fulfillment of domestic psychological and political components of low-intensity warfare. By creating a bipartisan commission of influential Republicans and Democrats,

President Reagan was seeking to defuse opposition to his Central American policy.

To a great extent Reagan has succeeded. Even with the Iran-contra scandal, there are numerous Democrats, among them Presidential hopefuls, who state that "while they are opposed to funding (publicly or privately) the contra war, they remain an opponent of the Sandinista regime." President Reagan has framed the debate in such a manner that most Democratic political figures feel it politically necessary (at present) to paint the Sandinista government as evil, that is, undemocratic, totalitarian, heavily influenced by Moscow and Havana. In short, most Democratic Party political leaders refer to the Nicaraguan government as Marxist-Leninist.

According to President Reagan and, then U.S. Ambassador to the United Nations Jeane Kirkpatrick, the Report issued by the Commission accurately reflected the Administration's security concerns in the region. The Report was given increased legitimacy precisely because it was written by a bipartisan group of twelve of the nation's "best and brightest", rather than being written by political evangelicals of the Reagan right.

IGNORING HISTORICAL REALITY

The Bipartisan Commission Report acknowledges that the violent upheavals in Central America are rooted in poverty and repression, but the main thesis underlying the Report is the charge (based on assertion rather than evidence) that the Soviet Union is the manipulator of indigenous revolution in the region.

In examining the common threads running through the Report of the Bipartisan Commission, the main thrust of the document is clearly stated:

> --The roots of the crisis are both indigenous and foreign. Discontents are real, and for much of the population conditions of life are miserable... But these conditions have been exploited by hostile outside forces---specifically by Cuba, backed by the Soviet Union and now operating through Nicaragua---which will turn any revolution they capture into a totalitarian state, threatening the region and robbing the people of their hopes for liberty. (Report, p. 4)

> --Indigenous reform, even indigenous revolution, is not a security threat to the United States. But the intrusion of aggressive outside powers exploiting local grievances to expand their own political influence and military control is a serious threat to the United States, and to the entire hemisphere. (Report, p. 4)

> --We have stressed before and we repeat here: indigenous reform movements, even indigenous revolutions are not themselves a security concern of the United States. History holds examples of genuinely popular revolutions, springing wholly from native roots. In this hemisphere Mexico is a clear example. But during the last two decades we have faced a new phenomenon. The concerting of the power of the Soviet Union and Cuba to extend their presence and influence into vulnerable areas of the Western Hemisphere is a direct threat to U.S. security interests. (Report, p. 84)

From these quotations it is evident that the Bipartisan Commission accepted the view of President Reagan that the crisis in Central America today is rooted in the Soviet Union's and Cuba's exploitation of local conditions in a concerted move to expand their political and military capabilities in the Western Hemisphere.

However, not wanting to appear insensitive to indigenous economic conditions as a cause of revolution, the Report implies that Mexican style revolutions would be acceptable today in Central America. This is a direct obfuscation of history. Historical evidence suggests that the United States did not support the Mexican revolution at the time it occurred.

Carlos Fuentes, the noted Mexican scholar and diplomat, writes that the Mexican Revolution was the object of constant harassment, pressures, menaces, boycotts, and even a couple of armed interventions (the U.S. intervened militarily in Mexico in 1914 and 1916).

If one examines U.S. policy towards Mexico from 1910-1932, it is clearly documented that administrations from President Taft to Hoover opposed Mexican programs for agrarian reform, secular education, collective bargaining and recovery of natural resources.

Fuentes, moreover, stresses the point that the Mexican revolution did not make an instant democracy out of his country. He states, "the first revolutionary government, that of Francisco I. Madero, was the most democratic regime Mexico has ever had. Madero respected free elections, a free press and an unfettered congress." What was the U.S. response to this growth of political democracy? Madero was promptly overthrown in February 1914, by a conspiracy of the American Ambassador, Henry Lane Wilson, and a group of reactionary generals. (Aguilar, 1968)

U.S. INTERVENTION IN NICARAGUA

The obfuscation of history continues with the Report's historical perspective on U.S. involvement in Central America. Admitting that the record of the past is a "mixed one," the Report goes on to state:

> For the most part, U.S. policy toward Central America during the early part of this century focused primarily on promoting the stability and solvency of local governments so as to keep other nations out. This was reflected in (President) Theodore Roosevelt's Corollary to the Monroe Doctrine, which held that the United States should take action to prevent situations from arising that might lead to interventions by extra-hemispheric powers. Theodore Roosevelt once defined the sole desire of the United States as being 'to see all neighboring countries stable, orderly and prosperous.' THIS FORMULATION REFLECTS BOTH A GREAT POWER INTEREST IN KEEPING THE HEMISPHERE INSULATED FROM EUROPEAN INTRIGUE AND THE CONCERN OF OTHERS' WELL-BEING THAT HAS OFTEN ANIMATED OUR FOREIGN POLICY. (Report, p. 34)

The above quotation takes a unilateral document, the Monroe Doctrine, and transforms it into a hemispheric one concerned only for the well-being of all Americans--North and South. Thus, it is not surprising that the Report covers U.S. intervention in Nicaragua between 1909 and 1933, in two sentences. (Report, p. 34)

The fact is that the United States has intervened militarily in Central America over thirty times since 1850, while the U.S. has militarily intervened in Nicaragua eleven times, including the extended occupations by the Marines from 1912-1925 and 1926-1933. To dismiss eleven direct military interventions with two sentences is to deny the historical reality of the Nicaraguan people. The occupation of Nicaragua, by U.S. Marines, from 1912-1933, with an interruption of only eighteen months, has earned Nicaragua the dubious distinction of enduring the longest U.S. occupation imposed on any Latin American country during the 20th century.

With regard to the U.S. creation of the National Guard in Nicaragua, the Report states "the immediate purpose was to provide stability." (Report, p. 34) Admitting that Anastasio Somoza used the instrument of the National Guard to impose a personal dictatorship, a most amazing statement is made:

> The ability of Somoza and later his sons to portray themselves as friends and even spokesmen of the U.S. began with the use they were able to make of the legacy of U.S. military occupation, thereby creating an identity between the U.S. and dictatorship in Central America that lingers, INDEPENDENT OF THE FACTS, to this day. (Report, p. 34)

The National Guard in Nicaragua was established as a result of increasingly negative public and Congressional opinion regarding President Coolidge's decision in 1926, to have U.S. marines return to Nicaragua to protect an unpopular regime that had become so dependent on U.S. dollars it could not govern with U.S. soldiers.

What the return of the marines accomplished in 1927, was to encourage the creation of a nationalist revolutionary movement. The name of the man who came to lead that movement was Augusto Cesar Sandino. His cause was to drive the United States out of Nicaragua. The number of U.S. troops in the country increased from 1200 in 1927 to 5400 in 1928 in an effort to combat Sandino's guerrillas. As the size of the U.S. force grew, however, there was increasing pressure in the U.S. Congress to force the President to withdraw the marines from Nicaragua. This latest intervention was, in short, becoming too costly politically and economically. The State Department argued that the troops should remain as Nicaragua had become an important test case. A State Department memorandum, written in 1927, but not declassified until the 1960s stated:

> Central America has always understood that governments which we recognize and support stay in power, while those we do not recognize and support fall. Nicaragua has become a test case. It is difficult to see how we can afford to be defeated.

The cry to bring home the troops persisted so the United States government created and trained a "native national guard" designed to act, according to U.S. officials, as a "politically neutral referee" in mediating future crises.

The United States appointed as the commander of the guard, Anastasio Somoza, when President Hoover announced the U.S. marines would come home in early 1933. At the urging of the United States Sandino and Somoza agreed to meet in 1934 in an effort to reach a negotiated political settlement. As the negotiations were opened, Somoza had Sandino and his top aides murdered in cold blood. (Gillgannon, 1983) In 1936, Somoza declared himself President of Nicaragua. Interestingly, the United States refused to support the civilian government in its efforts to keep Somoza from the presidency on the grounds that "the United States should not interfere in Nicaragua's internal affairs." (LeFeber, 1984)

According to conservative estimates, some thirty thousand Nicaraguans died in the four decades prior to the Sandinista

victory in 1979, for opposing the government of Anastasio Somoza
and his sons Luis and Anastasio II.

Nicaragua is the largest nation in Central America (an area
the size of the state of Illinois or roughly equivalent to the size
of England and Wales combined). It has a population of
approximately 2.9 million people (equivalent to the population of
the metropolitan area of Boston, Massachusetts). Thus, there are
no population pressures similar to El Salvador. Yet, when the
Somoza regime was toppled, the Somoza family alone owned 30 percent
of the nation's arable land, approximately 5 million acres of land
(an area the size of El Salvador); and, owned Nicaragua's twenty-
six biggest companies. From 1961 on, Somoza and his friends
funneled Alliance for Progress money into businesses they
controlled. Meanwhile, only two percent of the rural population
had potable water by the end of the 1960s, and only 28 percent of
Managua's residents had access to sewage services. Land and tax
reforms were never discussed by the Somoza regime. Over 200,000
peasant families had no land, while half of all the arable land in
the country was occupied by 1800 ranches. By early 1978, the
repression had become so brutal that a number of prominent
businessmen publicly sided with the Sandinistas, especially after
the assassination in January, 1978, of Pedro Joaquin Chamorro,
publisher of the opposition newspaper LA PRENSA. Even Alfredo
Pellas, the richest non-Somoza in Nicaragua, urged Somoza to resign
when he publicly stated: "Private enterprise and workers are
united in saying, 'No More Somoza!'"

Fearful of a Sandinista victory, the U.S. government proposed in November, 1978, a mediated settlement that would include Somoza's resignation, but exclude the Sandinistas from participation in any reform government. Predictably neither side accepted. Somoza refused to step down and any proposal that would exclude the Sandinistas was politically naive. (Lernoux, 1980)

The historical reality of U.S. intervention and occupation has, thus, bequeathed to Nicaragua two major legacies. The first is the memory of Augusto Cesar Sandino. Sandino fought against a U.S. Marine occupation of Nicaragua for six years and, by doing so, became a symbol of dignity for a Latin America that had been placed, without having sought the honor, under the stifling protection of the Monroe Doctrine.

The second legacy produced more practical consequences. When at last they departed Nicaragua in 1933, the marines left behind a national guard that held the monopoly of weapons and was led by a man who had favorably impressed U.S. government officials-- Anastasio Somoza.

President Reagan, in a speech last Spring before a group of Hispanic Americans stated "We cannot afford the consequences of passively watching guerrillas force communist dictatorships down the throats of the people of Central America." It is hypocritical on the part of any president of the United States, to talk of forcing dictatorships down the throats of peoples (such as the Nicaraguans) whose history has been a tale of U.S. sponsored oppression. Such present day oppression can be found in the U.S. policy of low-intensity warfare.

The fact is that there is no civil war in Nicaragua. Rather, that nation is being threatened and harassed by the United States' recruited, trained, financed and equipped band of counterrevolutionarios (contras) controlled by former National Guardsmen from the Somoza regime. Clearly, the contras are not the democratic loving people the Reagan administration makes them out to be. When President Reagan compares the freedom fighters (i.e., contras) in Nicaragua to the Founding Fathers of the United States (men such a George Washington and Thomas Jefferson) and later states "I am a contra," one can understand why anti-United States sentiment continues to grow in Nicaragua and among the oppressed in all of Central America.[1]

U.S. INTERVENTION IN EL SALVADOR

Another illustration of the failure of the Bipartisan Commission to grasp the historical reality of Central America, is

---

[1]On May 28, 1986 Honduran President Jose Azcona Hoyo told the National Press Club in Washington, D.C., that "We (Hondurans) believe the contras should be fighting inside Nicaragua...." Later that day Azcona told editors and reporters of The Washington POST that he "supports President Reagan's request for $100 million in new aid for the contras, "BECAUSE IT IS NECESSARY TO PREVENT THEM (CONTRAS) FROM BECOMING AN UNCONTROLLABLE GROUP OF BANDITS IN HONDURAS IF THEY LOSE U.S. BACKING." (San Antonio EXPRESS-NEWS, 1986)

the Report's one paragraph explanation of the origins of the
present crises in El Salvador:

> (In El Salvador) military based regimes that had been
> moderately progressive in the early 1960s had become
> corrupt and repressive by the 1970s. The annulment of
> the victory by civilian Christian Democratic candidate
> Jose Napoleon Duarte in the 1972 election ushered in a
> period of severely repressive rule. It was in this
> context, with its striking parallels to the developments
> in Nicaragua and Guatemala, THAT THE PRESENT CRISIS IN
> EL SALVADOR BEGAN. (Report, p. 22)

The Report's view of the source of the rebel movement in El
Salvador is made explicitly clear in the chapter on Central
American Security issues. This is yet another effort to gloss over
the reality of the United States' historic role in El Salvador:

> --Whatever the social and economic conditions that
> invited insurgency in the region, outside intervention
> is what gives the conflict its present character. Of
> course, uprisings occur without outside support, but
> protracted guerrilla insurgencies require external
> assistance. INDEED, IF WRETCHED CONDITIONS WERE
> THEMSELVES ENOUGH TO CREATE SUCH INSURGENCIES, WE WOULD
> SEE THEM IN MANY MORE COUNTRIES IN THE WORLD. (Report,
> p 87)

> --Propaganda support, money, sanctuary, arms, supplies,
> training, communications, intelligence, logistics, all
> are important in both morale and operational terms.
> WITHOUT SUCH SUPPORT FROM CUBA, NICARAGUA AND THE SOVIET
> UNION, NEITHER IN EL SALVADOR NOR ELSEWHERE IN CENTRAL
> AMERICA WOULD SUCH AN INSURGENCY POSE SO SEVERE A THREAT
> TO THE GOVERNMENT. (Report, p. 87)

With reference to the Report's conclusions let us examine some
recent historical experiences in El Salvador.

In El Salvador the oligarchs are the Fourteen Families that
have dominated the country since the 19th century. When the
Fourteen Families welcomed Alliance for Progress money and private
investment, it was always made clear that control would remain in

their hands, and that President Kennedy's demand for reforms would be given no more than lip service. Thus, although U.S investment in El Salvador rose from $31 million in 1960 to $76 million in 1971, the funds merely reinforced earlier trends. The mass of Salvadorans were fastened even more closely to: a dependent export economy; an increasingly mechanized productive system that increased unemployment; a land policy where officials seized plots from peasants in order to produce more export crops; and, a condition in which the majority of the population had neither work, land, nor sufficient food. By the mid 1970s, El Salvador was one of the worlds five most undernourished nations. Ninety percent of the peasants have no land and they comprise two-thirds of the population. Functional illiteracy among peasants approaches 95 percent. Two percent of the people own 58 percent of the arable land. The average monthly income of the peasants in 1980 was twelve dollars. The infant mortality rate in 1983 was 78.8 per 1000 live births. Eighty percent of all children are ill nourished. And, most startling, from 1961 to 1971, the decade of rapidly increasing economic assistance from the U.S., the number of landless Salvadoran families more than tripled.

Even since commercial coffee growing came to El Salvador in the 19th century, the large growers have been progressively squeezing the peasants off the land. El Salvador's peasant population protested time and time again, only to be slaughtered. In 1932, challenged by an uprising of poorly-led and poorly-organized peasants, the Fourteen Families worked with the military to exterminate more than 30,000 peasants. An alliance of the military and oligarchs has led real power in El Salvador ever since.

In 1969 a war broke out between El Salvador and Honduras. To the rest of the world it became known as the "soccer war," since the pretext was a dispute on the football field. However the real cause of the war which lasted two weeks and killed two thousand was the invasion of Honduran territory by 300,000 land-hungry Salvadoran peasants, an exodus encouraged by El Salvador's ruling military/oligarchs to free more farmland for export crops such as coffee and cotton.

Several thousand Salvadoran peasants were herded back over the border by Honduran troops in 1969, only to be met by increased repression by Salvadoran government officials. Although a formal peace treaty was signed by the two nations in 1983, bitter feelings remain; and, as the U.S. has increased the number of Salvadoran soldiers being trained by U.S. Army personnel in Honduras, the Honduran government has come under increasing pressure to respond. Within the past year the Honduran government has requested that the U.S. wind down the training of Salvadoran troops on Honduran soil. Memories of the 1969 war linger on, but the point to remember is that the origins of this conflict lie with the oligarchs of El Salvador--in their refusal to support land reform.

In mid-1976, President Molina, of El Salvador decreed a mild agrarian reform supported by AID and the Inter-American Development Bank. Had it ever gotten off the ground, the 1.4 million-acre project would have benefitted 12,000 landless peasants. Although the 250 families that owned the land would have received $53 million in compensation, the estate owners immediately denounced the project as "communist subversion," just as they had denounced the Alliance for Progress and the then U.S. ambassador as "communist-inspired." In the face of determined opposition from the Association of Private Enterprise and the Planter's and Cattlemen's Front, Molina quickly dropped the agrarian reform program. (Lernoux, 1980)

In May, 1984 issue of THE PROGRESSIVE there is an in depth expose on the U.S. role in creating the death squads of El Salvador. Among the activity over the past twenty years, officials of the State Department, the CIA and the U.S. armed forces have, according to author Allan Nairn: conceived and organized ORDEN, the rural paramilitary and intelligence network described by Amnesty International as a movement designed "to use clandestine terror against government opponents;" trained leaders of ORDEN in surveillance techniques; conceived and organized ANSESAL, the elite presidential intelligence service that gathered files on Salvadoran dissidents; and, provided American technical and intelligence advisers who often worked directly with ANSESAL.

For the Commission and Reagan administration to state that the crisis in El Salvador began in 1972, and that without aid from the Soviet Union, Cuba and Nicaragua the insurgency would pose no threat to the El Salvadoran government, is yet another classic example of the obfuscation of history. The fact that the

Bipartisan Commission consisted of twelve persons considered to be among the nation's 'best and brightest' makes this deliberate obfuscation of history all the more disturbing.

Today the United States holds a virtual veto power over El Salvador's internal and external policies. The major concern of the Reagan administration is the prosecution of the war by the Salvadoran government.

The Administration views tiny El Salvador as a vital strategic link in Central America. President Reagan believes the triumph of the FDR-FMLN would have a serious impact on Guatemala, and on Honduras. Thus the domino theory is alive and well in Washington, D.C., and El Salvador cannot be allowed to fall. If the FMLN were ever to appear close to victory there is little doubt that the United States would intervene with massive military force. (Anderson, 1986)

That there are Marxist factions within the rebel movement is not questioned. But the rebel movement issed of several political and military groups.

The political arm of the rebellion, the Democratic Revolutionary Front (FDR) is headquartered in Mexico City, under the leadership of Guillermo Manuel Ungo, a social democrat and head of the small National Revolutionary Movement (MNR). Ungo was Duarte's running mate in the 1972 presidential election. A number of important spokesmen for the FDR, like Ruben Ignacio Zamora Rivas, are in the Social Christian Movement, a group that broke off from the Christian Democratic Party (PDC) in 1980. Thus, while the

more radical rebel movements are also represented on the FDR
diplomatic political commission, which makes policy for the front,
the general tone of the FDR is one of moderation. (Anderson, 1986)

The fighting arm of the rebels is the Farabundo Marti Front
of National Liberation (FMLN), in which neither the MNR or the
Social Christians are represented. The five FMLN groups are the
Popular Revolutionary Army (ERP), the Popular Liberation Forces
(FPL), the Armed Forces of National Resistance (FARN), the
Communist Party of El Salvador (PCES) and the Central American
Revolutionary Workers' party (PRTC). The last two are small and
carry little weight on the general coordinating committee.
(Anderson, 1986) Since the death by suicide of the charismatic
Salvador Cayetano Carpio of the FPL in 1983, the dominant rebel
leader has been Joaquin Villalobos. Still in his mid-30s,
Villalobos heads the ERP, which is generally regarded as the most
radical rebel movement.

The saddest and most ironic aspect of continued conflict in
El Salvador, is the placing of the Salvadoran civil war firmly in
the East-West geostrategic struggle. Once again, the Reagan
administration is creating a self-fulfilling prophecy. U.S. policy
in El Salvador, if continued, will only succeed in eliminating
moderate voices from leadership positions thus polarizing the
people of El Salvador.

Today, the war in El Salvador which has gone on for 7 years,
has claimed an estimated 60,000 lives (including direct fatalities
and civilian casualties related to the war). The war is expected

to drag on many years more, with the outcome uncertain. With United States military assistance the Salvadoran Army has quadrupled in size over the past 6 1/2 years to more than 52,000 men.

Today in El Salvador, fifty percent of those who can work are unemployed or underemployed. In 1987, Salvadorans face a 40 percent increase in prices and inflation that is a growing source of discontent. Yet, the sons of the wealthy are safe because there is no draft and the Army "recruiters" do not pick up young men in affluent neighborhoods. The wealth of the rich in El Salvador is safe because taxes are collected irregularly and capital flight is estimated to have reached $1 billion. Even though the wealthy remove their money from El Salvador, their businesses remain safeguarded by U.S. aid that provides dollar credits and war insurance, accounting, in 1987, for 81 percent of El Salvador's national budget ($586 million). The economy is a shambles and is actually expected to shrink in 1987. Per capita income has fallen 32 percent since 1979. In ignoring the roots of the war in El Salvador, the Reagan Doctrine is doing more to harm what it seeks to defend than the Soviet Union could ever accomplish on its own.

MARCH 1987 UPDATE

In March, 1987, the U.S. Department of State issued a report to the President and Congress titled: "A Plan for Fully Funding the Recommendations of the National Bipartisan Commission on

Central America." In March 3, 1987 Presidential message to Congress included in the updated Report, Reagan states:

> Democracy is making great strides in Costa Rica, El Salvador, Guatemala, and Honduras. Their progress is building societies in which their citizens enjoy freedom of choice and equal justice under law stands in marked contrast to the totalitarian subjugation suffered by the Nicaraguan people.

President Reagan continued by forcefully stating the current unrest in Central America is the responsibility of the Soviet Union via Cuba via Nicaragua.

> This [economic] assistance is urgently required to help meet the great economic and social needs of the struggling democratic governments of the region. By generating conditions of violence in Central America that undermine prospects for economic growth, the communist government of Nicaragua works to discredit the democratic system.... The Soviet Union and its allies have provided the Sandinista regime military hardware and sufficient economic aid to keep Nicaragua's failed economy afloat. The United States must help those small nations in Central America that have chosen freedom.

The President is recommending a three year extension of the original Bipartisan Commission Report request: 1984-89. The Reagan administration is asking Congress to extend the program's execution until 1992. Additionally, Reagan is requesting that Congress approve an additional $300 for fiscal year 1987 as economic support fund assistance for Costa Rica, El Salvador, Guatemala and Honduras. To make this request more acceptable to Congress, or as Reagan states, "consistent with sound budget principles," the President asks that Congress allow him to transfer $300 million from "unobligated balances in such accounts as I may designate for which appropriations were made by the Department of

Defense Appropriations Act, 1985 (as contained in Public Lay 98-473); the Department of Defense Appropriations Act, 1986 (as contained in Public Law 99-190); the Department of Defense Appropriations Act, 1987 (as contained in Public Laws 99-500 and 99-591); and, the Department of State Appropriations Act, 1987 (as contained in Public Laws 99-500 and 99-591)."

The line between economic and military assistance becomes even more blurred. This is the strategy of low-intensity warfare. Even in the midst of the Iran-contra Congressional hearings, the Bipartisan Commission Report issued in 1984, continues to provide a framework for requests couched in nonpartisan language.

The reality is that the economic proposals in the 1984 and 1987 Reports were supporting narrow private interests in Central America at a heavy cost to U.S. taxpayers as a whole. Historical evidence would suggest that the recommended economic aid programs, managed by the current power elites in Central America, would continue to have a negative impact on the great majority of people in Central America.

Both Reports make much of a domino theory that suggests that revolutions spread like communicable diseases. U.S. influence in Central America depends not on quarantining ideas and programs of other countries, but on demonstrating a genuine interest in development and democracy in the region, rather than viewing the countries as so many pawns in a geostrategic chess game.

The fundamental flaw with the Bipartisan Commission Report, specifically, and low-intensity warfare, in general, is that both have as an ultimate goal, continued American domination of the region. The Bipartisan Commission Report reflects LIW theory by assuming the United States would take direct responsibility for organizing the economies, political structures, military structures and cultures of the region. U.S. personnel would train Central America's teachers, doctors and police. Experts from the U.S. would design the region's land and urban reform programs; U.S. union (AFL-CIO) representatives would guide Central American unions; U.S. political scientists would create Central American democratic institutions. A U.S. representative armed with veto power over $6.9 billion (the President's 1987 request for funding through 1992) worth of aid, would "negotiate" with representatives of the region's recipient countries for getting the money. The programs are fused with prevailing U.S. economic and political ideology. The emphasis is on free markets, with a heavy role for private enterprise, especially U.S. corporations. These new institutions would reinforce the strong influence over Central American economic development which the United States already exercises through its commanding position in the International Monetary Fund, the World Bank Group, the Inter-American Development Bank, and various bilateral aid and loan guarantee programs.

What the Bipartisan Commission Report recommended, and President Reagan continues to propose, is a program of U.S. responsibility for battered economies of Central America that is unprecedented in the post World War II era. The plan is more illustrative of the British East India company than the Marshall

Plan. The post-war Marshall Plan for Europe also had a political objective, but its success was due to its emphasis on eliciting regional initiative and planning. The local energies, institutions, experience, and political will were all in place. U.S. money and ideas served as the catalyst. In Central America, the U.S. role is not that of catalyst, but of reorganizer of chaos and repression. Even if U.S. geopolitical motives for undertaking this enormously expensive commitment were not so clearly revealed, such an intrusive role in internal affairs of the region would be bitterly resented and would feed the very nationalist currents which the Reagan administration is trying to contain. Any effort to "Americanize" Central America is predestined to failure.

The Bipartisan Commission Report, a major document in Reagan's low-intensity warfare doctrine, constructs an elaborate rationale for intensifying policies that have not worked and will not work. Because the 1984 Report was vital in defusing partisan political debate over the Reagan Doctrine, a more in depth look at the Report's assumptions and proposals would provide insight as to why Reagan's program is predestined to failure.

A closer examination of the Bipartisan Commission Report will also illustrate why it is not enough for United States citizens and Washington politicians to simply oppose aid to the contras and the militarization of Central America. There is a saying in Spanish "la paz comienza con la justicia" (peace begins with justice). If the United States is interested in peace in Central America, it must work for justice. Justice can never be created through a doctrine of low-intensity warfare designed to continue U.S. domination of the region. The ultimate formulation of any just solution for Central America cannot come from ideas imposed from outsiders, but instead must be rooted in Central Americans' own experience and interpretation of their historical reality.

CHAPTER 2

PROMOTING POLITICAL DEMOCRACY

According to the Bipartisan Commission Report the first principle the United States should use to guide our Central American foreign policy is the nurturing of democracy in this hemisphere. The Report states:

> The issue is not what particular system a nation might choose when it votes. The issue is rather that nations should choose for themselves, free of outside pressure, force or threat. There is room in the hemisphere for differing forms of governance and different political economies... The United States can have no quarrel with democratic decisions, as long as they are not the result of foreign pressure and external machinations. (Report, p. 12)

The essence of the U.S. effort is to be the legitimation of governments by free consent--"the rejection of violence and murder as political instruments, of the imposition of authority from above, the use of the state to suppress opposition and dissent." (Report, p. 13)

HISTORY OF POLITICAL DEVELOPMENT

The Bipartisan Commission Report's view of the historical development of Central America in the political arena is a classic obfuscation of history.

The period from 1890-1930, was labelled by the Report as the heyday of oligarchic rule. "A small group of families controlling the most productive land constituted the dominant elite. Export-oriented growth generated pockets of modernization and higher living standards in the urban areas. But the middle classes remain weak." (Report, p. 19)

The period of the 1930's was viewed as a "terribly disruptive" one in Central America with new dictatorships appearing in El Salvador, Honduras, Guatemala and Nicaragua. At this point the obfuscation of history appears:

> While they typically ruled with strong-arm methods, they also often represented previously excluded middle classes. HAVING RESTORED ORDER, THESE DICTATORS ENCOURAGED SOME ECONOMIC DEVELOPMENT AND SOCIAL MODERNIZATION, AND THEY ENJOYED A DEGREE OF POPULARITY---at least for a time. (Report, p. 20)

Citing Nicaragua as an example, the Report states that after the death of Anastasio Somoza Garcia (1896-1956), his eldest son Luis made various attempts to relax "the harsher aspects of the old authoritarianism--to allow a greater sense of pluralism and freedom." (Report, p. 21)

In Honduras, according to the Report, military and civilian parties rotated or else ruled jointly in an arrangement whereby "military officers controlled security matters and acted as political arbiters, while the civilian elites managed the economy, held key cabinet positions, and staffed the bureaucracy." (Report, p. 21)

In Guatemala, after the United States helped bring about the fall of the Arbenz government in 1954, politics "became more divisive, violent and polarized than in the neighboring states. But even there, there were efforts to combine civilian and military rule, or to alternate between them." (Report, p. 21)

In El Salvador a similar system operated from 1958 to 1972, according to the Report. There, "a group of younger more nationalistic officers came to power AND PURSUED POPULIST STRATEGIES." The Report states that these officers "allowed the major trade union organizations to grow and to have a measure of political participation. The (Salvadoran) Army created its own political party, modeled after Mexican PRI. It held elections regularly, IN WHICH THE OFFICIAL CANDIDATES GENERALLY WON; on the other hand, through a system of corporate representation within the party, MOST MAJOR GROUPS HAD SOME SAY IN NATIONAL AFFAIRS." (Report, p. 21)

In the understatement of the century regarding Central America, the Report goes on to say "none of these regimes was TRULY democratic, but the trend seemed to favor the growth of centrist political forces and to be leading toward greater pluralism and more representative political orders. This trend gave hope for peaceful accommodations and realistic responses to the profound social changes occurring in the countries of Central America." (Report, p. 21)

The Report then points out that in Nicaragua, El Salvador and Guatemala, the 1960s and 1970s saw increased repression, greed and corruption, which polarized these societies, "precipitating the crisis which has now spread throughout Central America."

THE U.S. REVOLUTION

The historian, Arthur Schlesinger, Sr., wrote an essay in 1959 entitled "America's 10 Gifts to Civilization." (La Feber, 1983) The first gift he observed was the right of revolution. However, with a single exception, all the foreign revolutionary leaders cited by Schlesinger, who referred to the United States as their example did so before 1850. By 1850, certainly by the end of the U.S. Civil War in 1865 and bloody suppression of the Philippine rebellion by U.S. troops in 1902, the "gift of revolution" had lost a good deal of its 1776 value.

In 1821, John Quincy Adams, the U.S. Secretary of State wrote the following regarding the growing independence of Latin American nations:

> I wished well to their cause; but I had seen and yet see no prospect that they would establish free or liberal institutions of government... They have not the first elements of good or free government. (La Feber, 1983)

In short, it was great that the Latin Americans were eager to rid themselves of European colonial powers. However, as they were ill equipped to develop "free and liberal" institutions, the United States would replace the European nations as the power in the Hemisphere. The Monroe Doctrine, issued in 1823, was the public announcement of Thomas Jefferson's private opinion that "America has a hemisphere to itself." This was the same Thomas Jefferson who, referring to Laws of Nature and "Nature's God," wrote, in 1776, of how people can "alter or abolish" any government that no longer derives its "just powers from the consent of the governed." The United States' Declaration of Independence, appealing to natural law, gives people the right to have a violent revolution once a government ceases to be based on the "consent of the governed."

What did Adams mean by "free and liberal?" In the United States' tradition these terms refer to the "liberal--Lockean" tradition which includes a powerful predilection for private property, and non-radical, constitutional, republican-representative, stable democratic governance. Representative government and capitalism as they are merged in the United States, constitute a major portion of the intellectual baggage U.S. policy makers carry with them in thinking about the problems in Central America and the Third World in general. Thus, the question becomes "Can a country born free and liberal," as was the United States, ever understand societies and politics where these premises do not apply? In Central America the U.S. historical experience is for the most part irrelevant. For example, Central American history illustrates and lends support to a belief that elections will not bring about the fundamental change in the structural and institutional system which perpetuates violence and oppression (Archbishop Camara's violence number one). Revolution, not elections, is needed.

There are some interesting facts about the U.S. revolution that Central Americans find interesting. The Reagan administration and the Bipartisan Commission Report constantly referred to the refusal of the Sandinistas to immediately hold national elections following their triumph in 1979. Five years passed prior to national elections in Nicaragua in November, 1984. Central Americans, especially Nicaraguans, point out that thirteen years passed from the time of U.S. revolution to the first national elections which put George Washington in the presidency. (Coffin, 1983)

The Reagan administration also attacks the current democratically elected government as a fraud since the counterrevolutionaries (Reagan refers to them a freedom fighters) were not invited to participate. Yet, following the U.S. revolution 80,000 counterrevolutionaries (supporters of Great Britain) fled to Canada. The newly independent nation quickly ruled that these counterrevolutionaries were thereafter "not allowed to vote, teach or preach in the United States." (Coffin, 1983)

Secretary of State George Schultz stated in 1983 that the United States would "not tolerate people shooting their way into power," in a reference to Central America. (La Feber, 1983) Nicaraguans are aware that in 1776 General George Washington shot his way to independence over such issues as "taxation without representation." The British troops were not engaged in the wholesale slaughter of civilians, torture of prisoners, or the creation of death squads--part of the history of El Salvador, Guatemala, Honduras and Nicaragua.

Furthermore, the United States has intervened militarily in Central America over 30 times since 1850, and a total of 70 times in all of Latin America since 1850. (DEFENSE MONITOR, 1984) These interventions have been in the words of the U.S. State Department "to protect American lives, property and interests in times of unrest." The United States has a proven history of supporting right-wing dictators shooting their way to power--for example, El Salvador 1932; Nicaragua 1933-36; Guatemala 1954; and, Honduras 1963. Today, the United States has recruited, trained and supplied the contras, who, at the urging of the United States, are trying to "shoot their way back into power" in Nicaragua.

The Bipartisan Commission Report and the Reagan administration argue that the crisis in Central America originates in Moscow and Havana, which now operates through Managua. However, saying the Sandinista led government in Nicaragua is exporting revolution is similar to arguing that France was responsible for the U.S. revolution. To argue that the El Salvadoran rebellion did not originate in El Salvador and is manipulated by an outside power is to utilize the logic of the Soviet Union in its accusations that the Solidarity movement in Poland originated in, and is manipulated by, the United States.

Carlos Fuentes, the Mexican diplomat and scholar, in a Harvard commencement address in 1983, asked his audience, "How can we (the U.S. and Latin America) live and grow together on the basis of such hypocrisy?" Fuentes asked the following:

> Why is the United States so impatient with four years of
> Sandinismo, when it was so tolerant of forty-five years

of Somocismo? Why is it so worried about free elections in Nicaragua, but so indifferent to free elections in Chile? And why, if it respects democracy so much did the United States not rush to the defense of the democratically elected president of Chile, Salvador Allende, when he was overthrown by the Latin American Jaruzelski, General Augusto Pinochet?

Regarding Nicaragua, Fuentes stated that "it is being attacked and invaded by forces sponsored by the United States. It is being invaded by counterrevolutionary bands led by former commanders of Somoza's national guard who are out to overthrow the revolutionary government and reinstate the old tyranny. Who will stop them from doing so if they win? These are not freedom fighters. They are Benedict Arnolds." (Fuentes, 1983)

Secretary of State George Shultz recently stated before the U.S. Senate that: "The future of democracy is precisely what is at stake in Central America. If we abandon those seeking democracy, the extremists will gain and the forces of moderation and decency will be victims." (Bell, 1985)

Why should Shultz and the Reagan administration be viewed as anything other than hypocritical? Is the United States truly interested in promoting democracy? Or, is the U.S., in reality, only interested in a facade of democracy--that is, a civilian, "democratically" elected government to mask the fact that the real power in the country continues to be held by the oligarchy/military coalition. Honduras has a civilian president, Jose Azcona del Hoyo, but every knowledgeable person understands that real power in Honduras remains in the hands of the armed forces commander. On March 31, 1984 there was a coup within the Honduran military which saw General Gustavo Alvarez Martinez replaced by General Walter Lopez Reyes. General Lopez, as the commander of the armed forces, was the real power in Honduras, until he was ousted in a coup in February, 1986 (which several reporters attributed to the U.S. embassy). (Robinson, 1987) Real political power in Honduras continues to reside in the office of commander-in-chief of the armed forces, not, unfortunately, in the civilian "democratically elected" president.

El Salvador is another example of a facade of democracy. The Reagan administration created much fanfare over the "democratic" election of President Jose Napoleon Duarte. The U.S. greatly increased aid to El Salvador as a result of Duarte's election. Yet, the press in the U.S. today (Washington POST, New York TIMES, etc.) often carries stories of how Duarte is essentially powerless.

Father Ignacio Martin Baro, Vice-Rector of Central American University in San Salvador, stated in a January, 1986 interview that the military is today the most powerful force in El Salvadoran politics--more powerful than the oligarchy. Two factors have contributed to this according to Fr. Martin Baro. First, is U.S. militarization of the Salvadoran crisis. For example in 1979 there were 400 military officers in El Salvador and "we had problems! Now there are over 3,000 and the number is growing." Secondly, since President Duarte negotiated the release of his daughter who had been kidnapped, the top military powerbrokers, according to Fr. Martin Baro, "no longer consult Duarte on major military decisions." Why doesn't the military pull off a coup? "Simple," states the Vice-Rector. "The Salvadoran military and the Reagan administration need a facade of democracy to keep the military aid flowing. But the fact remains that Duarte is, in reality, a puppet government." (Hufford, 1986)

The Reagan administration engaged in a highly visible disinformation campaign regarding the November, 1984 Nicaraguan elections. Although the U.S. supported candidate, Arturo Cruz and his party chose not to participate, the Administration harshly accused the Sandinistas of conducting an election that was a "sham," that is elections that did not allow all to participate. A more detailed examination of the Nicaraguan election will follow, but to illustrate the hypocrisy of the Reagan administration one can cite the 1984 Uruguayan elections. The Administration had only praise for Uruguay. Neither Reagan nor Shultz protested the arrest and detention by the military of the most popular politician in Uruguay upon his return from exile. Wilson Ferreira Aldunate, who had campaigned, in exile, for a return to democracy in Uruguay was not permitted to campaign for office and was not released from prison until after the elections. The military negotiated a formula for relinquishing power, which demanded that Mr. Ferreira not be a candidate, and that the military be exempt from purge or prosecution for past abuses. During the military dictatorship in Uruguay, the country had the largest number of political prisoners relative to its population in the world. (IHT Editorial, 1984)

As the civilian government took office on March 1, 1985, the Uruguayan army commander, Lieutenant General Hugo Medina warned:

"If we (the military) are obliged, we will have no choice but to carry out another coup d'etat." (Riding, 1985) The U.S. supported, conservative president, Julio Maria Sanguinetti knows he cannot alienate the military in his country. Nor would the Reagan administration want Sanguinetti to oppose the generals. Supporting democracy in Latin America has never been of major importance to the Reagan administration. The Administration's campaign to identify with the spread of democracy masks the extent to which it gives top priority to a shortsighted, negativistic anti-communism.

Upon entering office, President Reagan quickly sent retired General Vernon Walters (now the U.N. Ambassador), then U.N. Ambassador Jeane Kirkpatrick and high ranking military officers to show his goodwill toward the dictatorial regimes of Argentina, Brazil, Chile and Uruguay, as well as Guatemala, Honduras and El Salvador. This was a concerted effort to befriend military dictatorships.

In a New York TIMES editorial (in the INTERNATIONAL HERALD TRIBUNE) of February 27, 1985 the following was written regarding the Administration's relationship with General Pinochet of Chile:

> The Reagan administration is reconciled to four more years of military dictatorship in Chile and is not even embarrassed to say so. That is the incredible message delivered there by Assistant Secretary of State Langhorne Motley. He rests easy with the Pinochet regime's plan to permit no elections until 1989. NO ONE SHOULD BE FOOLED BY WASHINGTON'S RECENT REFUSAL TO VOTE FOR NEW INTERNATIONAL LOANS TO CHILE. THAT WAS ONLY AN EMPTY GESTURE TO IMPRESS LIBERALS IN CONGRESS. Mr. Motley's diplomacy is truly breathtaking. He was the highest ranking American visitor to Chile since General Pinochet

reimposed a state of siege last fall and ended all
pretense of liberalization ...

It should be apparent from only these few illustrations that
the Administration is primarily interested in a facade of democracy
to cover its support for right-wing generals who support Reagan's
negativistic anti-communism in Central and South America.
Democracy for Latin America is scarcely a Reagan concern.

GUATEMALA

The recent election of a civilian president in Guatemala,
Vinicio Cerezo, ending 30 years of brutal military dictatorship
should be welcomed by all. However, one must ask why the
Guatemalan military agreed to hold elections; and, whether the new
president will be strong enough to fundamentally challenge the
existing economic and military oligarchy; and, whether the Reagan
administration deserves credit for being sincerely interested in
promoting democracy in Guatemala?
The Reagan administration did indeed "lean" on the Guatemalan
military to hold elections. Why? According to a high-ranking
staff member of a key Congressional committee, "because unless
there is at least a facade of a civilian president, there is no way
the U.S. can send economic assistance." (Volman, 1985)

"The Reagan administration," says this observer, sees the
possibility of a politically conservative government allied with

a strong anti-communist military emerging from these elections."
(Volman, 1985)

Because of one of the hemisphere's worst records of human rights violations, it has been difficult for Reagan to receive Congressional backing for increased aid to Guatemala. Aid to Guatemala is not just a matter of politics. It has become a dire economic necessity. The fact is that Guatemala's military acceded to elections because it realized that Guatemala could not stay afloat without massive and rapid infusions of U.S. aid.

"The elections are basically a side show to the economic crisis," according to a key Senate Republican aide. "The country is broke, there is almost no foreign currency left. The Guatemalans have to pay (cash) for every shipload of oil as they receive it." (Volman, 1985)

Guatemala's military remains the most powerful political force in the country. President Cerezo has acknowledged this in stating, "At best, a civilian president will be able to stay in power by inching toward democracy." (Volman, 1985) The new civilian president would be faced with the very real possibility of a military coup or assassination attempt on his life if he strongly advocated basic structural reforms, that is, land reform and changes in the banking system. Such changes are crucial to any improvement in the lives of Guatemala's poor.

EL SALVADOR

When Reagan entered office there were approximately 4,000 rebels facing 17,000 U.S. trained and supplied army and security forces in El Salvador. Thus, Reagan advocated a military victory against the rebels as a way of illustrating his seriousness in restoring U.S. military credibility in an area he viewed as vital in the East-West conflict (Reagan was determined to overcome the Vietnam and Iranian syndrome). Within a few months, however, the war in El Salvador became stalemated, the right-wing death squads were murdering 300 to 500 civilians, on average, a month; and, in the year ending April 1981, over forty mayors and local councilmen who were members of the Christian Democratic Party (Duarte's) were killed by the right-wing. (La Feber, 1983)

Thus, with military victory an impossibility, President Reagan began to base his entire policy on an election scheduled for March, 1982. The election's purpose was to choose a constituent assembly that would write a new constitution and choose an interim president to govern until further elections were held in 1983 or 1984.

Duarte's government offered the rebels a place on the ballot if they would agree to lay down their arms and play according to the new political rules. The Reagan administration is continually citing El Salvadoran government offers to the rebels to lay down their arms and participate in the democratic process as proof the refusal to do so means they are Marxist-Leninists loyal to Moscow. The rebels fully understand that to do so, historically, has meant their physical as well as their political death. Their suspicions are well founded. Immediately following Duarte's offer to the rebels, the Salvadoran security forces' death-squads circulated a list of over one hundred rebels to be shot on sight. (La Feber, 1983)

Over one million voters turned out to cast their ballots in the 1982 election. As Reagan and the U.S. media pointed out, this was indeed an impressive number. What was not mentioned by Reagan or the U.S. media was that as peasants voted, their identity cards were marked and their thumbs stamped with ink. Authorities claimed these measures aimed at eliminating vote fraud, but rumors had been spread of ugly consequences for those lacking marked identity cards and thumbs stamped with ink. (La Feber, 1983) Also, the image given by Reagan and the U.S. media was that voting was by secret ballot. However, ballots were numbered and ballot boxes transparent. Salvadorans were casting their votes in full view of the government! (La Feber, 1983) Given the peasants fear of the military, a fear warranted by dead bodies left in streets, the fact that the right-wing parties, led by Roberto D'Aubuisson won thirty-six seats in the constituent assembly was not surprising. Duarte's Christian Democrats won only twenty-four seats.

The election proved an embarrassment for the Reagan administration. Prior to the election U.S. State Department officials had claimed that only Duarte could restore the nation, and denounced D'Aubuisson as the reported leader of "a right-wing terrorist group." The Carter administration had refused to issue

D'Aubuisson an entry visa based upon those reports. After the election, however, the Reagan administration had to accept D'Aubuisson as El Salvador's legislative leader--elected by the process the Administration had devised. The reality was summed by a Latin American expert at the conservative American Enterprise Institute in Washington, D.C., who stated: "Elections in Central America, with Costa Rica being the major exception, have generally been peripheral to the main areas of politics." (La Feber, 1983)

Perhaps even more embarrassing was the fact that the United States, primarily through the CIA, had provided Duarte with "information and capabilities" prior to the election. U.S. Senator Jesse Helms of North Carolina and a close friend of Roberto D'Aubuisson disclosed that the Administration had contributed over $300,000 to Duarte's campaign funds. (La Feber, 1983) Helms was angry the Reagan administration was working against D'Aubuisson, who received assistance during the election from McCann-Erickson, the largest U.S. public relations agency operating outside the U.S. In a well-run advertising campaign, McCann-Erickson spent $200,000 to sell the right-wing terrorist's brand of electoral politics. The money is alleged to have come from Miami-based El Salvadoran oligarchs. (La Feber, 1983)

The 1982 El Salvadoran election is only one case study of U.S. staged demonstration elections, the purpose being to demonstrate to the U.S. public that their government has enabled a friendly neighbor to take a "step toward democracy." In reality, these demonstration elections are a public relations device to reassure

the U.S. public, defuse domestic opposition to economic and
military aid for repressive governments, and to maintain support
for continuing U.S. interventionary strategies.

In a book, entitled DEMONSTRATION ELECTIONS: U.S.-STAGED
ELECTIONS IN THE DOMINICAN REPUBLIC, VIETNAM, AND EL SALVADOR
(1984), authors Herman and Brodhead, are highly critical of the
acceptance by the mass media of the scenario provided by
Washington. According to the authors the media becomes bedfellows
with the U.S. Administration in perpetuating a fraud on the U.S.
public by focusing on election day details (e.g. turnout), not on
the framework that makes elections meaningful.

It is as though the Reagan administration and U.S. policy
makers in general think of democracy as a virus--one can catch it
as easily as a common cold. But in a country like El Salvador,
with a history of corrupt elections and brutal military death-
squads, only a facade of democracy can be established overnight.
This fact is clearly documented by Raymond Bonner, former New York
TIMES correspondent from Central America and author of the book
WEAKNESS AND DECEIT - U.S. POLICY AND EL SALVADOR (1984). Bonner's
story is one of a U.S. foreign policy in Central America marked by
"hypocrisy and dual standards," of "weakness and deceit." Bonner's
comment on who holds real power in El Salvador is simple: "The
military runs the country, not Duarte." The recent (1985)
elections which gave Duarte's Christian Democratic Party a majority
of seats in the national assembly has not, and will not, mean a
change in real power in El Salvador. The military and oligarchs

continue to hold the power to effectively block any serious proposal for economic and/or land reform; or, to block any proposal to negotiate an end to the civil war. Bonnor's analysis remains valid.

New York TIMES reporter James Le Moyne, in a May 17, 1985 article, wrote that Duarte still is reported to have to "consult senior army officers on most major decisions." Duarte must further consider the reaction of the U.S. government which has sent over $1.9 billion in economic and military aid to El Salvador since 1980. Le Moyne also states that Duarte must continue to consider the views of the "powerful private sector." Although the appearance of democracy increased with the 1985 elections, the fact remains that the military and oligarchy continue to rule El Salvador.

NICARAGUA

The double standard in evaluating Latin American elections can be illustrated by comparing the coverage in the United States of the 1982 Salvadoran and the 1984 Nicaraguan elections. As has been stated, the Reagan administration heralded the Salvadoran vote as a giant step forward for democracy and condemned the Nicaraguan election as a "sham." There are five areas one can use for comparison. First, more than 700 journalists were in El Salvador in 1982 to cover the elections. Major newspapers dispatched two or three reporters. Election stories made the front pages and led off the national evening news programs for days. By contrast the media provided only minimal coverage of the Nicaraguan elections.

Second, most of the stories on the Nicaraguan elections focused on candidates and parties that were not participating. Nearly every article noted that the U.S. backed Arturo Cruz was not on the ballot. By contrast it was almost never mentioned that in El Salvador F.D.R. leader Guillermo Ungo, a social democrat, was not permitted to participate. Those stories which did mention Ungo generally stated that he and the F.D.R. were boycotting the election, even though confidential documents obtained by the press showed that the army would not permit him or other leftist candidates to run.

Third, coverage of the Nicaraguan elections also stressed that press censorship and a state of emergency restricting political activities were in effect.

Stories about the Salvadoran election rarely, if ever, noted that there is no press censorship in El Salvador, because there is no opposition press in the entire country; that opposition editors and reporters have been murdered and their plants bombed. Nor did many stories of the Salvadoran elections mention that a state of emergency limiting political activity was also in effect in El Salvador during both the 1982 and 1983 elections.

Fourth, a major theme of the coverage on the Salvadoran elections was news of guerrilla attacks aimed at disrupting the voting.

In contrast, contra raids in Nicaragua were rarely reported although the contras killed at least two election officials while they were registering voters, another was kidnapped and seven soldiers were killed by contras while transporting election-day materials.

Fifth, journalists routinely wrote and spoke of El Salvador's move toward democracy, while reporters routinely label Nicaragua as "communist" or "Marxist-Leninist." Those terms trigger negative responses among readers and oversimplify the complex debate going on at present over the future economic structure of Nicaragua. This point can be illustrated by a comment made by George Melloan, a senior editorial writer of THE WALL STREET JOURNAL, a paper that routinely uses the phrases "Marxist-Leninist" and "communist" in referring to the Sandinistas and rebels in El Salvador. At a discussion on press coverage in Central America, Melloan declared: "I don't have the foggiest idea what Marxism-Leninism is." (Bonner, 1984)

Why is there a double standard in the media coverage of Central America? This is a difficult question, but according to Raymond Bonner, "journalists like politicians (in the U.S.) don't want to be labeled as leftists, or as being "soft on communism." In short, journalists are not, for the most part, going to jeopardize their careers.

The Bipartisan Commission Report which was issued on January 10, 1984 stated the following regarding the Sandinistas and elections:

In Nicaragua the revolution that overthrew the hated
Somoza regime has been captured by self-proclaimed
Marxist-Leninists. In July of 1979 the Sandinistas
promised the OAS that they would organize 'a truly
democratic government' and hold free elections, but that
promise has not been redeemed... The Sandinista
Directorate has progressively put in place a Cuban-style
regime... This also produces an acute sense of insecurity
among Nicaragua's neighbors. (Report, p. 30)

A clearer illustration of U.S. thinking on elections in

Nicaragua is found later in the Commission Report:

Under military pressure from Nicaraguan rebels who
REPORTEDLY received U.S. support, and under diplomatic
pressure from the international community, especially
from the Contadora group, the Sandinistas have recently
promised to announce early this year a date and rules for
1985 elections... (Report, p. 31)

From the perspective of the Reagan administration the

Sandinistas would never have considered holding elections without

military pressure from the contras. In 1983 UN Ambassador Jeane

Kirkpatrick argued that the Administration was "waging covert war

to force free elections in Nicaragua." (NATION, 1984) Predictably

once the elections were scheduled, the Administration made every

effort to wreck the electoral process. Within three months after

the Sandinista's announcement that elections would be held in

November, 1984 a new U.S. policy on elections in Nicaragua had

crystallized.

According to a report by New York TIMES, correspondent Phillip

Taubman the new policy was as follows:

Since May, when American policy toward the election was
formed, the Administration has wanted the opposition
candidate, Arturo Cruz, either not to enter the race, or,
if he did, to withdraw before the election, claiming the
conditions were unfair... The Administration never
contemplated letting Cruz stay in the race...because then
the Sandinistas could justifiably claim that the

elections were legitimate, making it much harder for the United States to oppose the Nicaraguan Government. (LASA Report, 1985)

The principal instrument for implementing this policy, according to Taubman's official Administration sources, was COSEP, the Superior Council of Private Enterprise, "which was in frequent contact with the CIA about the elections," and whose mission was to prevent Mr. Cruz from reaching an agreement with the Sandinistas. (LASA Report, 1985)

According to the Latin American Studies Association Report on the elections:

"... in the six-month period leading up to the election, the Reagan administration used a combination of diplomatic, economic, and military instruments in a systematic attempt to undermine the Nicaraguan election process and to destroy its credibility in the eyes of the world. Within Nicaragua, the behavior of U.S. diplomats was clearly interventionist. This behavior included repeated attempts to persuade key opposition party candidates to drop out of the election, and in at least one case, to bribe lower-level party officials to abandon the campaign of their presidential candidate, who insisted on staying in the race. (LASA Report, 1985)

Much of the Reagan administration's public attention focused on the non-participation of Arturo Cruz and the Coordinadora. As Cruz had lived in Washington, D.C. since 1970, returning to Nicaragua for only one year, in 1979-80, it was amazing how the Administration so easily convinced the U.S. media that Cruz was THE significant opposition force to the Sandinistas.

In December, 1983, the Coordinadora issued a "nine points" statement amounting to a series of demands that the Sandinistas must meet before "free and open" elections could be held, that would include the candidacy of Cruz. The original demands of the Coordinadora were for political changes (such as dialogue with the contras) that had nothing to do with the elections, but signified an attempt to impose the Coordinadora's program before the elections were held. The Sandinista position on the Coordinadora's proposals for major changes in political structure and public policies was that they should constitute the Coordinadora's party platform for the elections, rather than the conditions for the Coordinadora's entry into the electoral process.

The Sandinistas also flatly refused the Coordinadora's key demand--initiate direct talks with the contras. In El Salvador there is a genuine civil war in process. In Nicaragua there is no civil war as the Reagan administration argues. The contras would not exist were it not for Reagan's administration. Regarding the Coordinadora's points having to do with creating appropriate conditions for free elections, the Sandinistas agreed to accept them.

Ultimately the issue of Cruz's participation came down to a demand to postpone the election so Cruz would not be unduly harmed by a late entry into the electoral process. The Sandinistas were understandably hesitant to agree to this, especially as there was mounting evidence the U.S. would not allow Cruz to participate even at a later date. In other words, if the Sandinistas agreed to postpone the election, there was a high probability the U.S. and

Cruz would find yet another reason to pull out at the last minute
in an effort to discredit the elections. (LASA Report, 1985)

What the Sandinistas did offer Cruz was extra television time
to take account of Cruz's late entry in the campaign. When Cruz
and the Coordinadora rejected this offer, the Sandinistas offered
to postpone the elections as Cruz requested provided Cruz could get
the contras to agree to a truce for the election period. Cruz said
he would agree to this; however, the following day he withdrew his
offer, unable to deliver the guarantees of the U.S. supported
right-wing members of the Coordinadora. At this point the
Sandinistas broke off the negotiations. It had become obvious the
U.S. and the far-right forces in Cruz's coalition had no intention
of legitimizing the elections. Why would the U.S., having given
such public attention to Cruz, allow him to participate and, in all
probability, do poorly at the polls. As previously stated Cruz had
lived in the U.S. thirteen of the fourteen years preceding the
elections. He had no visible solid base of mass support within
Nicaragua. (LASA Report, 1985).

Jonathan Steele, writing in the GUARDIAN on the Nicaraguan
elections stated:

> Some outsiders, here on their first visit, and led in
> advance by the enormous power of the bulk of the Western
> media to expect to see a dictatorship, found themselves
> in confusion. They could not bridge the gap between
> their prejudices and the reality they discovered...
> (Steele, 1984)

One of the original doubters in the British delegation was
David Ashby, Conservative MP from Leicester. Ashby told Steele

"There were no irregularities in the conduct of the electoral process or the counting... even if the Nicaraguan system as a whole was closer to my concept of democracy, the Sandinistas would still have won a majority." (Steele, 1984)

Steele concludes that "this is a revolution which seems to know how to maintain popular support, and is therefore a greater potential problem for the U.S. than a tear away extremist regime which would lose its backing at home and increasingly have to rely on repression to stay in power." (Steele, 1984)

How did Reagan and the U.S. respond to the Nicaraguan election in which seven political parties participated--three to the right of the Sandinistas and three to the left. The Administration orchestrated a highly successful disinformation campaign. The final results of the election were not even reported by most of the international media, which focused its attention on an avalanche of alarmist news reports, supposedly based on secret intelligence information deliberately leaked to U.S. television networks by Reagan administration officials, which portrayed a massive, Soviet-supplied offensive arms build-up in Nicaragua, allegedly aimed at giving the Sandinistas the capacity to invade neighboring countries. The reason for the alarm was the Administration "concern" over the possible delivery of MiG 21s to Nicaragua.

The intention of the Reagan Administration's disinformation campaign was quite simple. First, to distract attention from the Nicaraguan elections, with their 82% turnout, absence of irregularities, and competitiveness (a 33 percent opposition vote).

Second, according to a New York TIMES editorial the MiG scare provoked a barrage of Administration threats "that seemed less addressed to Nicaraguans than aimed at whipping up a security scare among the Americans. That would narrow the scope for diplomacy, and type as weaklings those in Congress and the State Department who prefer diplomacy to war." In short, the disinformation campaign was an effort to delegitimize the Nicaraguan elections, while building public and congressional support for a renewal of direct aid to the contras. (LASA Report, 1985)

The disinformation campaign continues. Listening to President Reagan or Secretary of State Shultz one would never imagine democratic elections were held in Nicaragua. For example, in a speech to 60 legislators from other nations of the Western Hemisphere, on January 24, 1985, President Reagan stated:

> A new danger we see in Central America is the support being given to the Sandinistas by Colonel Qaddhafi's Libya, the PLO, and most recently, the Ayatollah Khomeini's Iran... The subversion we're talking about violates international law. Support for Nicaraguan guerrillas is self-defense. (IHT, January 25, 1985)

In testimony before the House Foreign Relations Committee, February 19, 1985, Secretary of State George Shultz argued that the people of Nicaragua have fallen behind the Iron Curtain:

> I believe very strongly that we in the democracies simply cannot put up with a Brezhnev Doctrine. As you know the Brezhnev Doctrine, in effect, states that once a country has been taken into the socialist camp it can never leave... I think we have to support those who stand up for freedom and liberty... I see no reason why we should slam the door on people just because they have somehow BEEN TAKEN BEHIND THE IRON CURTAIN... (Gwertzman, 1985)

In his first news conference of this second term on February 21, 1985, President Reagan described Nicaragua as totalitarian. When he was asked whether his goal was to remove the Sandinista government, he replied:

> Well, remove it in the sense of its present structure, in which it is a Communist totalitarian state, and IT IS NOT A GOVERNMENT CHOSEN BY THE PEOPLE, SO YOU WONDER SOMETIMES ABOUT THOSE WHO MAKE SUCH CLAIMS AS TO ITS LEGITIMACY. (Smith, 1985)

Speaking in San Francisco on February 22, 1985, Secretary of State Shultz said the bottom line in Nicaragua was:

> Those who would cut off these freedom fighters from the rest of the democratic world are, in effect, CONSIGNING NICARAGUA TO THE ENDLESS DARKNESS OF COMMUNIST TYRANNY. And they are leading the United states down a path of greater danger. (Gwertzman, 1985)

In a March, 1985 news conference President Reagan declared that in backing the armed violence of the Nicaraguan contras, the United States was pursuing a "tradition to trying to help people who had A COMMUNIST TYRANNY IMPOSED ON THEM BY FORCE, DECEPTION AND FRAUD." (Wicker, 1985)

Reagan has stated on more than one occasion that there would be no problem in Nicaragua, "If the Sandinistas would let the contras BACK INTO THE GOVERNMENT. Then they could all get on with the original democratic aims of the revolution against Somoza." (Geyelin, 1985)

At a March 25, 1985 meeting at the White House with 180 Central Americans who flew to Washington from Miami to lobby Congress on behalf of the contras Reagan stated the Sandinista leaders have become "as they had always planned, eager puppets for the Soviets and Cubans." Reagan went on to say:

> The Soviets' plan is designed to crush self-determination of free people, to crush democracy in Costa Rica, Honduras, El Salvador, Guatemala and Panama. It's a plan to turn Central America into a Soviet beachhead of aggression... The government-directed relocation of Nicaraguans from a strip near the Honduran border in recent days can be compared to Stalin's tactic of Gulag relocation and is similar to forced relocation in the Ukraine, Vietnam, Cambodia, Afghanistan, Angola, Ethiopia, and Cuba. (Oberdorfer, 1985)

Who are the contras that President Reagan refers to as "freedom fighters" and compares to the Founding Fathers of the United States? In April 1985, the bicameral Arms Control and Foreign Policy Caucus released a report analyzing leaders of the Nicaraguan Democratic Forces--FDN (i.e., the contras) and their U.S. money sources. According to the report, 46 of 48 command slots in the FDN are held by former Somoza National Guardsmen. (NATIONAL CATHOLIC REPORTER, May, 1985) Unfortunately, it is painfully clear that the Reagan administration will continue a disinformation campaign in an effort to delegitimize the Nicaraguan elections. As the Latin American Studies Association Report concludes:

> Clearly, the Nicaraguan electoral process in 1984 was manipulated, as the U.S. Government so often charged. However, the manipulation was not the work of the Sandinistas--who had every interest in making these elections as demonstrably fair, pluralistic, and competitive as possible--but of the Reagan administration, whose interest apparently was in making the elections seem as unfair, ideologically one-sided and uncompetitive as possible. (LASA Report, 1985)

One of the vehicles to be utilized by the Reagan administration in its continued efforts to delegitimize the Nicaraguan Government is LA PRENSA, Nicaragua's largest opposition newspaper. In May, 1985, it was announced that LA PRESNA would receive $100,000 in aid from the U.S. government because of a grant from the National Endowment for Democracy. The NED is funded by the U.S. Information Agency and is jointly controlled by representatives from the AFL-CIO, the U.S. Chamber of Commerce and the Republican and Democratic parties. The NED is designed, according to the Reagan administration, to promote pluralism and democracy abroad. Critics argue, however, that the NED (established in 1983) has become one of the Reagan administration's most creative vehicles for involving private groups in the promotion of its foreign policy agenda (Charles, 1985). Regarding the grant to LA PRENSA, critics charge that the money has less to do with the promotion of democracy than with subsidizing anti-Sandinista forces in Nicaragua. According to Reggie Norton of the Washington Office on Latin America, "In giving money to LA PRENSA you are not giving money to a good newspaper, an independent newspaper. You're taking sides in a very open way." (Charles, 1985) The Sandinista government ultimately shut down LA PRENSA, arguing that it had become a CIA front.

72

SUMMARY

From the information presented it is obvious that the United
States fears a democratically elected, socialist oriented state in
Central America, which finds its justification for revolution more
in the Biblical story of Exodus than in Marxism; and, its
justification for a democratic socialist society more in the New
Testament than in Marxism. The United States is plainly more
comfortable with authoritarian, pro-capitalist governments,
although it has become necessary to create a facade of democracy
for these societies.

The United States not only refuses to recognize the historical
reality of Central America, it continues to engage in a bipartisan
distortion of the history of that region. The Bipartisan
Commission Report provides one with the classic illustration of
this fact. Such a blatant distortion of history is necessary if
one is to utilize current geostrategic (Cold War) arguments for
U.S. involvement in Central America; to justify continued
exportation of repression through the training of local police
units; to justify pushing U.S. economic and political programs in
the region that are grounded in liberal-Lockean, capitalistic
development models; and, to justify ignoring the voices of the
oppressed as they are empowered through grassroots organizations
such as the Christian base community.

The distortion of history along with the acceptance of U.S.
economic doctrine as an absolute, allows policy makers in the

United States to continue to believe that Central Americans have a problem "we" can solve without it being necessary to engage in any internal reflection on the root causes of the Central American crises. However, the fact remains that with or without the support of the United States, the oppressed of Central America will ultimately have their revolution and will ultimately restructure their societies as they deem necessary. The United States needs to recognize this fact and willingly export the Declaration of Independence, recognizing that the anti-capitalist sentiment in Central America is rooted in historical reality not Marxism.

CHAPTER 3

ECONOMIC AID PROGRAMS

The Bipartisan Commission Report prided itself on avoiding a single factor analysis of the Central America crisis. The section on "toward Democracy and Economic Prosperity" states that "the crisis in Central America has no single cause, but the troubled performance of the region's economies has been a major factor. They were among the most dynamic in the world in the 1960s and early 1970s. But that growth was unevenly distributed and poverty continued to plague most of the region's people." (p. 41)

For the return to the rapid economic growth of the 1960s and 1970s, along with a more equitable distribution of this increased wealth, the Bipartisan Commission Report recommends a program firmly rooted in the present vertically interdependent international economic order, that is, one rooted in the transnational corporate capitalistic model. Specifically, the Commission Report argues that for Central America to succeed economically the following will be required:

1. Economic growth goes forward in tandem with social and political modernization.
2. Indigenous savings are encouraged and supplemented by substantial external aid.
3. The nations of the region pursue APPROPRIATE economic policies.
4. In particular, these policies recognize that success will ultimately depend on the re-invigoration of savings, growth, and employment. (Report, p. 40)

The term "APPROPRIATE economic policy" is directly tied to the Report's strong emphasis on the private sector. An illustration of this point can be found in the following quote:

"The most successful efforts in the postwar period—including Central America's own sustained expansion during the 1960s and 1970s—were led by the private sector. In these cases governments provided appropriate incentives and eliminated roadblocks, rather than trying to make themselves the engines of growth. THIS MUST BE DONE AGAIN IN CENTRAL AMERICA." (Report, p. 41)

According to the Bipartisan Commission Report, the United States is presently preventing an even more serious deterioration in Central America's economic condition by making its influence felt in six ways:

1. By its own economic recovery, which should eventually be reflected in greater demand and better prices for Central American exports.
2. By the Caribbean Basin Initiative (CBI), which opens up favorable prospects for new Central American trade, and by the Generalized System of Preferences (GSP), which extends duty free access to the U.S. market for many Central American products.
3. By its bilateral economic assistance programs.
4. By its contribution to multilateral agencies, including the Inter-American Development Bank, the International Monetary Fund, and the World Bank which in turn provide financial support, policy advice, and technical assistance.
5. By its support of the international coffee agreement.
6. By initiative of the thousands of United States private citizens working in voluntary organizations and on their own to help improve living conditions in the region. (Report, pp. 45-56)

To encourage more private investors in the U.S. to consider projects in Central America the Bipartisan Commission Report recommends the formation of a privately owned venture capital company for the region called the Central America Development Corporation (CADC).

CADC, capitalized by private sector investors, would use its capital to raise funds which, in turn, would be lent to private companies active in Central America.

The U.S. government would support the CADC initiative through a long-term loan. Membership in the Central America Development Organization (CADO) as envisioned by the Bipartisan Commission, would initially be opened to the seven countries of Central America: Belize, Costa Rica, El Salvador, Guatemala, Honduras, Nicaragua and Panama; and, to the United States. Associate member status would be available to any democracy willing to contribute significant resources to promote regional development. The Commission Report then states that while "the Executive Secretary of CADO should be from Central America, THE ORGANIZATION'S CHAIRMAN SHOULD BE FROM THE UNITED STATES." (Report, pp. 56-57, 61)

Nicaragua would be encouraged to participate in CADO. However, its continued membership would be conditioned on continued progress toward "DEFINED political, social and economic goals." (Report, p. 62). But, while Nicaragua would be held strictly accountable, the Bipartisan Report states that the United States would NOT be bound to accept the judgments of CDO. The U.S. would be free to maintain a bilateral economic assistance program in a particular country, REGARDLESS OF PERFORMANCE (the model for CADO is CIAP--the Inter-America Committee for the Alliance for Progress, Report, p. 63).

Agriculturally, the Commission Report states that "where appropriate," programs of land reform should be initiated; however, the major thrust in the rural areas is to be a program to provide long-term credit at positive but moderate real interest rates to make possible the purchase of land by small farmers. (Report, p. 27). Thus improving land title registration and defending economic rights for farmers (i.e., private property rights) is the Reports' path to "land for the landless."

External financing needs up to 1990 have been estimated at $24 billion for the seven Central America countries. Half of this sum would, according to the Report, come from the World Bank, the International Monetary Fund, the Inter-American Development Bank, private investors, and commercial banks, "IF EACH CENTRAL AMERICAN COUNTRY FOLLOWS PRUDENT ECONOMIC POLICIES." The balance, as much as $12 billion, would have to be supplied by the U.S. (Report, p. 53)

The Commission Report proposes that U.S. economic assistance over the five year period 1985-1990 total $8 billion. (Report, p. 53) The recommendation is made that the U.S. congress appropriate these funds on a multiple-year basis, channeling most of the money through the proposed Central America Development Organization.

The economic analysis of the Bipartisan Commission Report is, therefore, firmly grounded in the international capitalistic economic structure, with emphasis on expending private ownership, increasing the size of the middle class and, in the final analysis, providing a middle class basis for the growth of democracy. The fact is, that for all the commission's efforts to be innovative in its economic analysis and proposed solutions, the proposals are little more than a stale rewrite of John F. Kennedy's Alliance for Progress.

ALLIANCE FOR PROGRESS

The success of the Cuban revolution and the coming to power of Fidel Castro in 1959 sent shock waves through Washington, D.C. In an effort to prevent future Cubas, president John F. Kennedy announced the Alliance for Progress in March, 1961.

The ten-year plan aimed to channel $100 billion into Latin American development in return for reforms (especially tax and land reform, carried out by the recipient governments). The United States pledged approximately $20 billion, with the remainder to come from the Latin Americans themselves (primarily the private sector). The Alliance aimed at an annual real per capita growth rate of 2.5%, or about 5.5% given the rate of the region's population increase. The actual target, however, was Castro. Kennedy accused the Republicans of losing Cuba, vowed not to lose another nation to communism during his presidency, and was determined to disprove Nikita Khrushchev's boast that the Monroe Doctrine was dead. Kennedy's plan was to use the alliance to develop stable economies and growing middle classes that would resist Castro-type revolutions. (La Feber, 1984) Military security and economic growth would develop hand-in-hand (the same logic used by the Bipartisan commission twenty-three years later).

Funds were channeled through governmental institutions, including the new Latin-American Development Bank, and were accompanied by increasing amounts of private capital. Investors were especially attracted by the Central American Common Market (CACM) which united the five small, limited markets in a larger regional marketplace after 1962. Most U.S. investment was in the banking and small manufacturing areas. Growth rates in Central America were impressive during the 1960s: the per capita increase of gross national product for the decade was 32.6% for Costa Rica, 25.8% for El Salvador, 21.2% for Guatemala, 11.7% for Honduras and 34% for Somoza's Nicaragua. (La Feber, 1984) On the surface it appeared as though increasing economic aid through the vertical interdependence model worked. In reality, the Alliance for Progress poured billions of U.S. dollars ($10 billion in 1961 dollars) into the hands of the Latin American oppressor classes, and over a decade ended up with more dictatorship, less real development and more insurgency than existed before the program began. In Central America the most important development of the decade was the appearance of significant revolutionary guerrilla bands in Guatemala, El Salvador and Nicaragua. Neither the U.S. nor the Central American oligarchs/military rulers were seriously trying to transform those growth figures into more equitable societies and political stability.

To illustrate this point, one can cite the Hickenlooper amendment of 1962, in which Congress aimed to end all aid to any nation that expropriated U.S. property without quick compensation. This amendment made impossible the redistribution of large amounts of property in Latin America unless these nations plunged into debt to pay for the redistribution. Congress also tied amendments to the Alliance for Progress that forbade the use of Alliance monies to purchase land for redistribution. (La Feber, 1984)

The oligarchs were eager to siphon off Alliance funds to relieve their own tax obligations. They also bought up additional land, with Alliance money, for producing more export crops, thus driving peasants off the land and forcing many to depend increasingly on more expensive imported food for survival. Ironically, in most areas the incidence of malnutrition rose with the amounts of food exports. Of each $100 per capita increase in Latin American income during the 1960s, only $2 reached the poorest 20% of the population. Moreover, the gains that the Alliance did produce only led the region to tie itself dangerously to foreign lenders. In 1958, Latin America's debt service was $1 billion, or 10.5% of its export earnings; a decade later, after seven years of the Alliance for Progress, it was $2 billion and 16% of export earnings. (La Feber, 1984)

EL SALVADOR

In El Salvador, ten years of the Alliance for Progress accomplished the following: El Salvadorans were fastened even more closely to a dependent export economy; an increasingly mechanized productive system that increased unemployment; a land policy where officials seized plots from peasants in order to produce more export crops; and, a condition in which the majority of the population had neither work, land, nor sufficient food. By the mid 1970s, El Salvador was one of the worlds five most undernourished nations. Ninety percent of the peasants, today, have no land and they comprise two-thirds of the population. Functional illiteracy among peasants approaches 95 percent. Two percent of the people own 58 percent of the arable land. The average monthly income of the peasants in 1980 was twelve dollars. The infant mortality rate in 1983 was 78.7 per 1000 live births. Eighty percent of all children in 1983 were ill-nourished. And, most startling, from 1961 to 1971, the decade of rapidly increasing economic assistance from the U.S., the number of landless Salvadoran families more than tripled. (La Feber, 1984)

Ever since commercial coffee growing came to El Salvador in the 19th century, the large growers have been progressively squeezing the peasants off the land. El Salvador's peasant population protested time and time again, only to be slaughtered. In 1932, challenged by an uprising of poorly-led and poorly-organized peasants, the Fourteen Families worked with the military to exterminate more than 30,000 peasants. An alliance of the military and oligarchs has held real power to El Salvador ever since.

The "green revolution's" agricultural advances hastened the land accumulation by families of military officers and the oligarchs, leading to the El Salvadoran peasant saying "Coffee eats men." (Lernoux, 1980) More and more peasants were becoming landless.

In mid 1976, President Molina, of El Salvador decreed a mild agrarian reform supported by the United States AID and the Inter-American Development Bank. Had it ever gotten off the ground, the 1.4 million-acre project would have benefitted 12,000 landless peasants. Although the 250 families that owned the land would have received $53 million in compensation, the estate owners immediately denounced the project as "communist-subversion," just as they had denounced the Alliance for Progress and the then U.S. ambassador as "communist-inspired." In the face of determined opposition from the association of Private Enterprise and the Planter's and Cattlemen's Front, Molina quickly dropped the agrarian reform program. But by then the land owners were accusing the Catholic church, El Salvador's priests, sisters and bishops, of being responsible for encouraging agrarian reform and of "inciting the people to revolt." Molina and his defense minister General Carlos Humberto Romero, promised to "clear the country of rebellious priests." Though each claimed themselves to be profoundly Catholic they ordered the arrest of five priests, expelled eighteen and, according to author Penny Lernoux, contributed to the deaths of two others.   (Lernoux, 1980)   Even U.S. sponsored plans to make peasants small land owners (i.e., capitalists) is met with strong resistance by the local Salvadoran ruling elite. Since this elite is staunchly anti-communist, the U.S. prefers dropping even mild land reform programs to alienating the ruling oligarchs.

What is U.S. foreign aid to El Salvador accomplishing in 1986? From 1980-85, the United States contributed $1.98 billion in economic and military aid to promote democracy and strengthen the private sector. An additional $486.2 million is included in the 1986 foreign-aid package of the Reagan administration. This money has neither defeated the rebels nor brought El Salvador prosperity nor helped to spark development. On the contrary, gross domestic product at the end of 1985 had fallen to 77% of what it was in 1978; per capita income had fallen to 73%; and, per capita consumption had fallen to 68% of 1978 levels. Unemployment (government figures) is 30% and underemployment is 60%. Inflation was 22% at the time of the 100% devaluation of the currency on January 21, 1986.   (Rosenthal, 1986)   The reality is that El Salvador, economically and militarily speaking, is completely dependent on U.S. assistance.   Officially 40 percent of El Salvador's government budget, in 1986, went for defense.

NICARAGUA

Nicaragua is the largest nation in Central America (equivalent to the size of England and Wales). It has a population of approximately 2.9 million people; therefore, there are no population pressures similar to El Salvador. What had the Alliance for Progress achieved by the time the Somoza regime was toppled in 1979? The Somoza family alone owned 30 percent of the nation's arable land, approximately 5 million acres of land (an area the size of El Salvador); and, also owned Nicaragua's twenty-six biggest companies. (Lernoux, 1980)

From 1961 on, Somoza and his friends funneled Alliance for Progress money into businesses they controlled. Meanwhile, only two percent of the rural population had potable water by the end of the 1960s, and only 28 percent of Managua's residents had access to sewage services. Land and tax reform were never discussed by the Somoza regime. Over 200,000 peasant families had no land, while half of all arable land in Nicaragua was occupied by 1800 ranches.

Specifically, between 1961 and 1967, the Alliance authorized nineteen loans for Nicaragua totaling $50 million. The Inter-American Development Bank injected another $50 million. Private enterprise from the U.S. increased its investment in Nicaragua from $18 million in the 1960s to $75 million in 1970. Private enterprise investment rose faster in Nicaragua in the 1960s than in any other Central American country. The country's GNP rose 6.2

percent annually between 1960 and 1970, the third best in all Latin America. (La Feber, 1983)

Alliance dollars went into agricultural projects that almost solely benefitted the oligarchy. Exports rose 20 percent annually between 1960 and 1965, yet imports rose faster, so the country began to pile up a large foreign debt. (La Feber, 1983) The Alliance aimed at diversifying the economy. The oligarchy, however, interpreted this to mean the building up of cotton instead of coffee production. Cotton was as exposed to wildly fluctuating world market prices as coffee, plus cotton was being replaced by synthetic fibers. What the cotton boom accomplished, therefore, was to evict small farmers from grain producing lands, thus, turning Nicaragua from being a net exporter to net importer of staple foods. (La Feber, 1983) In short, the Alliance for Progress was a statistical success (as success is measured by Western economists working within capitalistic development models). In reality, the Alliance for Progress played a major role in helping Nicaraguans lose the capacity to feed themselves.

The Alliance for Progress, as the Bipartisan Commission recommended twenty-three years later, called for both economic and military aid as stability was necessary for economic growth. By 1967 there were twenty-five U.S. military advisers in Nicaragua. The Pentagon supplied over $1.2 million or 13 percent of Somoza's annual defense budget. U.S. military relations with Somoza's forces were the closest in the hemisphere. Anastasio Somoza, Jr., became president of Nicaragua in 1967. A graduate of West Point in the United States, he required all his officers to spend one year at the School of the Americas in the Panama Canal Zone. The School trained more Nicaraguans during the fifties and sixties than officers from any other Latin American nation. (La Feber, 1983) The fact is that the Alliance did little or nothing for peasants driven off the land and laborers displaced by machines. The Alliance for Progress, a statistical success, accelerated Nicaragua's revolution.

In January, 1986, Nicaragua had a $4.5 billion foreign debt. President Daniel Ortega states that, to date, the U.S. financed contra war has cost Nicaragua's economy, directly and indirectly, $1.5 billion. Exports in 1984 were $365 million compared to $850 in imports. (ECONOMIST, February 2, 1985) Ironically, the U.S. economic boycott of Nicaragua, while hurting the country in the short run, may, in the long run, place Nicaragua in a better position to confront its economic crisis than its neighbors in Honduras, El Salvador, Guatemala and Costa Rica. Why? Nicaragua is forced to seek new trading partners and economic ties to countries throughout West and East Europe, the Arab nations, African nations such as Nigeria (oil), as well as strengthening ties to South American countries such as Brazil and Argentina. Nicaragua is also establishing economic trade agreements with China. Thus, in the long run, Nicaragua will have a more diverse trade base than the other Central American nations, which are becoming more economically dependent on the U.S. each day. For example, in the most peaceful country of Central America, Costa

Rica, the United States spends $1.2 million a day, the highest per capita U.S. economic aid program anywhere in the world. One prominent businessman recently commented that "Costa Rica's economic troubles would really begin if the Sandinistas in Nicaragua were overthrown, because the United States would then have no reason to continue Costa Rica's high level of economic aid." (Jones, 1985)

GUATEMALA

In Guatemala the Alliance for Progress pumped $50 million into the economy between 1962 and 1966. Direct private investment from the U.S. jumped from $13 million in 1960 to $186 million in 1970. (La Feber, 1983) Instead of redistributing wealth, the Alliance funds worsened the disparity between the rich and poor. After a decade of Alliance money, 80 percent of rural children received no schooling, the literacy rate was the lowest in the hemisphere next to Haiti and the average Guatemalan received one-third the requirements needed for a proper diet. The percentage of the Guatemalan government budget devoted to social service ranked among the lowest of the five major Central American nations in 1966, while the percentage spent on the military was the highest. By the mid-1960s Guatemala's trade balance and gross national product were rapidly improving, yet 66 percent of the people actually dropped in average per capita income from $87 to $83 a year. Alliance money was used to increase farm and ranch land in the northeastern jungle area. However, because economic growth depended on exports and because exports came from large commercial farms, the Alliance money turned the newly opened land into huge cattle ranches and plantations of 62,000 acres each. Once again the peasants were the losers in the midst of an "economic boom." (La Feber, 1983)

An economic upsurge in the mid-1970s made multimillionaires of several dozen politicians, industrialists and planters, as well as a handful of generals who took over vast tracts of oil-rich property in the Northern Transversal region. None of this prosperity trickled down to Guatemala's 4 million Indians, whose standard of living declined during the 1970s. (Perera, 1984)

Unemployment today is over 40 percent; and, illiteracy remains constant at around 70 percent. When it came to power, January 14, 1986, the government of President Vincicio Cerezo inherited an economy in which investment was 40% lower than in 1981; a slump in exports of around 30% has been matched by a contraction in imports of around 50% since 1981; and, the country's foreign exchange reserves of $740 million in 1978 have evaporated, while a foreign debt of $2.5 billion has been run up. Capital flight remains a problem, with $700 million known to have left the country for foreign banks between 1981-85. (ECONOMIST, February 2, 1985)

HONDURAS

Honduras provides, perhaps, the most interesting case study regarding the Alliance for Progress. In 1960 United States citizens controlled 95 percent of all foreign investment in Honduras, a country which lagged behind other Central American nations in economic development.

Dr. Villeda Morales, who became the Honduran president in 1957, was a liberal who was sensitive to private property. Thus, Washington looked to Villeda Morales to set an example for Alliance programs. Morales had already sponsored a labor code, social security and modest agrarian reform. Morales initially took the Alliance objectives seriously. In 1961 he drafted an agrarian reform law which threatened massive uncultivated lands owned by United Fruit and Standard Fruit. The U.S. ambassador Charles R. Burrows told Morales not to allow the proposed reform to become law UNTIL THE U.S. STATE DEPARTMENT GAVE ITS APPROVAL. (La Feber, 1983) The Honduran president, however, signed the reforms into law prior to a State Department response. United Fruit retaliated and many Hondurans lost jobs. Morales was pressured into meeting with United Fruit officials to work out an agreement cutting back on the law's effects.

A military coup successfully placed Oswaldo Lopez, the army commander, in the presidency of Honduras in 1963 (the fourth military coup in two years in Latin America--the others being Peru, Guatemala and the Dominican Republic). Although Kennedy condemned the coup (which occurred ten days prior to scheduled elections) and initially broke off relations with Honduras, the coup meant additional Alliance money and private investment for the country.

U.S. direct investment declined in Honduras during 1960 and 1961, rose slightly in 1962 and 1963, and then doubled between 1963 and 1971 to well over $200 million. Despite this inflow of capital, U.S. companies took more out of Honduras after 1963 than they put in. For example in 1968 the outflow reached $22.4 million and in 1969, $17.7 million. (La Feber, 1983) Honduras was exporting more than it was importing, yet this negative outflow was causing higher debts. U.S. companies controlled the banana industry, the largest mining companies, and key parts of the nation's infrastructure--including the two most important railroads.

Also, the two largest commercial banks in Honduras, Atlantide and Bank of Honduras came under the respective control of Chase Manhattan Bank in 1967 and National City Bank of New York in 1965. (La Feber, 1983) Financially speaking, U.S. banks were in control of the Honduran economy. The Alliance for Progress failed to diversify the Honduran economy. Instead it led to an expansion of an export economy, increased its indebtedness, lessened Honduras' control over its own economy, and paradoxically pulled wealth from the country while doubling U.S. investment. Today Honduras is, next to Haiti, the poorest nation in the hemisphere. More than 20,000 families live on the brink of starvation. Infant mortality rates are among the highest in the world. Illiteracy stands at over 70%. (La Feber, 1983)

In November, 1984, the Honduran government, faced with a 1983 trade deficit of over $250 million, requested a total of $1.3 billion in U.S. economic aid over a four year period beginning in 1985. This would have meant a doubling of U.S. aid. (Cody, 1984)

While the Reagan administration did not double economic assistance to Honduras immediately, such aid was substantially increased. The Administration realized Honduras should receive an increase in economic aid when the Honduran government began to state publicly the increased threat to their security as a result of their hosting constant U.S. military maneuvers, and the U.S. backed contras. (Cody, 1984) Given the history of Honduras, it is doubtful that any substantial increase in economic assistance will reach the oppressed in this, the poorest nation in Central America.

RECIPE FOR FAILURE

The economic proposals put forth in the Bipartisan Commission Report are predestined to failure for the same reasons the Alliance for Progress failed. The most obvious reason is that no amount of economic aid can buy economic development in the middle of a war. But there are far more basic reasons the recommendations put forth by the Bipartisan Commission will, if implemented, go the way of the Alliance for Progress.

The United States in viewing the Central American crises primarily in ideological terms--that is, in the East/West geostrategic framework--is refusing to acknowledge the historical reality of that region, as experienced by the mass population. In addition, the United States is once again, as it did in the Alliance for Progress, proposing solutions based upon the historical experience of the United States, that is, liberal-Lockean notions that place an overriding emphasis on private property, political democracy, stability, anti-communism and pro-Americanism; and proposed solutions grounded in first world capitalistic development theory (for example, the works of W.W. Rostow, Seymour M. Lipset and Karl W. Deutsch).

These authors focused on the economic and social prerequisites of democracy, suggesting that democracy and pluralism were the inevitable result of socio-economic modernization. Their error, and that of policy makers using their theories, was to mistake correlation for causation, to assume that since most democracies in the world were often the most economically developed, the latter was the CAUSE of the former. It followed than that political democracy and development (in most of the literature the terms were used synonymously) would be a product of economic development and that democracy and political development would proceed inevitably from the force of economic growth. That approach is not only logically flawed, it is culturally imperialistic. The fact is that programs (such as those proposed by the Bipartisan Commission

Report) that derive from imperial sensibilities can never promote self-reliant development.

The problem remains that, in the United States, governmental leaders and policy makers--Republican or Democrats--accept as doctrine the belief that capitalism and freedom are synonymous. That is to say, capitalism IS freedom. Doctrine continues with the commonly held belief that capitalism and military security go together. All this is not surprising given the fact that the U.S. revolution of 1776 stressed the individual's right to private property and personal liberty above all else.

The crucial point is for the United States to recognize that from the perspective of the oppressed in Central America, capitalism is anti-revolutionary. Capitalism, in Central America has been associated with a brutal oligarchy/military supported by the United States. The view of capitalism is that it threatens the freedom of the many. What the United States must come to grips with is that this perspective does not find its origin in Marxist ideology. Rather, the origin lies in the historical reality of Central America, including the role the United States has played in that region. The simple fact is that even if Karl Marx had never lived, Tsars still ruled Russia, and Batista still ruled Cuba, the United States would be facing a revolutionary situation in Central America today that had clear anti-capitalist, anti-U.S. sentiments.

The belief of policy makers in the United States (whether one is referring to Kennedy's Alliance for Progress, or the Bipartisan

Commission Report of the Reagan administration), is that if the U.S. only gives enough economic aid to strengthen the private business sector, thereby creating a large middle class in Central America, the result will be greatly increased political stability, strong economic growth, increased support for democracy, and, increased anti-communism.

The United States clings to this belief--capitalism and freedom as synonymous terms--which leads policy makers to introduce new versions of old recipes for U.S. economic aid packages to Central America. The belief is doctrine.

Historically speaking, the idea that increased U.S. economic aid will increase political stability, democracy and anti-communism in Latin America is without foundation. For example:

> -- Costa Rica developed as a democracy before any U.S. aid was offered.
>
> -- The Dominican Republic received more U.S. economic aid per capita in the early 1960s than any Latin American nation, yet exploded in revolution in 1965 (the response of the U.S. was to send in 22,000 troops).
>
> -- Chile received more economic aid per capita in the late 1960s than any other Latin American nation, yet democratically elected Salvador Allende, a Marxist, as president in 1970 (the U.S. response was to destabilize Chile economically and finance the revolt against Allende). (Wiarda, 1984)

Similarly lacking in historical support is the U.S. belief that democracy cannot exist without a large middle class of property owners. It is not possible to find any data supporting this thesis. Rather, the evidence in Central America indicates that the new middle class tends to adopt the behavior/values of the traditional oligarchy. The new middle class in Central America has been very supportive of the military, for example, in opposing sharing any of their new wealth and power with the poor.

Economic aid proposals which emphasize rapid economic growth within capitalistic developmental models are, quite obviously, viewed with suspicion by the oppressed of Central America. Historically speaking, U.S. economic aid has increased the dependency of donor countries, as it has strings attached. U.S. aid loans, for example, normally require their recipients to buy U.S. goods with that money, often at inflated prices Secondly, U.S. economic aid in Central America has fluctuated with the changing political climate in donor countries. Thirdly, U.S. economic aid has often generated greater debts, for example, aid to Central American nations has normally been in the form of loans, not grants. Loans must be repaid with interest. The fact is, that in many Third World countries, new foreign aid loans are often used to repay previous foreign aid loans. Lastly, from a Central American perspective, the amount of economic aid represents a negative flow for the region. Central America has been supplying the U.S. with cheap agricultural goods and raw materials for decades while being expected to purchase more expensive U.S. manufactured goods.

Also, from a Central American perspective it is vitally important in the future to reject any program emphasizing export cropping (increasing the production of key export crops such as coffee, bananas, cotton, at the expense of production of basic food staples).

Export cropping has traditionally meant the following:

1. Less food is produced for local consumption,
2. Local food staples begin to cost more,
3. As more acreage is devoted to export cropping, basic food staples must be imported,
4. Export cropping often disrupts the ecological balance of the land,
5. Single export economies are vulnerable to widely fluctuating commodity prices and have often had to sell at prices lower than the world market price,
6. Foreign exchange earnings, if any, have benefitted the wealthy oligarchs not the poor,
7. People are driven off the land into urban areas where there is not adequate housing, employment, food staples, etc.,
8. Agricultural production is on a larger scale and becomes concentrated in fewer hands,
9. Export cropping is more mechanized, which means fewer jobs. In labor surplus nations this creates more problems; and,
10. The debt spiral locks the nations into an increased emphasis on export cropping. (McGinnis, 1979)

Finally, one should mention that the Bipartisan Commission is recommending an economic aid program based primarily upon private investment at a time when private investment has stopped and disinvestment has begun on a massive scale. Accurate figures on capital flight are not available, but balance of payment data suggest that $2.5 billion to $3 billion in private capital flowed out of Central America between 1979 and 1982. (La Feber, 1983) The reality is that by channeling economic aid through existing oligarchs/military rulers in Central America, much of that money would end up in Miami banks rather than in Central American development projects. The Alliance for Progress should provide a historical lesson for U.S. policy makers.

HORIZONTAL INTERDEPENDENCE

If injustice in Central America is to be overcome there is a need for the United States to reject the solutions of the Alliance for Progress and Bipartisan Commission Report that are consistent with the present day international economic order, that is, vertically interdependent model. Solutions which would go to the heart of the problem in Central America would be the product of a new international economic order based upon horizontal interdependence and self-reliant development models. (See Appendices A and B.)

Any redistribution of goods without a corresponding redistribution of power is paternalism. Vertical inter-dependence involves a relationship of inequality in wealth and power--it is a master-slave relationship. Even if the economic situation of the oppressed would improve with the economic aid package recommended by the Bipartisan Commission, a questionable assumption, the master-slave relationship is no longer acceptable to the oppressed in Central America.

Self-reliant development emphasizes meeting the basic human needs of the masses of people in a country through strategies geared to the particular human and natural resources, values, and traditions of communities and regions within a country, and through strategies maximizing the collective efforts of people within each country and among Third World countries. This model of self-reliant development is expressed eloquently by Mahbub ul Haq:

> ... Not self-reliance in the same sense of cutting our links completely from the world, but self-reliance in the sense of being so self-confident as a nation as to base our development on our own cultural values. Self-reliance is a very comprehensive concept which cuts across all walks of life. It implies not only reliance on our own domestic resources or technology. It is relying on OUR OWN THINKING AND OUR OWN VALUE SYSTEMS without being defensive OR apologetic. (Mc Ginnis, 1979)

Self-reliant development is grassroots, process oriented development consisting of four basic components:

1. Sufficient Life Goods--food, shelter, clothing, health care, skills development, work (ECONOMIC RIGHTS).
2. Dignity/Esteem--recognizing, affirming and calling forth the value/uniqueness of each person and each people (CULTURAL RIGHTS).
3. Participation--the right of individuals and peoples to shape their own destinies (POLITICAL RIGHTS).
4. Solidarity--the corresponding duty to promote these rights with and for others (DUTIES AS WELL AS RIGHTS). (McGinnis, 1979)

How sufficient life goods are provided is just as important as that they are provided. The process must always be one that empowers people. Goods must be provided and programs must be structured to combat paternalism, domination and negative dependency.

Specific actions which could be taken in the short-term to begin a process of evolution towards a model of horizontal interdependence are:

1. Emphasis on local production of food staples to reduce food imports and guarantee national and regional food security.
2. Reform of land tenure, tax and labor laws, combined with equitable enforcement.
3. Emphasis on developing agro-processing and labor-intensive productive sections.
4. Development of expanded domestic markets once incomes and land distribution are more equitable.
5. Emphasis on use of locally available resources to produce goods and services to meet domestic demand.
6. Encouragement of regional trade and cooperation along decentralized and horizontal lines.
7. Coordination with global efforts to relieve Third-World debt obligations, securing more favorable and equitable terms of international trade, while simultaneously leading to decreasing dependence on present international banking and lending agencies and institutions.

The major problem of course is that self-reliant development and horizontal interdependence threatens transnational corporate capitalism. If both were to be realized, radical change in existing structures and processes would need to occur in both the United States and Central America. The greatest mistake made when working within the vertical interdependence model, as the Alliance for Progress and Bipartisan Commission Report did, is detaching change in Central America from change in United States. Once again, programs that derive from imperial sensibilities cannot promote self-reliant development. To avoid further disaster in Central America, the revolutions of that region must be brought home to the United States. If a viable economic assistance package is to be created for the Central American region, then the political, economic and cultural basis for U.S. policy must be challenged and changed.

SUMMARY

The prospects for the development of a United States economic aid package based upon horizontal relationships with Central American nations remain quite remote. Although this is the approach most likely to promote self-reliant developments while attacking structural or institutionalized economic oppression, the fact remains that it runs counter to United States doctrine that capitalism IS freedom; that capitalism and military security go together; and, that economic growth and development precedes political democracy and development.

Realistically, the United States will not accept economic structures and political systems in Central America that do not share the values of the United States--the recognition of the right of private property being the most important. The prospect for Central America is one of continued U.S. dominance; of governments supported economically and militarily by the U.S.; of continued U.S. economic aid programs that work to increase the wealth of the ruling oligarchs/military rulers, therefore working against the empowerment of the oppressed; and, of increased efforts to destabilize Nicaragua and remove the Sandinistas from the government, as they are perceived to be a threat to U.S. economic doctrine.

As this approach will lead to increased insurrection and revolution the United States will remain increasingly involved militarily in Central America. Instead of promoting freedom and democracy the United States is pursuing a path which could turn Central America and Mexico into the "Eastern Europe" of the Western Hemisphere. United States economic doctrine as gospel--as an absolute--will continue to place the U.S. on the side of the oligarchs/military rulers. The U.S. should realize by now that it can win wars, but it cannot win revolutions. The alternative to disaster is to recognize that U.S. economic doctrine is not an absolute and to promote policies in Central America grounded in self-reliant development models. The key to a viable economic policy in Central America is a fundamental change in the manner in which the Central American economic crisis is perceived in the United States. From this perspective, the economic future of the oppressed in Central America does not appear to be an exceptionally bright one.

CHAPTER 4

CULTURAL INSENSITIVITY

In analyzing the Bipartisan Commission Report from a cultural perspective one must conclude that from an educational, political, military and religious perspective, the document is culturally undemocratic. That is to say, the cultural right of Central Americans to self-reliant decision making processes in search of solutions to the structural and institutional violence experienced by the oppressed, is ignored.

The Report begins the chapter on Human Development by stating that "a comprehensive effort to promote democracy and prosperity among the Central American nations must have as its cornerstone 'human development'."

> The burden of action in these areas, even more than in some others, lies primarily on the Central Americans themselves. However well-intentioned, no foreigner can feed, educate, doctor, clothe and house another country's people without undermining its government or creating cultural conflicts. (Report, p. 68)

Had the Commission members made recommendations based upon the above quotation, a foundation might have been laid for a political settlement to the regional conflict. Unfortunately, this was not the case.

EDUCATION

The Report recognizes that, in Central America, educational advancement for the children is directly tied to malnutrition.

Instead of recommending the immediate need for the U.S. to support agricultural programs designed to make Central America once again self-sufficient in food, the Report recommends that in the short run the United States and members of the European Community provide additional food aid.

To assist in overcoming illiteracy the Report recommends that the U.S. Peace Corps establish a "front-line" group of teachers to serve in a new Literacy Corps. The number of Peace Corps volunteers in Central America should be increased from the "the current 600 to a figure of six times as great." A Central American Teacher Corps would expand Peace Corps activities at the primary, secondary and technical level.

The Peace Corps expansion program has begun in Costa Rica, Guatemala, Belize and Honduras. However, gone is the philosophy that the Peace Corps should help the most needy. Today the Peace Corps is the "Peace Corporation" where the emphasis is on private enterprise and on the psychological/political component of low-intensity warfare. In 1980 there were 354 Peace Corps volunteers in all Central America. By 1989, in line with the Bipartisan Commission Report recommendations, the Peace Corps will have added an additional 1500 volunteers to the region.

The Peace Corps expansion campaign is known as the Peace Corps' Initiative for Central America. It has been proposed that the expanded Peace Corps include, for example, a "literacy corps" in Guatemala to "teach Spanish to Mayan Indian dialect speakers." (Barry & Preusch, 1986) This will complement the Guatemalan army's

U.S. sponsored plan (part of low-intensity warfare strategy) to incorporate the Indian population into "the national identity." A similar plan is now in effect in Honduras. The Bipartisan Commission Report recommended the literacy corps as an apparent response to the highly successful "literacy brigades" that produced spectacular increases in Nicaraguan literacy rates after 1979. Peace Corps director Ruppe kicked off the organization's drive to find new Spanish-speaking volunteers with a speech at the Miami Chamber of Commerce. Miami was selected, she said, because of its large bilingual population (Cuban Americans). (Barry & Preusch, 1986)

New Peace Corps volunteers, as part of low-intensity warfare strategy, are given a series of lectures on "ideology" to prepare them for their experience in Central America. Among the topics, the trainees receive instruction on, is the "philosophy, tactics and menace of Communism." (New York TIMES, September 24, 1984) Former Peace Corps director Sargent Shriver said that ideological instruction has grown more intensive since he left the agency." We didn't think we ought to make them (Peace Corps volunteers) into philosophical Green Berets," commented Shriver.[2] (Barry & Preusch, 1986)

---

[2]A recently formed organization called "The Returned Peace Corps Volunteers Committee on Central America" opposes the Peace Corps expansion in Central America. Francine Dionne, a spokesperson for the group, said, "They have declared the Peace Corps an instrument of U.S. foreign policy and a tool of the Reagan administration." (New York TIMES, September 24, 1984)

Vocational education would be primarily concentrated in agriculture, according to the Report. In a statement illustrating the lack of education promoting self-reliant development and decision-making the Report states:

> "Drawing on its own agricultural experience, the United States can offer increased technical support to help Central Americans improve production and productivity of both cash and food crops." (Report, p. 71)

The Bipartisan Commission, instead of being innovative in its approach to hunger, malnutrition and the effects of emphasis on export cropping, has followed U.S. economic doctrine in recommending agricultural education and assistance that is consistent with the technological view--as opposed to the socio-political view held by the oppressed of Central America. The technological view defines the problem in Central American agriculture as one of inadequate production. There is not enough food, not enough fertilizer, irrigation, modern equipment, not enough know-how, not enough efficiency.

The solution offered by the technological view is to rapidly increase production--a modernized 'green revolution'. Thus more and better scientific farming is the approach, e.g. new seeds, fertilizers, pesticides, etc. More technical education is needed and the approach to the New International Economic Order is one that redistributes the latest technology.

The socio-political view of the oppressed of Central America defines the agricultural problem in terms of land ownership and use. Arable land is controlled by the few and used to produce non-essentials and export crops for profit. The maintenance of colonial patterns of trade work to perpetuate the system.

The solution, according to this view is a socio-political revolution. The key is a land reform program that gives priority to self-sufficiency in food, that is, local food needs first. Thus, the socio-political view of a New International Economic Order is one that redistributes decision-making power in international economic and political institutions, so that these institutions can be fundamentally changed, paving the way for the creation of a new global horizontal interdependence. In short, the Central American perspective would argue that as long as hunger is viewed as a technological problem rather than socio-political one, the hungry of the region will remain hungry.

To support an economic recovery and human development program founded in private enterprise, the Report stresses the need for education programs in the business and public administration sections. The Report calls for the strengthening of existing institutions such as the Central American Institute for Business Administration (INCAE). Along with this, the Report recommends expansion of the International Executive Service Corps (IESC). (Report, pp. 71-72)

The IESC is a private, voluntary organization of retired U.S. business executives. The IESC would be asked to give particular attention to training managers of small businesses. According to the Report "this would strengthen the economy, while also contributing to the development of the middle class." (Report, p. 72)

The Bipartisan Commission argues that it is imperative to offer young Central Americans the opportunity to study in the United States, "both to improve the range and quality of educational alternatives and to build lasting links between Central Americans and the United States. This was in response to the United States Information Agency figures that in 1982, total Soviet, Eastern European and Cuban university scholarships to Central Americans reached 7500. The USIA stated that while overall Central American enrollment in U.S. universities was "around" 7200 in 1982, only 391 Central American students were supported in universities by U.S. government sponsored scholarships. Thus, most Central American students in the U.S. come from families with high incomes. According to the USIA, the key factor which distinguished Cuban and Soviet educational strategy from that of the United States is the targeting of students from lower income families. The Bipartisan Commission stated that the political and academic leaders they spoke with "emphasized the long-run cost of having so many of Central America's potential future leaders--ESPECIALLY THOSE FROM DISADVANTAGED BACKGROUNDS--educated in Soviet block countries." (Report, p. 72)

The Report, therefore, recommends a program of 10,000 U.S. government sponsored scholarships to bring Central American students to the U.S. Half of these would be four to six year university scholarships, while half would be two to four year vocational-technical scholarships. Special targeting would assure all social and economic classes participated.

The Bipartisan Commission recognized a need for the United States, "in close partnership with the Central American governments and universities, to develop a long-term plan to strengthen the major universities in Central America." The commission's analysis of the present state of universities in Central America is as follows:

> Universities suffer from over-extended facilities, over-emphasis on traditional fields such as law) at the expense of applied disciplines (such as business, management, natural sciences, engineering and agriculture), poorly trained instructors, and extremely high attrition rates. Moreover, many of the universities have become highly politicized, MORE CONCERNED WITH POLITICAL ACTIVISM THAN WITH EDUCATING STUDENTS TO MEET THE CONCRETE NEEDS OF THEIR COUNTRIES. (Report, p. 69)

The principal thrust of the U.S. assistance effort is this area should be, according to the Report, an effort to "help improve the quality of Central American universities." The program of assistance would include:

-- Technical assistance to provide immediate improvements in undergraduate teaching and curriculum.

-- Selective investments in improving libraries, laboratories and student facilities.

-- An innovative effort to recruit and train junior faculty and young administrators

-- A complementary program of refresher training and upgrading of existing faculty and administrative staff.

-- An expanded program of pairing U.S. and Central American colleges and universities.

> -- A significant expansion of opportunities for
> faculty, students, and administrators to visit
> the United States for periods which may range
> from a few weeks to several years. (Report,
> p. 73-74)

Such an analysis of the educational system, along with the
solutions that logically arise from this analysis, are culturally
undemocratic. That is to say they are culturally imperialistic.
What is needed are expanded opportunities for U.S. university
faculty, students and administrators to visit the rural areas of
Central America for periods ranging from a few weeks to several
years. If peace is to come to Central America, it is the
curriculum in U.S. universities that needs improving; in the way
the history of Central America is presented, and, in changing the
First World technological approach academics and researchers in the
U.S. use in "problem-solving" the crises in the region. The United
States needs to move beyond the mentality that "THEY" have problems
to which "WE" can find technological solutions.

HEALTH CARE

Central America, according to the Bipartisan Commission
Report, must develop a system of health care suitable "to its own
needs;" yet, the Report requests that existing technical assistance
programs supported by the United States AID be expanded. Broader
concentration should "be placed upon health care systems,
management health care planning and health economics." Although
the Report called on the Central American nations to develop a

health care system based on its own needs, the Bipartisan
Commission stated:

> From our (U.S.) own experience we can advise them that
> what is needed is not service alone....but the
> development of alternative systems of health care
> delivery and an expanding effort in preventive medicine.
> (Report, pp. 76-77)

Voluntary private organizations funded by the American Schools
and Hospitals Abroad (ASHA)--the section of AID which supports such
efforts--would be used to accomplish the Report's goals, along with
private sector business ventures in the health care field.   To
quote the Report:

> Many urban centers in Central America now have well-
> equipped and well-staffed private medical institutions.
> In considering the development of private sector
> enterprises, as well as the fulfillment of local needs,
> a health insurance could be provided so that these
> (private) institutions could help bear the load...
> (Report, p. 79)

The Report argues that the lessons of experience from Medicare
and Medicaid and from private insurance systems in the United
States should be brought to bear on the development of
demonstration finance systems. (Report, p. 79) One must raise the
question as to whether the experiences over the past twenty-five
years in a post-industrial, capitalistic, first world nation are
in any way relevant to the needs of the Central American nations.

Specifically, the Report sees a need to address the problems
of malnutrition, malaria, dengue fever and lack of immunization
programs for childhood diseases, maternal and infant mortality
along with continuation of current population and family planning

programs supported by the U.S. Agency for International Development.

The Bipartisan Report fails to mention the health care system that has been created in Nicaragua since the overthrow of the Somoza regime. The Nicaraguan system has been successful in addressing most of the problem areas cited in the Report. Funds diverted to fight and defend against the contras have prevented the program from accomplishing more. However, even with a shortage of funds, the World Health Organization, in 1983, selected Nicaragua as one of seven countries world-wide to serve as a model of how "to provide health to all by the year 2000." Specifically, the WHO referred to Nicaragua's Health Days that have contributed to drastic reductions in child morbidity and mortality. (Donahue, 1983)

Health care in Nicaragua, since July 1979, is delivered primarily through health care centers, with a physician in charge of each center, assisted by a staff of nurses and trained paramedics. There were 177 care centers opened in 1979. By 1983 there were 446 such centers with an additional 50 opened the first half of 1984. In 1979 there were 37 hospitals in the country. In 1983 and 1984 seventeen new ones were opened. The last year of the Somoza regime 3 percent of the national budget went for health care. In the 1984 budget 13 percent went to health care. Medical care is total. It includes medical care, dental care, eye-glasses, hearing aids and free prescriptions. (Whitman, 1984)

Since 1979, infant mortality has been reduced from 121 per 1,000 live births to 80. The system is currently attempting to make inroads into the largest cause of infant deaths in the first year of life--which is diarrhea. (Whitman, 1984)

Women are encouraged to deliver their children in a hospital and to breast-feed their infants. Prenatal and postnatal care have a high priority.

Immunization programs have resulted in the virtual elimination of polio and reduced the number of diphtheria to only three new cases in 1983. Measles, whopping cough and tetanus have also been lowered. Parasitic diseases remain prevalent, although malaria is down 40 percent in five years.

Along the Honduran border, health care clinics are one of the prime targets of the contras. In 1984, for example, two volunteer European doctors (one West German and one French) were slain by contras near the Honduran border. (Whitman, 1984)

Nicaragua lacks one of the essentials for self-reliant development in the health care area, that is, the lack of an indigenous pharmaceutical industry. With the exception of a Bayer aspirin plant in Managua, all drugs and medications have to be imported. The U.S. efforts to destabilize Nicaragua's economy make the achievements of that nation in the health care field all the more remarkable. That the Bipartisan Commission Report failed to even mention the progress being made in Nicaragua in basic health care delivery is but one more illustration of the hard line ideological approach being taken by the Reagan administration against Nicaragua.

LIBERATION THEOLOGY

The most obvious and glaring omission of the Bipartisan Commission Report is the failure to mention, anywhere in the document, liberation theology. That twelve of the "best and the brightest" minds in the United States could approve a document on Central America without a discussion and analysis of the role of the Catholic Church in empowering the oppressed of the region, is truly remarkable. Discussing the revolutionary movement in Central America without reference to cumunidades de base (Christian grass roots communities) and their role in empowering the oppressed through the use of Paulo Freire's technique of conscientization (consciousness-raising) is comparable to preparing a report on the Middle East and making no reference to Jewism or Islam. The question becomes "why would the Bipartisan Commission omit any reference to liberation theology?"

The most probable thesis is that the omission was an intentional obfuscation of the reality of the crises in Central America today. Given the Commission's a priori acceptance of: the belief that Nicaragua already is a hard line Marxist-Leninist state; that the origins of the Central American crisis lie in Moscow working through Havana and Managua; the total commitment to the United States economic doctrine; and, the opposition to any development model that is critical of, or provides an alternative to, corporate capitalism, the Bipartisan Commission had to omit a discussion of liberation theology. To admit that a large number of Latin American bishops, priests, nuns and lay religious workers are supportive of efforts to bring about radical and fundamental structural economic and political change within a Christian, democratic socialist framework, would result in undermining the rationale for U.S. intervention in the region. Liberation theology, in confronting the root cause of the oppression and injustice in Central America poses a direct threat to U.S. interests in the area.

In the October 1973 issue of FOREIGN AFFAIRS Panama's Archbishop Marcos McGrath wrote the following:

> Great doubt has been cast on the possibility of achieving the necessary reforms for the integral development of our people within the capitalist structure of the international, and particularly the inner-American economy, when the terms of trade and foreign investment are still colonialist in structure and thus contribute to the continuing impoverishment of the poorer nations.
>
> Ironically the efforts of the prime producers --for instance of crude oil--to extract a higher price from buyers to the north have roused pious cries of protest: 'Extortion!' Suddenly Northerners fear that they may have to 'depend' on foreign producers. DO THEY IGNORE THE EXTORTION AND ECONOMIC DEPENDENCE THEY EXERCISE UPON THE POORER LANDS? This is 'an eye for an eye and a tooth for a tooth' in international economics. But who sets the rules of the game? The Christian nations to the north. (La Feber, 1983)

Rather than viewing the crisis in Central America as originating in Moscow, liberation theologists speak of the 'spiral of violence' as outlined by the longtime Catholic Archbishop of Recife, Brazil, Dom Helder Camara.

Camara describes three types of violence. Violence number one he labels INJUSTICE. This is most often referred to as 'structural' or 'institutional' violence. Such violence may be seen in landless peasants, malnourished children, or when innocent persons are arrested and tortured for political or religious dissent. Camara refers to this as invisible violence, because it is invisible to all to save its victims. (I should add that if persons in the United States and other developed nations have trouble understanding institutional violence, that says more about the narrowness of our perspective than about the breadth of the definition.)

Violence number two, REVOLT, breaks out when injustice becomes too widespread, too intolerable.

Violence number three, REPRESSION, occurs when those with authority respond to revolt. In other words, when the National Guard, the police, the army, are used to repress the revolt and restore order to ensure the maintenance of the pre-revolt status quo. (Brown, 1981)

The United States response to rebellions and revolutionary movements in Central America has been to concentrate on repression, that is, violence number three. Revolts, especially if perceived to be Moscow inspired, must be repressed at all costs. The position of policy makers in the U.S. has been to argue that "order must precede justice."

There is a saying in Central America, "La paz comienza con la justicia" (Peace begins with justice). Thus, Camara stresses that repression only increases the injustice to the point where a future revolt will break out that will be larger than the previous one. This, in turn, leads to increased repression and what Camara refers to as the 'spiral of violence'. Camara's message is that the ONLY place the spiral of violence can be broken is by addressing violence number one--injustice. Only by changing the unjust structures that serve to perpetuate oppression and violence, and, in Camara's words "devastatingly and relentlessly destroy human personhood," can the crisis in Central America be peaceably resolved. This reinforces an earlier point that even if Marxism, the Soviet Union and Cuba did not exist, there would still be, today, anticapitalist, anti-U.S. revolutionary activity in Central America. That these sentiments are, to such a large extent, found in liberation theology poses a unique problem for the United States.

Viewed historically, the Latin American Catholic Church would seem the least likely institution to oppose the structural oppression of the U.S. and Central American oligarchs/military rulers. Long before the appearance of Latin American military dictatorships there was the Inquisition. By the time of the wars of independence at the beginning of the nineteenth century, the Catholic Church was the largest landowner in all of Latin America. It was also the most conservative political force on the continent.

At its best, Catholicism was a benevolent paternalism, reinforcing the colonial system through praise of patience, obedience, and the virtue of suffering. The poor believed the missionaries when they said it was God's will or destiny, that they should be poor. Thus, the oppressed embraced fatalism on the promise of a better hereafter. Until the 1960s the Catholic Church was the major institution in convincing the oppressed to "accept their fate," that is, rule by the oligarchs and military. The church openly collaborated with corrupt dictatorships in exchange for power and material privilege.

What caused the Catholic Church to begin to question its traditional alliance with the oligarchs and military dictators? Originally it was Fidel Castro, the Cuban revolution and a fear of communism. (Lernoux, 1980) The Cuban revolution forced many Latin American bishops, priests and nuns to clearly see that the seeds of revolution lay in the extremes of Latin America's poverty and wealth. However, in the early 1960s the Catholic Church viewed the growing crisis in Latin America as the U.S. government did. Therefore, the primary goal of reform was to counter and defeat left-wing political movements and guerrilla groups. The Church became so involved in devising strategies to defeat communism that it continued to overlook the real cause of the people's misery: The injustice that stemmed from five centuries of social and economic oppression--(Camara's violence number One).

An illustration of the Church's strategy in the early 1960s can be found in Chile (similar approaches were being made throughout Latin America). The Vatican sent Belgian Jesuit Roger Vekemans to Chile in the late 1950s to establish the Center for Research and Social Action in the School of Sociology at the Catholic University of Santiago. Vekemans' job was to train Jesuit specialists in social reform (e.g., how to start housing projects, workers' cooperatives, etc.) and they, in turn, would work with politicians in Chile's Christian Democratic Party. How did Vekemans finance his program? By 1963 the West German bishops and government were contributing $25 million a year, while U.S. AID and the CIA were making major contributions ($1.8 million farm AID and up to $5 million covert aid from the CIA). Vekemans stated he saw nothing wrong with using CIA money to promote, in Chile, the National Association of Farm Workers and the Union of Christian Peasants among others. (Lernoux, 1980)

Similar programs were implemented throughout Central and South America. What the Catholic Church and the U.S. government tried to do failed, as these strategies were attempts to put a modern facade on an outdated society, without attacking its fundamental defects. Liberation theologists argue that Vekemans' approach failed because it was based, not on Christian values, but on political advantage.

The foundation for the formulation of liberation theology is to be found in the Vatican's Second Ecumenical Council (1962-65). Pope John XXIII had set the Church on a new path with his encyclicals MATER ET MAGISTRA (1961) and PACEM IN TERRIS (1963), which emphasized the human right to a decent standard of living, education and political participation. (Lernoux, 1980) Pope John XXIII also questioned the absolute right to private property and the Church's unswerving allegiance to capitalist individualism. (Lernoux, 1980)

In 1966, a declaration signed by fifteen Third World bishops went far beyond Vatican II in calling for a church comment to the world's poor and oppressed. The leader of this group was Dom Helder Camara. Soon after Pope Paul VI wrote POPULORUM PROGRESSIO, specifically directed at Latin America--encouraging Latin American bishops to hold a hemispheric conference to examine the conclusions of Vatican II in light of Latin America's own particular situation. Latin America was approaching a religious-political turning point, where the ideas of liberation theology would be approved by the Church's Latin American hierarchy. (Lernoux, 1980)

The turning point was the 1968 Latin American bishops meeting in Medellin, Colombia. According to the Medellin documents, the mass of the people in Latin America were oppressed by "institutionalized violence of internal and external colonial structures that, seeking unbounded profits, foment an economic dictatorship and international imperialism of money."

The Medellin documents further stated that "capitalism was as bad as communism; both systems are affronts to the dignity of the human being." Technocrats and "developmentalists" were attacked by the bishops for "placing more emphasis on economic progress than on the social well-being of the people," and "for failing to encourage popular participation in government."

The bishops at Medellin also addressed the issue of class conflict, stressing the polarization between rich and poor. The bishops placed the blame for social and economic injustice in Latin America squarely on those with "the greater share of wealth and power, who jealously retain their privileges, thus provoking revolutions of despair." Key words at Medellin were liberation and participation. (Lernoux, 1980)

One of the founders of liberation theology, Peruvian Father Gustavo Gutierrez writes that liberation is a more appropriate word than "development" in the context of poverty and repression, because liberation suggests that "man can begin to change himself as a creative being, directing his own destiny toward a society in which he will be free of every kind of slavery: WHEN HISTORY IS SEEN AS THE PROCESS OF MAN'S EMANCIPATION, THE QUESTION OF DEVELOPMENT IS PLACED IN A LARGER CONTEXT, A DEEPER, MORE RADICAL ONE. Man is not seen as a passive element but as an agent of history." (Lernoux, 1980)

According to liberation theology the Church becomes an institution of social criticism and a stimulus for liberation. The key difference in this approach to previous attempts at reform in Latin America is that the Church does NOT lead or organize the struggle for liberation; it is done by the people themselves. The Church is a prod from within, not a superstructure imposing its ideas from without, the goal is to empower people to be their own change agents.

A theology of liberation also transcends theology of revolution. The latter concerns itself with "freedom-from" while the former incorporates a "freedom for" philosophy. Under liberation theology freedom becomes the power to transform one's society and to create continually a new future. This requires the development of a new consciousness, that is, the acceptance of a new model of human nature. The oppressed consciousness must be liberated.

The reference book for this process is the Bible which is viewed by liberation theologians as a very revolutionary book which is from first to last the account of Jahweh's liberation of his people. The Exodus story is the paradigm event: Jahweh frees his people from oppression. This is not just the oppression of personal sin, but also the oppression of structural/institutional sin--that found in unjust social structures, enforced by oligarchs and dictators, grounded in a repressive economic order. The theme is one of political and economic liberation. Old Testament prophets along with Jesus, are seen as prophets constantly opposing the rich exploiting the poor, opposing religious leaders who side with the rich, while themselves proclaiming the gospel of "freedom to captives" and "liberation to the oppressed." Society is the object of liberation theology. One starts with humankind, not with God. Faith is not truth; rather, faith is a process of becoming. The starting point is Latin America under domination. (Lernoux, 1980)

The Bible becomes, therefore, a powerful instrument of what Paulo Friere called conscientization--the consciousness raising technique used in liberation theology. The priest, nun or lay religious worker moves into the midst of the oppressed in order to share the experience of daily oppression. Communication becomes a two way process whereby the poor instruct the teacher, who functions as a coordinator, while learning more about themselves and their reality, thus acquiring a desire to change that reality. Freire's message is to enter into dialogue with humility, that is, "How can I converse if I always see ignorance in others and never perceive my own?" Dialogue implies trust in, and love for, all humankind. (Lernoux, 1980)

Conscientization is awareness building; it is an opening of the eyes to the present situation. As the poor and exploited learn through this process, the historical reality of their existing socio-economic, political conditions and relate this to the gospel call to freedom, they are motivated to act against dehumanization. This does not lead to fanaticism. Instead it empowers people to enter into the historical process as responsible subjects. Freedom, if it is to be anything other than private self-adulation, has to be according to liberation theology, embodied in community life. True freedom is never a private affair. "Liberation from" requires the overthrow of those institutions designed to oppress humankind. "Liberation for" requires the creation of institutions which enable all human beings to reach their fullest potential.

In creating a new future, new dimensions of freedom will be discovered. Faith is a process of becoming.

The building blocks of a new society are the COMUNIDADES DE BASE or Christian grass-roots communities. These base communities are grounded and rooted in the local community. They are the creation of a Church without hierarchy and privilege. A Church without privilege implies the liberation of truth or, a struggle for the liberation of truth as the freeing of truth on a cultural level that is tied to the freeing from privilege on a subcultural level.

The base communities also discourage individualism. Participants, who number from 12-25 in each base community, are urged to pool their experiences and feelings, thus liberating themselves from the sense of isolation and insecurity caused by political and economic repression. Sharing is then extended to other Christian based communities, so that there is mutual support, each encouraging the others and exchanging experiences. Thus, these communities become strong antidotes to defeatism and fatalism.

The creation of a horizontal, decentralized, politically activist Church in Latin America has met with strong opposition--especially from the Vatican and the U.S. government. The reasons for the U.S. government's fear of these Christian base communities has been explained. The Vatican's fear is the erosion of a hierarchical Church that speaks in a united voice--albeit vertically, from the Vatican down. (Lernoux, 1984) Thus Pope John

Paul II in his trips to Central and South America has attempted to coopt the language of liberation theology, while criticizing what he sees as a Marxist analysis used by liberation theologians, and, above all else, stressing to the Latin American bishops their need to make certain the base communities work within the established Church hierarchy. From Pope John Paul II's perspective the 'base' in the communities must refer to their base in the institutional Church. (Kelly, 1984) To liberation theologians the 'base' refers to the process whereby the Church reaches out to the poor with the Gospel message and is in turn evangelized. (Kelly, 1984)

Pope John Paul II and other traditionalist theologians, in arguing against secularism, materialism, atheism, and class conflict argue that the Church must evangelize in order to humanize. (Kelly, 1984)

Heading the Vatican's attack on liberation theology is Cardinal Lopez Trujillo of Colombia, secretary-general of the Latin American Episcopal Conference (CELAM), Cardinal Joseph Ratzinger of the Vatican, and Belgian Jesuit Roger Vekemans, who remains one of the most influential opponents of liberation theology in Latin America.

Liberation theologians argue that the Church must be humanized BEFORE it can evangelize. They further argue that traditional theology tends to isolate itself from the social conditions and concrete situations of the poor. It tends to understand spiritual as something outside the material world of humanity. Liberation theologians feel that the Church in Central and South America is being challenged to become victims WITH the oppressed, to get involved with life and take part in the process of humanization that is needed. It is for this reason they say the Church must humanize to evangelize. (Kelly, 1984)

NICARAGUA AND THE CHURCH

Understanding the meaning of liberation theology and the struggle over its social movement is important for any meaningful understanding of present-day Nicaragua. In that country the Catholic Church is deeply divided, with the traditional hierarchy under the leadership of Cardinal Miguel Obando y Bravo (strongly supported by Pope John Paul II and the U.S. government) strongly opposing the Sandinistas. The "popular" Church in Nicaragua, Catholics supporting liberation theology through the Christian base communities, works closely with the Sandinista led government and is very supportive of the revolution.

Shortly after the triumph of the revolution the Nicaragua bishops in November 1979, issued a joint letter of support:

> Any social program that guarantees that the country's wealth and resources will be used for the common good, and that improves the quality of life by satisfying the basic needs of all the people, seems to us to be a just program. If socialism means that the injustice and traditional inequalities between the cities and the country and between the remuneration for intellectuals and manual labor will be progressively reduced, and if it means the participation of the worker in the fruit of his labor overcoming economic alienation then there is nothing in Christianity that is at odds with this process ... If socialism implies that power is to be exercised by the majority and increasingly shared with the organized community so that power is actually transferred

> to the popular classes, then it should meet nothing in our faith but encouragement and support. (Mac Eoin, 1983)

In short, the Church hierarchy, in 1979, supported the Sandinistas. In 1980, Nicaraguan bishops and Church leaders were put through a "process of reorientation" by theologians under the direction of Cardinal Lopez Trujillo. (Mac Eoin, 1983) Speaking about threats to the authority of bishops; the fear of a simpler, horizontal, democratic Church; and, concerns over Marxist concepts in liberation theology the Church hierarchy "persuaded" the Archbishop of Managua, Miguel Obando y Bravo to change his tune. By 1981, Obando was warning that "the revolution was falling into a 'Cuban model'; that the popular Church risked a split because the Catholic priests holding ministerial positions in the Sandinista government remained deaf to the call of the Vatican Council which explicitly urged them 'to assume a politically neutral attitude'; and, that the popular Church was tied to Sandinista ideology and married to the revolution." (Mac Eoin, 1983) The past year has witnessed a major effort by Obando and the traditionalist Church hierarchy to transfer priests and nuns who are living liberation theology, i.e., who are politically active supporters of the Sandinistas. Several have been completely removed from any pastoral activities with the poor.

Particularly disturbing to the Reagan Administration and Pope John Paul II is the fact that four influential Catholic priests joined the Nicaraguan government (following the revolution in

1979). Father Miguel D'Escoto (Maryknoll), Minister of External Affairs; Father Ernesto Cardenal (Trappist), Minister of Culture; Father Fernando Cardenal (Jesuit), head of the literacy campaign and currently Minister of Education; and, Father Edgar Parrales (diocesan) former Minister of Social Welfare and present Ambassador to the Organization of American States.

The Reagan administration has taken steps to establish closer ties to the Vatican than any other President in U.S. history. A U.S. Ambassador has been appointed to the Vatican, as President Reagan established diplomatic relations with the Vatican in 1984. This action marks the first time since 1867 that the United States and the Vatican have had full diplomatic ties (NATIONAL CATHOLIC REPORTER, May 24, 1985).

In 1981, the Vatican announced that the four priests in government were being suspended from their priestly functions (although they remained in their orders). No serious theological objections were brought against them as canon law clearly states there are "emergency situations in which priests could accept a political leadership role because there was no one else competent." The four priests were neither in heresy nor schism.

The real reason they were supposed to leave their government posts was political. It was difficult for the Reagan administration to point to the Nicaraguan government as a hard line Marxist-Leninist state when four Catholic priests served in such prominent positions. The NATIONAL CATHOLIC REPORTER's Vatican Affairs Writer, Peter Hebblethwaite wrote that it was "too much of a coincidence that the illegitimate mining of Nicaraguan ports should happen at the same time as Cardinal Ratzinger's denunciation of liberation theology in Rome, and President Reagan's anti-liberation theology speech at Santa Fe, New Mexico (which Hebblethwaite states could have been written in Ratzinger's office).

Father Fernando Cardenal often stated that the importance of the Nicaraguan experiment was that, for the first time in Latin American history, a people's revolution had been carried out WITH Christians rather than against them. (Hebblethwaite, 1984) This was liberation theology in practice and, according to Cardenal, the Church could only gain from it. The question Cardenal asked was "Would it be Christian to order Christians out of the revolution?" Pope John Paul II, in 1984, answered Cardenal by forcing him to leave the Jesuits. Fernando Cardenal wrote: "From my vantage point, the political stance of the Vatican toward Nicaragua coincides with that of President Reagan. With my withdrawal, they are training to delegitimize the revolutionary process." (Cardenal, 1985) Fernando Cardenal continues as Minister of Education and the other three priests continue in their government positions and as members of their religious orders.

During 1984 Archbishop Obando y Bravo, according to reports in the NATIONAL CATHOLIC REPORTER was engaged in clandestine efforts to solicit financial support in New York City, thus calling into question the neutral political role of several lay organizations in Nicaragua that are under his control. (Hedges, 1984)

Four of the Archbishop's principal financial supporters have been, according to the NCR, repeatedly linked with CIA operations and anticommunist Church organizations in Latin America in the past. These contributors are: the U.S. Agency for International Development, W.R. Grace, Misereor and Adventiat.

The Archbishop denied his programs have a political agenda, yet he has consistently denied funding or support to church groups sympathetic to the Sandinistas. (Hedges, 1984)

W.R. Grace, with vast investments in Latin America, founded the American Institute for Free Labor Development (AIFLD) and, for some time, Grace Chairman Peter Grace headed it. AIFLD was created in 1962 with financial help from AID, the U.S. State Department, W.R. Grace, ITT, Exxon, Shell, Kennecott, Anaconda, American Smelting and Refining, IBM, Koppers, Gillette and 85 other large corporations with interests in the region. The Institute, in the words of Peter Grace, "teaches workers to increase their company's business." It has become the most effective means for replacing independent labor unions with dummy labor organizations loyal to U.S. interests. (Hedges, 1984)

For example, AIFLD unions in El Salvador now constitute President Jose Napoleon Duarte's base of support. When U.S. Marines invaded the Dominican Republic in 1965, the AIFLD union was the only one to welcome their arrival. And, the AIFLD's National

Workers Confederation was once the chief labor voice for Chile's military junta. (Hedges, 1984)

Misereor and Adveniat are West German organizations through which the West German Catholic Church funnels money into Nicaragua and the other countries of Central America. Adveniat, along with AID, has long been a major supporter of the work of Belgian Jesuit Father Roger Vekemans.

Also, according to an April, 1985 report issued by the bicameral Arms Control and Foreign Policy Caucus entitled "Who are the Contras," three U.S. based religious groups are among the more prominent groups providing financial assistance to the contras. The religious groups named are the 900 year old Catholic Knights of Malta, the Christian Broadcasting Network's "Operation Blessing," and the Reverand Sun Myung Moon's Unification church-backed International Relief Friendship Foundation. (NATIONAL CATHOLIC REPORTER, May 17, 1985)

The strategy of Archbishop Obando y Bravo is to form "lay communities" modeled after liberation theology's Christian based communities. The study guides used by these groups are produced in Europe, written by traditionalist European church leaders. The lay organizations of Managua's archbishop have received strong support from the Vatican. The emphasis in these groups is upon adherence to hierarchial authority, both within the Church and family. They also insist upon the separation of political leaders and religion, although the leaders of these "nonpolitical" organizations are trained to speak out against the "Marxist ideology of the popular church." (Hedges, 1984) Pope John Paul II's plea is for a politically "neutral" church. To the believers in liberation theology in Central America this position is viewed as hypocrisy. The oppressed of Central America are now conscious of the fact that the Church in that region has always taken sides- -it has never been neutral. Historically the side the Church chose to support was that of the rich. Liberation theology argues that the plea is not that the Church should take sides for the first time but simply that it should CHANGE sides. The liberation theologians' answer to Pope John Paul II's argument that they are promoting class conflict which is Marxist and unChristian, is to say that while it is true God loves both the just and the unjust, his love for the oppressor is revealed in his concern for righteousness, WHICH INVOLVES HIS IDENTIFICATION WITH THE OPPRESSED, because only after the oppressed are liberated can the oppressor know and experience liberation. As Father Gustavo Gutierrez writes: "one cannot be FOR the poor and oppressed if one is not AGAINST all that gives rise to man's exploitation by man." (Lernoux, 1980)

Even with its enormous power and wealth, the Vatican's efforts to "win the hearts and minds" of Nicaraguan (and all the oppressed of Latin America) people is predestined to failure. Conscientization has gone too far. The oppressed are not going to be convinced by traditional hierarchical authority, that is, a Church which speaks TO and FOR them. Efforts by the U.S. government to work with the Vatican (traditional Church) places the

U.S. once again on the wrong side of the conflict in Nicaragua and Latin America. The reason the horizontal Church of liberation theology will ultimately triumph is that it uses a process which enables and empowers the oppressed to become the artisans of their own liberation, making their voice heard directly—without intermediaries. This is the voice of the people themselves in the process of self-liberation.

President Reagan recently proposed that the Nicaraguan government negotiate with the contras at meetings in which the Catholic hierarchy would serve as the arbitrator. Such a proposal is great for domestic politics in the U.S., but any informed observer knows that the Catholic Church is not a neutral party in Nicaragua. The hierarchical church is conducting a highly partisan and overt campaign to undermine the legitimacy of the Sandinista led government. This serves as yet another example to illustrate the fact that the Reagan administration is not seriously interested in a negotiated settlement in Central America. Pope John Paul II's opposition to liberation theology and the support the Sandinistas have received from "liberation" priests and nuns was evident in the elevation of Archbishop Miguel Obando y Bravo to Cardinal on May 25, 1985. (Koo, 1985)

SUMMARY

The tragic aspect of this struggle is that the United States is refusing to recognize that the opportunity to implement an economic program based upon models of horizontal interdependence and self-reliant development is present in Nicaragua and Latin America today. By this I mean that the U.S. could approve economic programs which would work with and through existing Christian based communities--comunidades de base. The U.S., in supporting economic programs designed BY the oppressed within these base communities could promote self-reliant development and a grass-roots democracy that is participatory in a meaningful sense. Unfortunately, given U.S. ideology in foreign policy and its absolute belief in corporate capitalist economic doctrine this golden opportunity will remain, for the foreseeable future, a missed opportunity.

Central Americans' cultural right to empowerment through the creation of self-reliant decision-making processes in search of indigenous solutions to the structural or institutional violence which has been at the core of the oppression in the region, is a right the United States' government has never seriously considered exporting.

CHAPTER 5

PROMOTING REPRESSION

The Bipartisan Commission Report accepts a long held U.S. myth about support for police/military organizations in Central America. The myth is that through U.S. police training and military assistance programs the United States can create police/military forces in Central America that are professional, apolitical, civil action oriented, pro-democratic and anti-communist.

First of all, it is not possible to be both apolitical and anti-communist. Secondly, and most importantly, the simple fact is, that the more "professional" training the U.S. has given Central American police/military forces the greater the abuses of power and human rights have been--that is, increased training has actually increased support for anti-democratic forces in the region.

According to the Bipartisan Commission Report a major obstacle to the effective pursuit of anti-guerrilla strategy is a provision of current U.S. law under which no assistance can be provided to foreign law enforcement agencies. The Report states that this law "dates back to a previous period WHEN IT WAS BELIEVED THAT SUCH AID WAS SOMETIMES HELPING GROUPS GUILTY OF HUMAN RIGHTS ABUSES." (Report p. 96) The Commission then states, "The blanket legal prohibition against the provision of training and aid to police organizations has the paradoxical effect, in certain cases, of inhibiting our efforts to improve human rights performance." (Report, p. 96) For example:

While it is now understood in the Salvadoran armed forces
that human rights violations endanger the flow of U.S.
assistance in the police organizations THERE IS NO
TRAINING TO PROFESSIONALIZE AND HUMANIZE OPERATIONS. And
in Costa Rica where the police alone provide that
country's security, we (U.S.) are PREVENTED FROM HELPING
THAT DEMOCRACY DEFEND ITSELF IN EVEN THE MOST RUDIMENTARY
FASHION. (Report, pp. 96-97)

The recommendation of the Bipartisan Commission was,
therefore, to suggest that Congress examine this question
thoroughly and consider whether Section 660 of the Foreign
Assistance Act should be amended so as to permit "under carefully
defined conditions" the allocation of funds to the training and
support of law enforcement agencies in Central America. The
concern of the Bipartisan Commission over the inability of the U.S.
to overtly assist Costa Rican police units found a sympathetic ear
in the U.S. Congress. Section 711 of the 1985 Foreign Assistance
Act, written specifically to justify U.S. action in Costa Rica,
allows the United States "to train police forces in any country
with no human rights violations, a standing army and a long-
standing democratic tradition". (Golphin, 1985). As a result, in
May, 1985, twenty U.S. Green Berets (members of the U.S. Army
Special Forces) arrived in Costa Rica to train the 700 member Costa
Rican civil guard--the national police force--in counterinsurgency
techniques. (Golphin, 1985)

Any present or future U.S. program to "professionalize and
humanize" Central American police/military forces will continue to
be viewed with suspicion by the oppressed given the historical role
of the United States in the organization, training and supplying
of forces of internal repression in their homelands. Once again

the Bipartisan Commission Report has engaged in the obfuscation of history.   The   United   States   government   simply   refuses   to acknowledge the historical reality of Central America.

HISTORY AND REPRESSION

The United States first became involved in the supply of repressive technology to Third World police departments in the early 1960s.   The catalyst was, as in the Alliance for Progress, Fidel Castro and the Cuban revolution. President John F. Kennedy's strategists argued for a policy of "counterinsurgency," stating that the police in areas such as Central America, constituted the first line of defense against insurgency in the region.

Kennedy proposed supplementing military aid funds with direct assistance to civil security forces. The result was the creation of the Office of Public Safety, in 1962. The agency remained in existence until 1974. During this period the OPS provided training to an estimated one million foreign policemen and funneled some $325 million worth of arms and riot gear to selected Third World Countries. (Klare, Arnson, 1981)

Local police forces were viewed as the key to a successful counterinsurgency program for three reasons: (1) police are regularly interspersed among the population and, thus, were considered well-placed to detect and neutralize anti-government organizations while they are still small and vulnerable; (2) police can employ violence selectively against individual dissidents, while the military tended to use force indiscriminately against whole communities or neighborhoods, thus alienating the population at large; (3) the Vietnam experience, according to General Maxwell D. Taylor and Under Secretary of State U. Alexis Johnson (1971) illustrated the need for the U.S. to develop a policy of "preventive medicine." Effective policing is preventive medicine in that it can detect and suppress dissident organizations in their early stages of development, preventing the outbreak of full-scale insurgency, thus precluding the need for military intervention.

The police units that most readily fit the preventive medicine model are, naturally, intelligence and surveillance units, the special branch or political police, riot squads, and paramilitary commando units or S.W.A.T. (Special Weapons and Tactics) teams.

The Office of Public Safety aided foreign police agencies in three ways: (1) by making direct grants of police hardware (revolvers, shotguns, rifles, tear gas grenades, riot sticks, helmets, patrol cars, communications gear, computers, etc.); (2) by providing advanced training to foreign police officials; and, (3) by sending "Public Safety Advisers" to foreign police headquarters to provide training, advice, and technical support. (Klare, Arnson, 1981)

Advanced training for foreign police officers in the United States took place at the International Police Academy in Washington, D.C. Special training was provided in subjects such as: prison design and management (at Southern Illinois University); police records management (at the FBI Academy); maritime law enforcement (at the U.S. Coast Guard Academy); and, in the design and manufacture of homemade bombs and assassination devices (at a CIA-staffed school at the Border Patrol Academy in Los Fresnos, Texas). (Klare, Arnson, 1981)

The foreign police trainees were later so overtly involved in internal repression of dissent in countries with right-wing dictators (e.g., Brazil, Argentina, Chile, Uruguay and Paraguay) that Congress began to dismantle the OPS in 1973. Under the Foreign Assistance Act of 1973, OPS was prohibited from entering into any new police training programs abroad, and a year later Congress voted to abolish the Public Safety program altogether. On July 1, 1975 when Section 660 of the Foreign Assistance Act of 1974 took effect, it became illegal to use aid funds "to provide training or advice, or provide financial support, for police, prisons or other law enforcement forces for any foreign governments..." (Klare, Arnson, 1981) This has been amended, as stated previously, by Section 711 of the 1985 Foreign Assistance Act. However, the fact is that such training never ceased as a result of the 1974 Congressional action.

THE TRAINING CONTINUES

The dissolution of has not resulted in the termination of support for foreign police forces. The U.S. government, through the State Departments' International Narcotics Control Program (INC) and the Justice Departments' Drug Enforcement Agency (DEA), continues to provide equipment, training and advisers to the same police units it previously aided through OPS. The narcotics program, as did OPS, stresses the development of infrastructural elements: training, communications, intelligence, surveillance and mobility. INC has specialized in developing the intelligence gathering and sharing capabilities of Central American and other Third World nations.

Theoretically, equipment provided under INC programs can only be supplied to professional anti-drug units. However, a GAO report to Congress in 1976 revealed that it was not uncommon for foreign governments to arbitrarily label regular police units as narcotic squads in order to qualify for INC grants. (Klare, Arnson, 1981) Also, there is no effective monitoring system to insure that equipment given to narcotics units is not diverted for other purposes. Computer systems designed for intelligence networks can obviously be used by the political police as well as narcotics units. In short, the United States began a program of organizing, training and supplying repression in Central America in 1962 and continues this program today, albeit, under different agencies. What was overt aid to foreign police forces from 1962-74 has become more covert. But the result is the same.

In accordance with the national security doctrine of the U.S., direct grants of arms and equipment has been given through the Military Assistance Program (MAP), while training of foreign military personnel is done through the International Military Education and Training Program (IMET). During the 1960s, MAP grants to Latin America included large quantities of anti-guerilla hardware: helicopters, cross-country vehicles, surveillance gear, etc. In 1967, then Secretary of Defense Robert McNamara explained the MAP program in Latin America "will provide no tanks, artillery, fighter aircraft or combat ships. The emphasis is on vehicles and helicopters for international mobility and communications equipment for better coordination of incountry security efforts." (Klare, Arnson, 1981)

MAP aid peaked at $4.2 billion in 1973 as MAP aid came to be viewed by many in Congress as both a drain on the U.S. economy and itself as invitation to more Vietnams. Congress voted ultimately to abolish the MAP program, although permitting continued aid to a few "favored" countries which house U.S. bases or otherwise support U.S. military operations. As a result MAP appropriations declined from $4.2 billion in 1973 to $265 million in 1976. They remained at that level until Reagan took office and his Administration immediately asked for an additional $100 million in MAP funds to be used at its discretion in international emergencies. (Klare, Arnson, 1981)

The Executive branch of government has succeeded in circumventing the Congressional abolishment of MAP by greatly increasing military sales--both for cash and credit and to preserve the training and advisory elements of MAP by financing them separately under the IMET program (International Military Education and Training Program). IMET falls under Section 541 of the Foreign Assistance Act, which gives the Department of Defense authorization to furnish "military education and training to military and RELATED CIVILIAN PERSONNEL of foreign countries," under terms and conditions established by the President.

IMET training involves both military (e.g., tank maneuvers, infantry operations, amphibious warfare, etc.) and internal security instruction in subjects of particular relevance to counterinsurgency and anti-dissident operations (e.g. urban counterinsurgency, intelligence interrogation, civil disturbance, etc.).

The three major ways IMET supports anti-dissident operations are: (1) training military officers who are then transferred to police duties; (2) training military units which perform police functions on a "contingency" basis; and, (3) continuing to supply and train military forces even when countries are under martial law. (Klare, Arnson, 1981)

Arms may also be obtained through the Foreign Military Sales (FMS) program and the Commercial Sales (CS) program. FMS sales are negotiated by the U.S. government and typically involve major weapons systems used by the U.S. arms firms and usually involve light weapons and combat-support equipment (e.g. pistols, revolvers, tear-gas grenades, chemical "MACE", armored cars, etc.).

Under the Arms Export and Control Act of 1976, any firm wishing to export an item on the U.S. Munitions List through CS channels must first apply for an export license from the Office of Munitions Control in the Department of State as these sales are, in theory, subject to human rights standards applied to FMS exports. However, unless transactions exceed $1 million, they are not even reported to Congress. The Reagan Administration has, in addition, adopted a generally permissive attitude towards CS sales. (Klare, Arnson, 1981)

CS sales are important as these are weapons intended specifically for civil security purposes. Sale of internal

security hardware to the police and security forces of
authoritarian regimes clearly represent a form of U.S. involvement
in repression abroad. In some instances these weapons have been
used in the torture, assassination, incarceration and disappearance
of political dissidents. In Central America there are clear
examples of how U.S. programs designed to professionalize
police/military forces have assisted in creating a climate of
terror.

EL SALVADOR

The landmark event in the formation of the national security
apparatus in El Salvador and the rest of Central America was the
Declaration of San Jose, issued on March 19, 1963, at the
conclusion of a meeting proclaimed: "Communism is the chief
obstacle to economic development of the Central American region."
(Nairn, 1984)

The Declaration of San Jose triggered a series of follow-up
meetings among Central American ministers of the interior, who held
jurisdiction over police and internal security. These meetings--
organized and run by the U.S. State Department with assistance from
the CIA, AID, the U.S. Customs Bureau, the Immigration Service and
the U.S. Justice Department--"were designed to develop ways of
dealing with subversion," according to William Bowdler, who
represented the State Department at the sessions. (Nairn, 1984)

For El Salvador, Washington assigned a central role to General
Jose Alberto Medrano. Gen. Medrano stated in an interview with

journalist Allan Nairn, "ORDEN and ANSESAL grew out of the State Department, the CIA and the Green Berets during the time of Kennedy." (Nairn, 1984)

ORDEN is the rural paramilitary and intelligence network described by Amnesty International as a movement designed "to use clandestine terror against government opponents." Out of ORDEN grew the notorious MANO BLANCO, the White Hand, which former U.S. ambassador to El Salvador, Raul H. Castro, has called "nothing less than the birth of the death squads." (Nairn, 1984)

ANSESAL, the Salvadoran National Security Agency, gathers files on Salvadoran dissidents. The U.S. supplied ANSESAL with electronic, photographic and personal surveillance of individuals who were later assassinated by Death Squads. Colonel Nicolas Carranza, then director of the Salvadoran Treasury Police, told Allan Nairn in early 1984, that such intelligence gathering by U.S. agencies "continues to this day." According to General Medrano, "The State Department and AID's Public Safety office in El Salvador had administrative responsibility for establishing the ANSESAL network, but the substantive day-to-day intelligence work was coordinated by the CIA." Medrano admitted to Nairn that he was on the CIA payroll. (Nairn 1984)

ORDEN had the dual mission of teaching anti-communism and gathering information on individuals deemed suspicious. Medrano describes how dissidents were discovered:

> You discover the Communist by the way he talks. Generally he speaks against Yankee imperialism, he speaks against the oligarchy, he speaks against military men... In this revolutionary war, the enemy comes from our people. They don't have the rights of Geneva. They are

> traitors to the country. What can the troops do? When
> they find them they kill them. (Nairn, 1984)

Between October 1979 and January 1984 the Salvadoran military and rightwing terrorists killed at least 40,000 civilians in an effort to stop the spreading revolution. Such a bloodbath is equivalent to the U.S. government killing more than 1.5 million of the U.S. population. Fifty years earlier the Salvadoran military killed a similar number of peasants for similar reasons. (Bonner, 1984)

The close relationship between Salvadoran security forces and the U.S. government continues to this day. Reporter William R. Long, of the Los Angeles TIMES, wrote in March, 1985, that "Salvadoran authorities are creating an urban paramilitary police unit to fight increased attempts by leftist rebels to bring the guerrilla war to the capital." According to Long the unit is to be trained by U.S. military experts and will be part of the National Treasury Police (an agency linked in the past to rightist death squads). The U.S. Congress has barred foreign aid for police training, but a U.S. embassy spokesman, Don Hamilton, said "the restriction did not apply in this case because the Treasury Police unit would have NO REGULAR LINE LAW ENFORCEMENT RESPONSIBILITY. The unit would report to the army chief of staff." (Long, 1985)

The Bipartisan Commission Report requests that Congress alter the law so the U.S. can once again overtly train and supply Central American police forces in order to "professionalize and humanize" them. Logically one would have to conclude that to humanize Salvadoran internal security police/military forces the United

States government would first have to humanize itself. The Salvadorans have been very good students.

GUATEMALA

Between 1954 and 1983, 80,000 Guatemalans died violently, almost all at the hands of government forces. (Collins, 1983) At the height of one bloody repression in 1971, twenty-five U.S. officers and seven former U.S. policemen worked with the Guatemalan police/military forces. Colonel Carlos Arana Osorio, who had been selected by the military to win the 1970 presidential elections, stated that year that he would eliminate all guerrillas even "if it is necessary to turn the country into a cemetery." (La Feber, 1983) So thereafter, Arana's troops and such rightwing vigilante groups as MANO, raided the National University, assassinated three law professors, arrested 1,600 and murdered as many as 1,000 people in twelve weeks. In 1980 Guatemala's civilian vice-president resigned in protest remarking that "there are no political prisoners in Guatemala, just political assassinations." (La Feber, 1983)

The 1984 Amnesty International REPORT expressed concern that in Guatemala:

> the regular security and military forces, as well as paramilitary groups acting under government orders or with official complicity, continued to be responsible for massive human rights violations including large-scale torture, disappearance and extrajudicial executions. Victims included individual leaders of public opinions such as clergy, teachers and students at the Universidad de San Carlos, lawyers, doctors, trade unionists,

journalists and community workers, as well as peasants and Indians and urban poor.

Between 1978 and 1983, thirteen Catholic priests--more than in any other country in the world--were murdered by government-sponsored executioners in Guatemala. The first Cardinal in Central America, Mario Casariego (who died in 1983), was ultra-conservative. He was a close friend to three dictators--General Carlos Arana Osoris, Kjell Laugarud Garcia, and Fernando Lucas Garcia. The three referred to Cardinal Casariego as their "spiritual guide." (Day, 1983)

In 1979 a group of religious order priests met with Casariego demanding he break his silence and denounce the killing of priests. Casariego, who had a reputation for turning the names of persons involved in peace and justice groups over to government officials, told the priests at the 1979 meeting, "I told the government, if you're bad to kick you out (of Guatemala) but not to kill you." (Day, 1983).

The process of "professionalizing" the Guatemalan police/military forces began in the mid-fifties, following the CIA backed overthrow of the democratically elected Arbenz government. The early 1960s saw a rapid increase in U.S. efforts to recognize the Guatemalan army, teach political as well as military tactics, and develop a centralized communication and transport system. U.S. training to professionalize the military played a major role in the 1963 coup establishing the military dictatorship under Colonel Enrique Peralta. Evidence later surfaced that U.S. officials had encouraged the military to keep Juan Arevalo, a civilian candidate for the presidency, out of power. (La Feber, 1983)

Between 1966 and 1968 the future Guatemalan president then, Colonel Carlos Arana organized the slaughter of 8,000 Guatemalans in a counterinsurgency campaign. The U.S. government sent 1,000 Green Berets to assist Arana as advisers in this campaign. (Lernoux, 1980) According to Penny Lernoux, "U.S. pilots flew U.S. planes to drop napalm on the peasants and under the leadership of U.S. military attache, Colonel John Webber, paramilitary/groups composed of large landowners were encouraged to collaborate with the Army in hunting down subversive peasants." These groups were the forerunner of the Mano Blanca (White Hand) and Ojo por Ojo (Eye for an Eye), right wing vigilante groups consisting of off-duty police and retired military men, which, according to Amnesty International were responsible for thousands of deaths. (Lernoux, 1980)

The U.S. cannot escape responsibility for its role in creating a monster through programs designed to professionalize the Guatemalan police/military forces. What has the U.S. learned from its experience? Very little. The Reagan Administration requested U.S. military assistance to Guatemala be increased from $300,000 to $35.5 million, in his 1986 budget. (Washington POST, February 6, 1985). In addition, the Guatemalan military, with assistance from organizations such as U.S. AID is currently engaged in a "humanitarian relocation program" for Indian peasants in remote rural, jungle areas. The peasants are rounded up and forcibly moved to newly constructed "model" villages allegedly to improve their standard of living and health. In fact, it is a pacification program to combat present and future insurgency. (Millets, 1984) The hypocrisy of the U.S. in designing and supporting such a program can be illustrated in the very vocal campaigns the U.S. carried on before the world's media, attacking Sandinista efforts to relocate Miskito Indians in Nicaragua. According to the Reagan Administration this amounted to a gross violation of basic human rights. (Reagan, April 27, 1983) Little wonder the Administration remains silent on its role in, and support of, Guatemala's relocation program.

COSTA RICA

In May, 1985 officials at the State and Defense Departments announced that at the request of the Costa Rican government, twenty-four U.S. Army Special Forces advisers were to begin training four companies of the Costa Rican Civil Guard in "basic military skills." This training is being conducted to combat "Nicaraguan-trained terrorists and insurgents," according to U.S. officials. (Brinkley, 1985)

Costa Rica dismantled its army in 1949 after units participated in a civil war between the two main political parties. Since that time Costa Rica has been the most stable democracy in Central America. Many Costa Ricans argue that the absence of any force able to carry out military coups has been a major factor in keeping the country democratic. According to Joel Brinkley, a reporter for the New York TIMES, several U.S. military and diplomatic officials in the Reagan administration have been "urging the Costa Ricans to arm themselves."

In 1983, the Reagan administration gave Costa Rica $2.4 million to upgrade its two-tier, 8,000-10,000 member national police forces. The money was used to purchase such things as U.S. automatic machine pistols and antitank weapons, and 750 Costa Ricans were trained to use them. (Jones, 1985) The Administration argues such assistance is needed to help Costa Rica defend itself from internal subversion and an external attack from Nicaragua.

In 1984, the U.S. sent an additional $9.4 million for Costa Rica "security," a gift the Costa Rican government is not in a position to refuse even if it wished, as the U.S. is supporting Costa Rica economically at the rate of $1.2 million a day. This is the highest per capita U.S. economic aid program anywhere in the world. (Jones, 1985) This provides a clear illustration of the fact that the Reagan administration is more interested in overthrowing the Sandinistas in Nicaragua than in preserving democracy in Costa Rica. It would be ironic if in undermining a democratically elected government in Nicaragua, the U.S. training of Costa Rican forces led to the overthrow of democracy in Costa Rica.

COUNTERTERRORISM AID IN 1986

The Bipartisan Commission Report requested that the U.S. Congress lift the restrictive 1974 ban on the police-training program. Lifting the ban would enable the U.S. military to once again overtly train and supply Central American police forces in order to "professionalize and humanize" them.

In 1985 Congress granted a few special exceptions to allow limited help to the police in El Salvador. Under these exceptions U.S. advisers trained a Salvadoran police urban commando team, an urban counterterrorism unit of the treasury police and a special investigating unit to be used in politically sensitive crimes. (Le Moyne, 1986)

In December, 1985, Congress passed legislation ending the decade-old ban on the police training program. The Reagan administration moved swiftly. In January of 1986, U.S. military advisers began a $5 million program to train and equip the Salvadoran national police, national guard and treasury police. The training will concentrate on urban terrorism. (Le Moyne, 1986) There was strong criticism from human rights groups in the United States, but according to U.S. officials "if the United States hopes to professionalize the Salvadoran police and keep them from abusing prisoners, it must train and equip them." (Le Moyne, 1986)

Also, the Reagan administration announced in December, 1985, that it would request a total of $54 million to initiate a new counterterrorism assistance program in five Central American nations. The Administration is seeking $27 million to establish a specialized military counterterrorism program in El Salvador, Honduras, Panama, Guatemala and Costa Rica; $26 million for separate police antiterrorist training programs there; and, $1 million to protect individuals helping to prevent terrorist activities.

Democratic U.S. Senator John F. Kerry, of Massachusetts responded to the request by stating, "The fact is the death squad apparatus has not been dismantled in El Salvador. The Administration is deluding itself or deluding Congress because civilians continue to be killed by right-wing death squads although obviously at a reduced rate." (Ottaway, 1985)

An official of Americas Watch, a U.S. human rights monitoring group, told the Senate Foreign Relations Committee that death squad killings in El Salvador in the first six months of 1985 reached 81, more than double the number for the previous six months. (Ottoway, 1985)

SUMMARY

Washington's preoccupation with a military response to national security has served to reinforce the belief that in Central America all rebellion was, and is, bad by definition. The result has been the automatic defense of reactionary governments. The Bipartisan Commission Report, in its proposal to "humanize" Central America police/military forces should have recommended specific changes in the curricula of U.S. courses designed for Central American students. Course 0-47 on urban counterinsurgency operations, taught for years, at the U.S. Army School of the Americas in the Panama Canal Zone illustrates how one is to detect the presence of communist guerrillas:

1. The disappearance or movement of youths possibly indicates the recruitment to form guerrilla bands in the area. You should report

the reluctance of families of said mission
youths to speak about them.

2. The refusal of peasants to pay rents, taxes,
   or agricultural loans or any difficulty in
   collecting these will indicate the existence
   of an active insurrection that has succeeded
   in convincing the peasants of the injustices
   of the present system, and is directing or
   instigating them to disobey its precepts.

3. Hostility on the part of the local population
   to the government forces, in contrast to their
   amiable or neutral attitudes in the past. This
   can indicate a change of loyalty or of behavior
   inspired by fear, often manifested by children
   refusing to fraternize with members of the
   internal-security forces.

4. Short, unjustified, and unusual absences from
   work on the part of government employees.

5. Networks of police and informants don't provide
   the kind of reports they should. This could
   indicate that the sources of information have
   become allied with the insurgents or their
   sympathizers.

6. A growing hostility against governmental
   agencies and agencies of public order...
   (Lernoux, 1980)

Subversion, according to Course 0-47, is not limited to armed

insurrection; it can also take the form of non-violent action

similar to consciousness raising work by liberation theologists,

demonstrations, strikes and "compromised social sciences."

(Lernoux, 1980)

It should be simple to comprehend the basic truth that

repression and terror have been, and are today, being exported by

the United States to Central America. In fact, one could argue

that over the past twenty-five years repression and terror have

been the United States' chief exports to the region. Again, the

U.S. approach is "they" have a problem "we" can solve. This

approach, applied to the Central American police/military forces,

is a one way road to disaster. It is a no-win situation—everyone loses. By continuing this approach the United States remains its own worst enemy.

CHAPTER 6

PRIVATIZING FOREIGN POLICY

In 1975-76 the United States' Senate Intelligence Committee conducted a comprehensive investigation into the Central Intelligence Agency's covert operations. Known by the name of its chairperson, Senator Frank Church, the committee examined the secret "successes" as well as the public fiascoes. The Church Committee reported on efforts to assassinate foreign leaders, to overthrow democratically elected governments and to spread disinformation. It considered the effects on foreign policy as well as the implications for constitutional government. The Committee also described how the C.I.A. had come home and spied on Americans. The conclusion of the Church Committee was that the covert operations had not contributed to the national security but rather had posed a threat to American democracy.

The Church Committee noted in its final report that it had seriously considered recommending that Congress forbid such operations. But instead it proposed a series of measures, some of which were later included in the Intelligence Oversight Act of 1980, designed to insure that the C.I.A. would conduct covert operations only in "extraordinary situations" and after full consultation in the executive branch and with Congress. (Halperin, 1987)

Members of the Reagan Administration, the most ideologically rigid Administration in the Cold War period, ignored the limits imposed by Congress as a result of the Church Committee findings.

The structural vehicle used to bypass the U.S. Congress was the National Security Council, which in the Nixon-Kissinger years was turned into an operational agency for secret military operations. The evolution of the National Security Council into an operational agency, along with the national security adviser assuming the dominant role as the President's main adviser and spokesperson on foreign policy has created a structural problem that only Congressional legislation will rectify.

EVOLUTION OF THE NSC

The National Security Council was established in 1947, partly as a Republican-controlled congressional reaction to the manner in which President Roosevelt and the military chiefs had dominated policy-making during World War II.

The National Security Act established the NSC; unified the Army, Navy, and the Air Force (as separate services) under a single new Department of Defense; created the Central Intelligence Agency; and, prescribed the NCS's chief function as "advising the president with respect to the integration of domestic, foreign and military policies relating to the national security."

Beyond the statutory listings of its members--the president, vice president, and the secretaries of state and defense--THE LEGISLATION DID NOT DELEGATE ANY OPERATIONAL POWERS. Staffing arrangements were left to the discretion of the president.

Harry Truman moved quickly to establish his authority over the NSC by integrating it into the executive office of the president.

Truman was determined that the NSC be dominated by the Department of State, not the Department of Defense. President Truman used the NSC as an advisory forum to coordinate military and political responses to the North Korean challenge.

Dwight D. Eisenhower continued the policy established by Truman, using the NSC as an advisory forum, strictly under the wing of Secretary of State John Foster Dulles. Eisenhower, however, did expand the staff and responsibilities of the NSC. Especially significant was Eisenhower's creation in 1953 of the position of special assistant for national security.

Kennedy seldom used the NSC as a forum for obtaining policy advice. However, during the 1962 Cuban missile crisis, he established an ad hoc body of high-level officials called the Executive Committee of the NSC, to serve as his personal advisers for drafting alternative responses to the Soviet attempt to place missiles in Cuba.

Kennedy enhanced the role of the special assistant. Under JFK's Special Assistant, McGeorge Bundy, the NSC became the principal adviser to the president, with the responsibility of managing day-to-day national security affairs. Thus the special assistant of the NSC, under JFK, gained major influence over foreign policy at the expense of the secretary of state.

LBJ ignored the NSC as a major advisory council. He relied on the Tuesday lunch group (the secretaries of state and defense, special assistant of the NSC, director of the CIA and chairman of the Joint Chiefs) for advice and counsel on foreign affairs—especially the conduct of the Vietnam War. Although he depended heavily on McGeorge Bundy until Bundy resigned in 1966, LBJ wanted to demonstrate to the American people that he was capable of managing national security affairs himself. Thus, he replaced Bundy with Walt W. Rostow, while denying Rostow the same title as Bundy.

President Nixon, with Henry Kissinger as his special assistant for national security affairs, developed a highly formal White House-centered system of management of national security policy making and coordination. There was no doubt, under President Nixon that Kissinger displaced Secretary of State William Rogers as the chief architect of foreign policy. Eventually Rogers resigned.

The result of the Nixon-Kissinger system was to convert what had originally been a staff position, the special assistant for national security affairs, into the major operator of foreign policy (e.g., running a secret air war in Cambodia). Under Nixon and Kissinger, the NSC assumed many functions involving policy implementation and interagency coordination formerly performed by the State Department.

In 1973, Kissinger became the secretary of state, while retaining the position of special assistant for national security affairs.

The structural rivalry resurfaced again during the Carter presidency. Secretary of State Cyrus R. Vance and Zbigniew Brzezinski, the special assistant for national security affairs, were publicly at odds over who was actually the chief spokesperson for U.S. foreign policy. Vance ultimately resigned, having lost in his opposition to a military operation to try and free the hostages in Iran.

Reagan, in appointing Gen. Alexander M. Haig as secretary of state, suggested that primary responsibility for foreign policy implementation would return to the State Department. Nevertheless, due to the structural problem of the NSC versus the State Department, Haig resigned after two years over policy differences with the special assistant for national security affairs.

Haig's replacement, George Shultz, entered office determined to be the spokesman for foreign policy in the Reagan administration. Nevertheless, as the Iranian arms deal and links to the Contras have shown, the special assistant for national security affairs has held the real power in the operational arena of U.S. foreign policy.

EXCERPTS FROM THE TOWER COMMISSION REPORT:

ORGANIZING FOR NATIONAL SECURITY
Ours is a government of checks and balances, of shared power and responsibility. The Constitution places the President and the Congress in dynamic tension. They both cooperate and compete in the making of national policy.
National security is no exception. The Constitution gives both the President and the Congress an important role. The Congress is critical in formulating national policies and in marshaling the resources to carry them out. But those resources—the nation's military personnel, its diplomats, its intelligence capability—are lodged in the Executive Branch. As Chief Executive and Commander in Chief, and with broad authority in the area of foreign affairs, it is the President who is empowered to act for the nation and protect its interests.

THE REAGAN MODEL
President Reagan entered office with a strong commitment to cabinet government. His principal advisors on national security affairs were to be the Secretaries of State and Defense, and to a lesser extent the Director

of Central Intelligence. The position of National
Security Advisor was initially downgraded in both status
and access to the President. Over the next six years,
five different people held that position.

The Administration's first National Security Advisor,
Richard Allen, reported to the President through the
senior White House staff. Consequently, the N.S.C. staff
assumed a reduced role. Mr. Allen believed that the
Secretary of State has primacy in the field of foreign
policy. He viewed the job of the National Security
Advisor as that of a policy coordinator.

President Reagan initially declared that the National
Security Council would be the principal forum for
consideration of national security issues. To support
the work of the Council, President Reagan established an
interagency committee system headed by three Senior
Interagency Groups (or "SIG's"), one each for foreign
policy, defense policy, and intelligence. They were
chaired by the Secretary of State, the Secretary of
Defense, and the Director of Central Intelligence,
respectively.

Over time, the Administration's original conception of
the role of the National Security Advisor changed.
William Clark, who succeeded Richard Allen in 1982, was
a long-time associate of the President and dealt directly
with him. Robert McFarlane, who assumed the position of
national security adviser in 1983, although personally
less close to the President, continued to have direct
access to him. The same was true for OVADM John
Poindexter, who was appointed to the position in December
1985.

President Reagan appointed several additional members
to his National Security Council and allowed staff
attendance at meetings. The resultant size of the
meetings led the President to turn increasingly to a
smaller group (called the National Security Planning
Group or "N.S.P.G."). Attendance at its meetings were
more restricted but included the statutory principals of
the N.S.C. The N.S.P.G. was supported by the S.I.G.'s,
and new S.I.G.'s were occasionally created to deal with
particular issues. These were frequently chaired by the
National Security Advisor. But generally the SIG's and
many of their subsidiary groups (called Interagency
Groups or "I.G.'s") fell into disuse.

As a supplement to the normal N.S.C. process, the
Reagan Administration adopted comprehensive procedures
for covert actions. These are contained in a classified
document, NSDD-159, establishing the process for
deciding, implementing, monitoring, and reviewing covert
activities.

N.S.C. STAFF AND SUPPORT FOR THE CONTRAS
Inquiry into the arms sale to Iran and the possible
diversion of funds to the contras disclosed evidence of

substantial N.S.C. staff involvement in a related area:
private support for the contras during the period that
support from the U.S. Government was either banned or
restricted by Congress.

There are similarities in the two cases. Indeed, the
N.S.C. staff's role in support for the contras set the
stage for its subsequent role in the Iran initiative.
In both, Lt Col North, with the acquiescence of the
national security adviser, was deeply involved in the
operational details of a covert program. He relied
heavily on private U.S. citizens and foreigners to carry
out key operational tasks. Some of the same individuals
were involved in both. When Israeli plans for the
November HAWK shipment began to unravel, Lt Col North
turned to the private network that was already in place
to run the contra support operation. This network, under
the direction of Mr. Secord, undertook increasing
responsibility for the Iran initiative. Neither program
was subjected to rigorous and periodic interagency
overview. In neither case was Congress informed. In the
case of contra support, Congress may have been actively
misled.

The board had neither the time nor the resources to
conduct a full inquiry into the role of the N.S.C. staff
in the support of the contras that was commensurate with
its work on the Iran arms sales. As a consequence, the
evidence assembled by the board was somewhat anecdotal
and disconnected.

THE BID FOR PRIVATE FUNDING
Because of Congressional restrictions, the Executive
branch turned to private sources to sustain the contras
militarily. In 1985 and 1986, Mr. McFarlane and the NSC
staff repeatedly denied any direct involvement in efforts
to obtain funds from these sources. Yet evidence before
the board suggests that Lt Col North was well aware of
these efforts and played a role in coordinating them.
The extent of that role remains unclear.

In a memorandum to Mr. McFarlane dated April 11, 1985,
Lt Col North expressed concern that remaining contra
funds would soon be insufficient. He advised that
efforts be made to seek $15 to $20 million in additional
funds from the current donors which will "allow the force
to grow to 30-35,000." The exact purpose to which these
private funds were to be put was unambiguous. A number
of memoranda from Lt Col North make clear that the funds
were for munitions and lethal aid.

Asked by the board about the source of such funds, Mr.
McFarlane provided a written response that indicated that
"without solicitation" a foreign official offered $1
million a month from what he described as "personal
funds." At Mr. McFarlane's request, Lt Col North

provided the numbers of a contra bank account in Miami. Mr. McFarlane wrote that in 1985, the foreign official doubled his contribution to $2 million a month, a fact confirmed by two other U.S. officials.

Contributions appear to have been channeled through a series of nonprofit organizations that Lt Col North apparently had a hand in organizing. A diagram found in Lt Col North's safe links some of these organizations to bank accounts controlled by Richard Secord and others known to be involved in purchasing and shipping arms to the contras.

Other documents and evidence suggest that private contributions for the contras were eventually funneled into "Project Democracy," a term apparently used by Lt Col North to describe a network of secret bank accounts and individuals involved in contra resupply and other activities. In a message to VADM Poindexter dated July 15, 1986, Lt Col North described "Project Democracy" assets as worth over $4.5 million. They included six aircraft, warehouses, supplies, maintenance facilities, ships, boats, leased houses, vehicles, ordinance, munitions, communications equipment and a 6,520-foot runway. The runway was in fact a secret airfield in Costa Rica. Lt Col North indicated in a memorandum dated Sept. 30, 1986, that the airfield was used for direct resupply of the contras from July 1985 to February 1986, and thereafter as the primary abort base for damaged aircraft.

COORDINATING THE RESUPPLY OPERATION

The C.I.A. headquarters instructed its field stations to "cease and desist" with action which can be construed to be providing any type of support, either direct or indirect, to the various entities with whom we dealt under the program. The chief of the C.I.A. Central American Task Force added that in other respects the interagency process on Central America was in disarray in October 1984 and that "it was Ollie North who then moved into that void and was the focal point for the Administration on Central American policy until fall 1985."

As early as April 1985, Lt Col North maintained detailed records of expenditures for contra military equipment, supplies and operations. On April 11, 1985, Lt Col North sent a memorandum to Mr. McFarlane describing two sealifts and two airlifts" as of April 9, 1985." The memorandum set out the kind of munitions purchased, the quantity, and in some instances the cost. Lt Col North also noted that from July 1984 to April 9, 1985: "$17,145,594 has been expended for arms, munitions, combat operations and support activities."

Evidence suggests that at least by November 1985 Lt Col North had assumed a direct operational role, coordinating logistical arrangements to ship privately purchased arms to the contras. In a note to Poindexter on November 22, 1985, he described a prospective delivery as "our first direct flight [of ammo] to the resistance field [in] Nicaragua." This shipment was delayed when Mr. Secord was asked to use the aircraft instead to deliver the 18 HAWK missiles to Iran in November 1985.

In 1986, North established a private secure communications network. North received 15 encryption devices from the National Security Agency from January to March 1986, provided in support of his counterterrorist activities. One was provided to Mr. Secord and another, through a private citizen, to a C.I.A. field officer posted in Central America. Through this mechanism, North coordinated the resupply of the contras with military equipment apparently purchased with funds provided by the network of private benefactors. The messages to Lt Col North from Mr. Secord and the C.I.A. officer: (a) asked him to direct where and when to make contra munitions drops; (b) informed him of arms requirements; and (c) apprised him of payments, balances and deficits.

At least nine arms shipments were coordinated through this channel from March through June, 1986. The C.I.A. field officer in Costa Rica outlined his involvement in the resupply network and described the shipments: "This was all lethal. Benefactors only sent lethal stuff."

THE TOWER COMMISSION'S OVERSIGHT

In April, 1987, after five months of maneuver and study, someone admitted criminal guilt for arming the contras at a time when Congress prohibited it. Carl Channell, a flourishing fund raiser for ultra-conservative causes, confessed to misusing a tax-exempt organization as a conduit for arms and has identified Lt Col Oliver North, formerly of the National Security staff, as a fellow conspirator.

It has been obvious for some time that the Iran-contra scandal involved political offenses hatched in the White House. President Reagan condoned, perhaps also directed, paying ransom to Iran for hostages in Lebanon. That broke his political word and shattered public trust.

President Reagan bitterly disagreed with the Congressional ban on contra funding and let White House opposition, and secret funding, reach intolerable lengths. Colonel North and Carl Channell, teaming up to raise millions for the National Endowment for the Preservation of Liberty, took big donors into the Oval Office to receive Mr. Reagan's personal thanks. North has written: "The President obviously knows why he has been meeting with several select people to thank them for their 'support for Democracy' in Central America." (New York TIMES, May 1, 1987) The White House press secretary said on April 30, 1987 that the President was thanking the donors for sponsoring pro-Administration "support the contra funding" television advertisements (which were heavily used in the Congressional Districts of Congressmen who were key swing votes in the House of Representatives).

Mr. Reagan's presidency has shown once again that covert operations undertaken on White House authority alone risk more than they can deliver. Such actions presuppose a small, secret action group around the president, which may not fully consider dissenting views and skeptical analysis, and some of whose members may have a career or ideological stake in a proposed operation.

Even mere notification of Congressional committees would increase the opportunity for such dissent and analysis by critics with no personal commitment to the operation. Members of the Congress generally have a better sense of public acceptability, if any, of a covert operation, should it become public, than the bureaucrats, spooks and Presidential aides who conceived it.

If notification of Congress results in a leak to the public, the leaker most probably considers the operation unwarranted to unworkable or both, and he or she may well be right. President John Kennedy came to wish that press leaks had saved him from the Bay of Pigs debacle.

When a covert operation is exposed, as is all too likely in this age of information and communication, it can damage the public's confidence in a President's judgment. And since a covert operation will almost always force a President and his spokespersons to lie, its exposure erodes the public's trust in his integrity.

Public trust in a President's good judgment and integrity is an essential ingredient in his ability to lead. But that is precisely what he puts at risk when he turns to secrecy and covert operations to achieve aims he cannot share with the nation.

Beyond good judgment, integrity and trust in the President and his advisers, the structure must be analyzed as well. In the case of the Iran-contra scandal, the culprit appears to be the National Security Council. The Tower Commission Report let this issue get away. The Commission missed a great opportunity to recommend a fundamental overhaul of what the Report called the "N.S.C. System."

The Commission recommended that "no substantive change be made in the provisions of the National Security Act (of 1947) dealing with the structure and operation of the N.S.C. System"; that "overprescription" as to its "structures and processes" and "legislative restriction" as to its size would "destroy the system or render it ineffective."

Also, on the issue of accountability for the national security adviser in the form of Senate confirmation, the Tower Commission let the White House safely off the hook. As to the national security adviser or the N.S.C. staff being involved in covert operations, the Commission recommended that "each Administration formulate precise procedures for a restricted consideration of cover action and, that once formulated, those procedures be strictly adhered to."

The "president and adviser aberration" line neatly compartmentalizes the affair, which means there is no need to go to deeper, systemic issues. However, it should be clear by now that Presidential cover action, bypassing the Congress, breeds intemperate policy and chaos, from Cuba, to Vietnam, to Iran, Central America, and Soviet-American relations.

What is the point of having a Secretary of State if national security advisers such as McGeorge Bundy, Walt Rostow, Henry A. Kissinger (in his first Nixon administration incarnation) and Zbigniew Brzezinski, let alone N.S.C. subalterns like Lt Col Oliver North can, again and again, administration after administration, seize effective control of foreign policy and operations? (Janeway, 1987)

The problem is whether foreign policy-making without accountability (as illustrated by low-intensity warfare in Central America) in the office of the national security adviser is to continue to be sanctioned, as has been the trend for the past twenty-five years. The United States needs to have a very open, public debate on the systemic issue of whether or not the office of the White House, as it is presently structured, is safe for democracy? This is the most crucial foreign policy issue facing the United States today, and, it was the Tower Commission's biggest oversight.

PRIVATIZING FOREIGN POLICY

> I believe he [Gen. John K. Singlaub] was undoubtedly sent by the Lord Almighty to help save freedom and the United States from Russian totalitarianism. Our government's not doing it yet, but with General Singlaub given the go-ahead by God and President Reagan, freedom in our country may possibly survive...
> Ellen Garwood
> U.S. Council of World Freedom
> World Anti-Communist League

The privatization of foreign policy in the Reagan administration is a part of the theory of low-intensity warfare. If the U.S. Congress does oppose the President, Administration support for private aid offers the Legislature the specter of U.S. foreign policy run by franchise. The alternative for Congress is to approve Administration requests for CIA-managed official aid.

On May 15, 1987, President Reagan stated that he was deeply involved in private efforts to aid the contras in Nicaragua, even

during a two year period when Government aid to the contras was
barred by the U.S. congress.   Indicating he was proud of this
action, President Reagan stated:

> I was kept briefed on that. As a matter of fact, I was
> very definitely involved in the decisions about support
> to the freedom fighters. It was my idea to begin with.

Asked specifically what "idea" the President was referring
to, a senior White House official said "Central American policy,
support for the contras, from the very first."   (Roberts, 1987)
Asked if the President's support for the contras covered the period
when Congress banned Government aid to the rebels, the White House
official replied, "That's correct." (Roberts, 1987)

The White House staff and the President of the United States
is bluntly stating that what the Congress intended does not matter.
If the President decides the law does not apply to him, it does not
apply to him.   This sort of reasoning stated an editorial in the
May 17, 1987 AUSTIN AMERICAN-STATESMAN, "pervades the [Reagan]
Administration, whether it is 'spinning' the ABM treaty to permit
what it does not permit or twisting the Boland Amendment to permit
what it clearly does not permit.   The law, it appears, is the law
when that is convenient, and not when it is not convenient."

As President Reagan has perceived, private aid to the contras
may be more important politically than materially.   Reagan's
prosecution of the contra proxy war (part of LIW theory) against
the Nicaraguan government has tapped a wellspring of U.S. culture:
the tradition of rugged individualism and vigilante justice. Never
absent from U.S. culture, there is, today, a surfeit of Rambo

types--lonely mavericks, tough sheriffs, "quick on the trigger and ready to take offense," full of hatred for the Soviet Union and communism and--after the pain and frustration of Vietnam--anxious to settle scores. (Mathews, 1986) The contra war against the Sandinistas offers them a second chance.

While most unofficial military aid to the contras comes through third countries (specifically, Saudi Arabia, Israel and Taiwan), domestic military support is not insignificant. General John Singlaub, the principal private figure in orchestrating the private aid drives within the United States, was the right-hand man of Lt Col Oliver North, the National Security Council official charged with implementing the Administration's private aid strategy. Although General Singlaub claims he is not on the CIA payroll, the agency, according to his own admission, does approve of his activity. Singlaub stated "I try to communicate, sometimes by telephone [with Washington]," he says, informing them, "this is what I am about to do. If you object to it, send me a signal." (Matthews, 1986) According to Singlaub there have been no orders to stop yet. In 1984-85, he boasted of raising an average of $500,000 a month (both lethal and non-lethal aid) for the contras. (TIME, May 27, 1985)

On December 21, 1982, Congress passed the first "Boland amendment" prohibiting the Department of Defense and the Central Intelligence Agency from spending funds to overthrow Nicaragua or provoke conflict between Nicaragua and Honduras. The following year, $24 million was authorized for the contras. On October 3,

1984, Congress cut off all funding for the contras and prohibited DOD, CIA, and an other agency or entity "involved in intelligence activities" from directly or indirectly supporting military operations in Nicaragua.

The 1984 prohibition was subject to conflicting interpretation. Its Congressional supporters believed that the legislation covered the activities of the NSC staff. On the other hand, VADM Poindexter received legal advice from the President's Intelligence Oversight Board that the restrictions on lethal assistance to the contras did not cover the NSC staff. The NSC staff's role in support of the contras was not in derogation of the CIA's role because CIA involvement was expressly barred by statute. (TOWER COMMISSION REPORT, 1987)

The origins of citizen support for the contra war are rooted in the proliferation of right-wing Washington organizations and lobbies that flourish in the Reagan era. An obscure group, which has since receded to the background, kicked off the idea in 1982. In September of that year Charles Moser, secretary-treasurer of Free Congress and Education Foundation, proposed creating a new committee, modeled on the existing Committee for a Free Afghanistan and the free Angola Committee, to support "anti-communist struggle in Nicaragua." On it were representatives of four long-established ultra conservative policy and research institutions: Francisco Enrique Rueda of the Free Congress Foundation; Reed Irvine, founder of Accuracy in Media and a member of the Council for the Defense of Freedom; and Lynne Francis Bouchey, then executive vice president of the Council for Inter-American Security." (Clarkson, 1984)

By 1984, however, the original concept had developed far beyond the loose association of Washington-based groups to embrace a web of ultra conservative organizations stretching across the country, working together in a hierarchy that ended in the White House.

In April 1984, President Reagan and NSC adviser, Robert McFarlane, decided to coordinate all private aid to the contras, and promptly tapped anti-communist zealot Gen. John Singlaub as the chief fund-raiser. Singlaub at this time became the right-hand man of Lt Col Oliver North. The functions of the private support network were divided into four general categories: 1) lobbying and propaganda; 2) fund-raising; 3) provision of non-lethal assistance; and 4) arms acquisition and training.

PARTIAL LIST OF KEY PRIVATE ORGANIZATIONS FUNDING CONTRAS

-- Operation Blessing, the aid and relief arm of the Christian Broadcasting Network, Inc., (CBN). It has sent millions of dollars to Nicaraguan and other Central American refugees through paramilitary and other groups with connections to the contras.

-- Friends of the Americas, a Louisiana based organization founded by a conservative Democrat serving in the state House of Representatives, Louis Jenkins. Friends of the Americas has close ties with the Misura contra faction, which is allied with the FDN, the largest contra group.

-- PRODEMCA, somewhat atypical of contra aid groups in that it was sponsored by the Reagan administration in order to enlist Cold War liberals, particularly in the AFL-CIO, in support of U.S. policy. Elie Wiesel, recent Nobel

Prize winner sits on the board which is replete with members of the Democratic Socialists of America. Albert Shanker of the American Federation of Teachers, Norman Podhoretz of COMMENTARY and Jeane Kirkpatrick are members. The White House supports PRODEMCA by way of the federally funded National Endowment for Democracy. PRODEMCA gave LA PRENSA (Nicaragua) $100,000.

-- Nicaraguan Refugee Fund, created by a fund raising arm of the FDN, and supported by President Reagan, and his close supporters, business magnates J. Peter Grace and Joseph Coors.

-- World Anti-Communist League, headed by retired Army Maj. Gen. John K. Singlaub. The league has raised and funneled millions of dollars for military aid to the contras.

-- The Air Commando Association, based in Florida, which has about 1,600 members, almost all of them retired Air Force, Army, Navy and Marine Corps pilots, medical, or special operations personnel. It conducts "humanitarian efforts in support of President Reagan's policies in Latin America."

-- Nicaraguan Patriotic Association, based in Houston, Texas, raises money and other aid for the contras and their families.

-- The Carribbean Commission, led by New Orleans physician Alton Oschner, Jr., raises funds for the contras and hosts press conferences for contra leaders in New Orleans. Dr. Oschner is also associated with Friends of the Americas and the Nicaraguan Refugee Fund.

-- International Relief Friendship Foundation and Causa International, both arms of the Unification Church, and the Nicaraguan Freedom Fund of the Washington TIMES, the Unification Church-owned newspaper.

-- Civilian-Military Assistance, the Alabama based group that sends military equipment and volunteer American soldiers to the contras.

-- Americares Foundation and the Knights of Malta, whose contributors include CBN and whose leaders include business executives, Robert C. Macauley, J. Peter Grace, and the former Treasury Secretary William Simon, also of the Nicaraguan Freedom Fund.

-- The Christian Emergency Relief Team, with headquarters in Auburn, Washington. Its medical personnel are reported to interact closely with the Misura contras. And,

-- The Nicaraguan/Salvadoran Defense Fund and Refugee Relief International, programs of Soldier of Fortune magazine. The defense fund raises money for uniforms and equipment for Salvadoran government soldiers and the contras. (Kemper, 1985)

-- Bay of Pigs (2506 Brigade) Veterans Association: Miami, Florida. Anti-Castro group contributing food and clothing to the contras as well as mercenaries. It has sent U.S. mercenaries to Costa Rica, using the ranch of Bay of Pigs veteran John Hull as a base for raids. Other Cuban exile groups supporting the contras include Freedom Fighters, Alpha-66 and the Movement for an Independent and Democratic Cuba (whose Commander Huber Matos has accompanied contras on combat missions inside Nicaragua).

-- Council for the Defense of Freedom: The Council coordinates the work of anticommunist committees concerned with Nicaragua, Angola, El Salvador, Afghanistan, Kampuchea, and Vietnam. Members of this Council include: Father Enrique Rueda of the Free Congress Foundation, Dan Fefferman of the Freedom Leadership Foundation, Reed Irvine of Accuracy in Media, and Lynn Bouchey of the Council for Inter-American Security.

-- Council for National Policy: An influential right-wing think tank, the Council (based in New Orleans) regularly sponsors speaking tours for contra leaders. Its advisory board is stacked with right wing fundamentalists such a Rev. Jerry Falwell of Moral Majority, Rev. James Robinson of the Robinson Evangelistic Crusade and Jim Groen of Youth for Christ International. Other principals are: Joseph Coors, Hebert and Nelson Bunker Hunt, Pat Boone, U.S. Senator Jesse Helms, Gen. Singlaub, Rev. Pat Robertson, and Woody Jenkins.

-- Nicaraguan Freedom Fund: Principal members are Jeane Kirkpatrick, William Simon, Medge Dector, Michael Novak. Funded by the Washington TIMES newspaper which is associated with Rev. Moon's Unification Church.

Sources: Vicki Kemper, "In the Name of Relief: A Look at Private U.S. Aid in Contra Territory," SOJOURNERS, October 1985; and, Barry & Preusch, THE CENTRAL AMERICAN FACT BOOK, 1986.

The private aid network, used to circumvent the intent of the U.S. Congress, has been an integral part of the psychological operations aimed at the U.S. public and the Central American population. "I think the most critical special operations mission we have today is to persuade the American people that the communists are out to get us, warns J. Michael Kelly, Assistant Deputy Secretary of the U.S. Air Force. "If we can win this war of ideas, we can win everywhere else." (Barry, 1986) Likewise George Tauham, former president of the Rand Corporation and counterinsurgency expert states: "To me, our most pressing problem is not in the Third World, but it is here at home in the struggle for the minds of people... If we lose our own citizens we will not have much going for us anywhere else." (IRTF, 1986)

Low-intensity warfare theorist Dr. Sam Sarkesian says: "National leaders and the public must understand that low-intensity conflicts do not conform to democratic notions of strategy or tactics. Revolution and counterrevolution develop their own morality and ethic that justify any means to achieve success. Survival is the ultimate morality." (Barry, 1986)

In LIW there is no sudden escalation, advances are not measured in numbers of casualties or battlefield victories, and the conflict can last as long as it takes to achieve the objective. The distinction between war and peace is obscured--because it is "total war," LIW often seems invisible.

The invisibility is the precise aim of what is perhaps the central component to winning LIW--changing the way people in the

U.S. think about the world and the role of the U.S. in the world. In the United States the battle for public opinion is critical to LIW doctrine. To this end the Reagan Administration has created an Office of Public Diplomacy in the State Department to propagate its beliefs. Certain major themes--terrorism, humanitarian aid, free elections, democratization--bombard the media, intended to alter the public perception of U.S. intervention in the world and the war in Central America.

The goal of these themes, a psychological operation on the part of Washington against the U.S. people, is to redefine the "threat" and create the sense of a wartime situation in the United States. "Terrorism" is now a basis for all discussions on U.S. foreign policy. The ability of the Reagan Administration to mobilize the U.S. public against the old enemy of "communism" while linking it with new enemies--the Third World and "terrorism"--will determine the success of LIW throughout the world for years to come.

The war to win the hearts and minds of the U.S. public has taken the form of an intensive public relations campaign to cure the Vietnam syndrome and create the support for U.S. intervention throughout the world. Computerized maps that turn red, charges of Sandinista drug trafficking, international "terrorist" conspiracies, and alarmist predictions of hordes crossing the U.S. border from Central America are all part of these efforts.

Moreover, within the United States the "war on terrorism" as a component to LIW doctrine has grave implications for traditional U.S. democratic structures--having given LIW proponents the excuse to launch new interagency programs which pass decision-making processes from elected representatives to appointed elites. One such example is the State Department Office for Counterterrorism and Emergency Planning which directs the Inter-Departmental Group on Terrorism, which in turn is made up of representatives of the State Department, the National Security Council, the Drug Enforcement Agency (DEA), the FBI, the CIA and others.

Private right wing organizations such as the Moral Majority, defense contractors, mercenary groups and corporate-controlled mass media also play a large role in implementing LIW. The involvement of churches, businesses and private relief agencies not only further the goal of LIW in building an "alternative social system" but, at the same time, help to build on the home front an image of public consensus and create the psychological conditions for that consensus to grow.

Until recently, anti-communist rhetoric has been directed towards foreign targets. But recent times have seen increasing coordinated attacks against Central American solidarity groups, religious sanctuary communities, churches and national legislators who have been accused of being communist "dupes" or agents.

As an illustration of this fact, in April, 1984, President Reagan signed a highly classified document called the National Security Decision Directive (NSDD). According to Daniel P.

Sheehan, attorney and investigator for the Christic Institute in Washington, D.C., the directive contemplates the president unilaterally declaring a "State of Domestic National Emergency" in the event of direct U.S. military intervention in Central America. Under the directive's provisions, the Federal Emergency Management Agency (FEMA) would then be called upon to enforce a domestic side of the Administration's Central America war plan.

In a state of "domestic national emergency," FEMA's role would be crucial in silencing dissent to the Administration's Central America policy. According to Sheehan, FEMA, with the assistance of all state National Guard units, would under the proposed plan, be authorized to summarily arrest, detain, and imprison undocumented Central American immigrants.

FEMA officials have also sought the authority to arrest, at the same time, U.S. citizens whose names are on a classified "Administrative index" kept by the FBI. Those arrested would be detained if FEMA gets its way, at ten national detention centers located on military bases in the United States. (SOJOURNERS, 1986)

More directly, the obsession with "terrorism" has prompted proposals for legislation that would allow the Attorney General to designate certain countries or organizations of its choice as "terrorist" and would allow for prosecution of U.S. citizens who "support" them.

As Michael Klare wrote in 1985 on LIW, "Indeed, perhaps the most frightening aspect of the Administration's public explanation of LIW doctrine is the degree to which language is distorted to justify a policy that is the opposite of the pro-democratic one the Administration claims to be pursuing in foreign relations. If that distortion is allowed to continue unchallenged, we could face a serious threat to our own rights and liberties." (IRTF, 1986)

REAGAN'S FREEDOM FIGHTERS

There is no civil war in Nicaragua. There is a U.S. recruited, trained, financed and equipped band of counterrevolutionaries called the contras. It is the contention of the Reagan administration that contra leaders and all but a small, insignificant minority, are not former Somoza supporters (Somocistas), or former National Guardsmen. Rather, Reagan's "freedom fighters" are "lovers of democracy." They are brave men who opposed the Somoza dictatorship and, in turn, now oppose the "totalitarian" Sandinistas. Assistant Secretary of State Elliot Abrams, has stated: "To continue to associate Nicaragua's resistance forces with Somoza is patently misleading." (Le Moyne, 1986) In a State Department report issued on February 28, 1986, it is stated that only 41 of 153 senior officials in the Nicaraguan Democratic Force are former members of Somoza's National Guard. The rest are, according to this report, either civilians or disenchanted Sandinistas.

By focusing on statistics the State Department report is highly misleading, because it fails to examine or reveal the way power is actually exercised in the contra army. The report also fails to mention that the contra army was formed from the remnants of the National Guard by the Central Intelligence Agency, which helped select the top contra leaders. (Le Moyne, 1986) The fact is that a handful of people around Adolfo Calero make most of the decisions and the top commanders are National Guardsmen.

Calero is a graduate of Notre Dame University and was, prior to the 1979 Sandinista victory, manager of the Coca-Cola bottling plant in Managua. According to several rebel and U.S. sources, Calero maintained close contact with the Central Intelligence Agency. Thus, when the CIA selected civilian leadership for the contras in 1982, Calero left Nicaragua to become the political head of the Nicaraguan Democratic Force. (Le Moyne, 1986)

According to the State Department's own report, the 41 former National Guardsmen in the contra command structure hold the most powerful positions. For example, the five most important military officials--the supreme commander, Col. Enrique Bermudez, and the heads of operations, logistics, intelligence and personnel--were all members of the National Guard. In addition, the report says, the heads of counterintelligence, air intelligence, the rebel air force, medical service and naval force are also former National Guardsmen.

The report states that "most of the officers commanding the largest and most important rebel units are former National Guardsmen." (The report treats all commanders as statistical equals, regardless of the power they exercise.)

The key decision making group around Calero includes his brother Mario Calero; his brother-in-law, Enrique Sanchez, and Mr. Sanchez's brother, Aristides Sanchez, as well as Col. Bermudez. All of these men, according to U.S. sources, were originally approved as contra leaders by the CIA who financed them. (Le Moyne, 1986)

The Sanchez brothers, Enrique and Aristides, were large landowners who were among the most committed backers of the Somoza dictatorship. The State Department report barely mentions them or their dominant influence as aides to Mr. Calero. Col Bermudez, served as military attache in Washington under Somoza. He too had close CIA ties. Col. Bermudez relied on another National Guard officer, Ricardo Lau, to set up counter-intelligence operations that Honduran officials say used death squads to kill dozens of people suspected of being leftists in Honduras. Mr. Lau, who became one of the most feared men in Honduras, was forced to leave the contras by U.S. officials because of numerous allegations of human rights abuses by his troops. Col. Bermudez continues to defend Mr. Lau. (Le Moyne, 1986)

Clearly, the contras are not the democratic loving people the Reagan administration makes them out to be. When President Reagan compares the freedom fighters (i.e. contras) in Nicaragua to the Founding Fathers of the United States (men such as George Washington and Thomas Jefferson) and later states "I am a contra," one can understand why anti-United States sentiment continues to grow in Nicaragua and among the oppressed in all of Central America.

By early Fall, 1986, the United States Drug Enforcement Administration office in Guatemala had compiled convincing evidence that the contra military supply operation was smuggling cocaine and marijuana back to the United States. The Guatemala office of the DEA is responsible for El Salvador. After dropping military supplies in El Salvador, rather than returning to the United States in empty cargo planes, crews would stop in Panama, a major drug transhipment center, to pick up cocaine or marijuana.

When the crew members, based in El Salvador, learned that Drug Enforcement Administration agents were investigating their activities, one of them warned that they had White House protection. (Brinkley, 1987)

Congressional investigations have shown that the covert arms supply operation was set up and managed with significant direction from Lt Col Oliver North. Congressional officials became increasingly concerned in the light of further disclosures that North had told the Federal Bureau of Investigations, in October, 1986, to stop investigating Southern Air Transport, the Miami-based air-freight company involved in the contra supply operation. (Brinkley, 1987)

Philip Shenon, reporting in the New York TIMES, January 30, 1987, wrote that the contras are the focus of seven different criminal investigations by federal agencies. The FBI opened a criminal investigation to determine what happened to most of the

$27 million for nonlethal supplies for the contras that Congress approved in 1985. The GAO also began a separate inquiry into the whereabouts of millions of dollars that were supposed to be funneled to the contras from the sale of American weapons to Iran. In addition, a special prosecutor and two Congressional committees examining the Iran-contra affair are investigating charges of illegality tied to the contras. Other open criminal investigations focus on charges the contras or their backers smuggled arms, trafficked in drugs, laundered money; or violated the Neutrality Act, which bars Americans from involvement in military efforts against countries not at war with the United States.

DEMOCRATIZING THE CONTRAS

With the negative image and press the contras have received, it was crucial for the Reagan administration to put a democratic face on the contras. The Administration's long-term LIW goal is to force the Sandinistas to relinquish control of the government in order to reestablish democracy. To this extent, the Reagan administration created several democratic fronts. From the beginning the man CIA director William Casey handpicked to head the contras was Adolfo Calero, the former Coca-Cola distributor in Managua.

Working directly under Calero, has been Enrique Bermudez, a former colonel in Somoza's National Guard. Bermudez has served as the commander of the contras' main military force (FDN) since it was first created by the CIA.

Realizing that the House of Representatives would not renew aid to the contras unless it could be argued that the political leadership offered a democratic alternative to the Sandinistas (which was necessary for psychological and political components of LIW) the Reagan administration created a new umbrella organization of disparate contra groups in 1985. Thus, the United Nicaraguan Opposition (UNO) was created, with a directorate consisting of Calero, Alfonso Robelo and Arturo Cruz.

Alfonso Robelo, is a wealthy chemical engineer, who was a member of the Sandinista ruling directorate from 1979-80, going into exile in 1982. Robelo is the political leader of the small band of contras operating out of Costa Rica. He was at one time closely associated with Eden Pastora. Arturo Cruz is a former president of Nicaragua's Central Bank. He was for a short time a member of the Sandinista directorate and was once the Nicaraguan Ambassador to the United States. Cruz is enormously popular among U.S. Congressmen--Democrat and Republican. Arthur Cruz is the man leaders of both political parties in the U.S., would like to see as president of Nicaragua, once the Sandinistas are removed from power. Thus, Cruz, more than Calero or Robelo, has been the key to the facade of democracy needed for continued Congressional funding for the contras.

In a major blow to the Reagan Doctrine in Central America, Arturo Cruz resigned from the UNO directorate on March 9, 1987.

On February 16, 1987 Adolfo Calero had resigned from UNO's directorate in an effort to appease Cruz. However, Calero would not relinquish any control over the main contra force (FDN). He, therefore, remained the most powerful contra leader and the man with the closest ties to the CIA.

Cruz's departure stemmed from his frustration in seeing his moves for more civilian control of contra military operations deflected by Calero, who refused to moderate the right-wing, Somoza image of the FDN.

Calero and his followers, meanwhile, hold a grudge against Cruz for having served as the Sandinista government's ambassador to the United States during the regime's early years.

Furthermore, observers familiar with contra affairs say that Cruz suspected that Calero knew about the diversion of some $30 million to the contras from U.S. arms sales to Iran and that this factor was a key in Cruz's decision to leave the UNO three-man directorate. Cruz, however, is not above reproach. In January 1986, Lt Col North and Gen Secord began paying Cruz $7,000 a month for the role Cruz has played in creating a facade of democracy for the Nicaraguan resistance movement. In July, 1987, a newly created six person directorate was announced. Calling themselves the Nicaraguan Resistance, the new directorate was supposedly "elected" by an assembly of Nicaraguan political parties in exile. Some of the directorate's six members have been sworn enemies of one another. They united in this latest Reagan administration created facade of democracy as a last ditch effort to persuade the

US Congress to continue funding the contras. By briefly listing the backgrounds of the new directorate, one can predict that it is predestined to suffer the same fate as the previous Calero/Robelo/Cruz directorate. The newly "elected" members are:

- Aldofo Calero, the most powerful contra leder from the beginning. Jailed briefly in 1978 for joining an anti-Somoza business strike (once it became clear Somoza was losing). Goal is a Nicaragua as it existed prior to 1979, only without a Somoza. Long ties to CIA. Called former CIA Director William Casey, "Uncle Bill." Once Gave Col. North $90,000 in travelers' checks.

- Aristides Sanchez, a member of Calero's key decision-making group. Aristides and his brother Enrique represent a powerful land owning family that was among the most committed supporters of the Somoza dictatorship right up to the time of Somoza's defeat. William Casey, early on, approved of Aristides Sanchez as a contra leader.

- Alfonso Robelo, a one time Sandinista who left Nicaragua in 1982. A wealth businessman, he first joined Eden Pastora in Costa Rica, then left Pastora to join forces with Calero and Cruz in a political directorate that broke up earlier this year. Has no political base inside Nicaragua. State Department considers Robelo inconsistent, not a team player.

- Maria Azucena Ferrey, a member of Nicaragua's Social Christian Party, although represented in Nicaragua's democratically elected Assembly, remains very small. Her participation on the new directorate will likely serve to decrease support for the Social

Christian Party within Nicaragua. Her presence on the directorate plays right into the hands of the Sandinista Party.

- Alfredo Cesar, a politically ambitious newcomer. A former Sandinista, once jailed by Somoza. Has a master's degree in finance from Stanford University. In 1979 became head of the Nicaraguan Central Bank. Left Nicaragua in 1982, leading a small contra group in Costa Rica, financed by the US. Has no political base inside Nicaragua.

- Pedro Joaquin Chamorro, whose father (same name) was murdered by Somoza. Left Nicaragua when Sandinistas stepped up censorship of LA PRENSA, the family newspaper, after it became public knowledge that LA PRENSA had accepted $100,000 from the Reagan administration funneled through the National Endowment for Democracy. His mother, Violeta, is an outspoken critic of the Nicaraguan government. He has no personal base for power inside Nicaragua, and comes from a family that is politically split. His Uncle Javier (father's brother) publishes EL NUEVO DIARIO, and independent pro-government newspaper. His brother is editor of BARRICADA the Sandinista Party newspaper, and a sister serves as the Nicaraguan ambassador to Costa Rica. The State Department states Chamorro has shown no talent for compromise and alliance building.

Missing is Arturo Cruz, the long-time NSC/CIA "chosen one." For years the Reagan administration told Congress and the American people that Cruz was the true democrat who would assume political power once the contras won militarily or forced a negotiated settlement. Cruz, once the Nicaraguan Ambassador to the US for the Sandinista government, never held a political base of support inside Nicaragua. Since 1970, Cruz has lived in Nicaragua only one year.

The obvious point is that the Nicaraguan Resistance is a political body with widespread political support among the Reagan administration and contra supporters in Congress, but with little, if any, support internally in Nicaragua. Contra directorates will come and go--all failing because the Reagan Doctrine in Central America is fundamentally flawed. The US continues to believe that it has the "right" to select the leaders of Central American nations, but the oppressed of that region are telling the US that when it comes to the interests of Central America "Uncle Sam does not know what is best."

CONTADORA

On September 21, 1984, the Nicaraguan government unexpectedly announced it would accept and sign a regional peace proposal put forth by the so-called Contradora group (Colombia, Mexico, Panama, and Venezuela). Initially the Reagan administration had given a blanket endorsement to the Contadora peace process, but as Joanne Omang of the Washington POST stated, the Administration had never expected Nicaragua to agree to sign the regional treaty proposal. When Nicaragua announced its acceptance, the Reagan administration began raising questions about security guarantees and the scheduling of troop withdrawals.

Honduras, at the urging of the United States, then summoned all the nations of the region to discuss modifications of the Contadora peace proposal. Nicaragua refused the invitation, asserting that the meeting in Honduras was taking place outside the Contadora process.

Honduras, El Salvador and Costa Rica, promptly reversed their position of support for the treaty and, along with the United States, now sought extensive modifications in the earlier Contadora proposal. According to a background paper prepared for a National Security Council meeting attended by President Reagan the first week of November 1984, the "Administration believes it has effectively blocked an unsatisfactory regional peace settlement in Central America..." Following intensive U.S. consultations with El Salvador, Honduras, and Costa Rica, a counterdraft was submitted to the Contadora states on October 20, that shifts concern within Contadora to a document broadly CONSISTENT WITH U.S. INTERESTS. (Guillermoprieto, 1984, emphasis added).

Such action on the part of the United States is consistent with the position taken by the Bipartisan Commission. Regarding the Contadora process, the Commission wrote:

> The Contadora nations do not have extensive experience in working together, and the Contadora process has not yet been tested in terms of crafting specific policies to provide for regional security. Thus THE UNITED STATES CANNOT USE THE CONTADORA PROCESS AS A SUBSTITUTE FOR ITS OWN POLICIES ... (Report, p. 120)

The Bipartisan Commission was laying a foundation for circumventing the Contadora process if, and when, that process ran counter to U.S. strategic interests. In discussing Nicaragua's original peace initiatives the Bipartisan Commission wrote that these initiatives have given "little cause for optimism." The Report then makes an "enlightening" statement:

Significantly, these Sandinista proposals would prohibit exercises and maneuvers of the type United States and Honduran forces have carried out... (Report, pp. 115-116)

On December 4, 1985, eight Latin American nations (Colombia, Mexico, Panama, Venezuela, Argentina, Brazil, Peru and Uruguay) began a new diplomatic effort to persuade the Reagan administration to resume direct negotiations with Nicaragua. This move was opposed by the United States, which initially persuaded three of the draft's original four co-sponsors to request its withdrawal from circulation. However, after intense negotiations during the meeting in Cartegena, Colombia, of the Organization of American States (in December of 1985), Mexico persuaded its three partners in the Contadora Group--Colombia, Venezuela and Panama--to once again back the draft. (Riding, Dec. 4, 1985)

Four other key governments agreed to co-sponsor the resolution--Argentina, Brazil, Peru and Uruguay.

The United States has consistently blamed Nicaragua for the failure of the Contadora process. However, as previously explained, Nicaragua has accepted the original Contadora proposal.

Robert J. McCartney reporting in the Washington POST (on February 11, 1985) stated that in the bilateral negotiations between the U.S. and Nicaragua, the Nicaraguan delegation had even offered to accept a U.S. military presence in Central America. What Nicaragua has consistently called for is a bilateral agreement with the U.S. in which the U.S. formally pledges to end its support for the contras.

What was the U.S. response to an offer to accept a U.S. military presence in Central America? The Reagan administration broke off the bilateral negotiations. A year later, on February 8, 1986, the Administration told Congress that it plans to spend more than $45 million on new bases in Honduras (Reagan states these will not be permanent military installations). There would also be money to improve the major air base at Palmerola, Honduras. Actions such as these lend credence to the Nicaraguan claim that the Reagan administration is not seriously interested in reaching a negotiated settlement.

When the eight Latin American countries released a 25-point Central American peace plan in December, 1985, the Reagan administration was requesting an additional $30 million from Congress to give direct military aid to the contras.

What were the major points called for by the eight Latin American nations?

1. A halt "to foreign aid to the irregular forces" operating in Central America (implying U.S. aid to the contras);
2. The suspension of international military maneuvers (a U.S., Central American, Caribbean

activity, even involving state national guard units);

3. The "progressive reduction" and eventual elimination of the presence of "foreign military advisers... and installations" in Central America;

4. Respect for human rights;

5. Reinitiate and finalize negotiations leading to the signing of the Act of Contadora for peace and cooperation in Central America;

6. A commitment to nonaggression on the part of the five Central American countries through unilateral declarations; and,

7. Foster the reinitiation of conversations between the governments of the United States and Nicaragua. (Jones, Jan. 24, 1986)

The Contadora support group also called for a "Latin American solution" to what are "Latin American problems" for self-determination, that is, the independence of each Latin American country to choose its own form of political and social organization internally so that "each population may freely decide" its government through "universal suffrage in pluralistic democracies," and "noninterference in the internal affairs of other states." (Jones, Jan. 24, 1986)

The Reagan administration response was to say the U.S.-Nicaraguan "impasse could be overcome IF the Sandinistas accepted the March 1985 proposal of the Nicaraguan Democratic Resistance (the contras) for a church-mediated dialogue, cease-fire and suspension of the state of emergency." (Jones, Jan. 24, 1986) With Cardinal Obando y Bravo being one of the major leaders of the internal political opposition to the Sandinistas, (see Chapter Four) a proposal by President Reagan to have the hierarchical Catholic church be the mediator of a dialogue between the contras and Sandinista government is totally unrealistic. Reagan knows this, but such a proposal is great for domestic consumption. What American, Democrat or Republican, would be opposed to a church mediated dialogue in Nicaragua? Once again, the President is fulfilling the domestic requirements of LIW.

The Nicaraguan response was accepting of the Contadora proposal but reiterated that the United States should sign the protocol of the Contadora treaty (produced by the original Contadora group in September, 1984, which Nicaragua agreed to sign without modifications), which would make the United States cease support of the contras. The Nicaraguan government also stated it would never talk with the contras (as the contras were created by the U.S. and are financed and supplied by the U.S. The Nicaraguan government's position is that clearly the conflict is not a civil war in Nicaragua).

The foreign ministers and leaders of the eight nations also supported the proposal by the new Guatemalan president, Vinicio Cerezo Arevalo, for the establishment of a Central American parliament to deal with regional issues. President Reagan responded by requesting $100 million in new aid for weapons, ammunition and other military supplies for the contras in 1986. (McCurdy, 1986)

In January, 1986, the foreign ministers of the eight nations met in Caraballeda, Venezuela to work on a revision of the regional peace initiative based on the December, 1985 25-point plan. This was followed by intense negotiations in May and June of 1986.

On May 27, 1986, Nicaraguan President Daniel Ortega stated that "Nicaragua was prepared to seek concrete agreements on arms control" in an effort to resolve a deadlock over a Central American peace treaty. The latest version of the proposed treaty contains a key section on limits on weapons and military manpower in the region. Arms reductions mentioned by Ortega included aircraft, airfields, tanks, large mortars, artillery and rocket launchers. Nicaragua continues to emphasize, however, that it is not willing to discuss disarmament as long as the United States continues to support the contras, establish permanent military bases in Honduras, keep its military advisers in the region and conduct military maneuvers in the region. The United States has conducted almost continuous joint military exercises with Honduras since 1983, often within twelve miles of the Nicaraguan border. The United States refuses to agree to these conditions, with Reagan accusing the Sandinistas of being "insincere in negotiating arms limitation agreements." (Le Moyne, 1986)

Another current stumbling block in negotiating a Central American peace treaty is the Reagan administration's insistence that any treaty include a section that each country's economic, political and social model be approved by the "freely expressed will of their people." (Le Moyne, 1986)

The Reagan administration interpretation of this language would force Nicaragua to hold new elections, while moving to strengthen a free enterprise economic structure. Interestingly, the 1984 Nicaraguan elections were the most democratic in the nation's history, and were more democratic than the elections of El Salvador, Honduras and Guatemala (see Chapter Two). Also at present, the Nicaraguan economy has a higher percentage of private ownership in business and industry than does Mexico, whose government we support.

On February 15, 1987, the Presidents of all the major Central American nations except Nicaragua met in San Jose, Costa Rica, in an effort to define a joint strategy on ending the conflicts in Central America. Costa Rica presented a plan for discussion that called for cease-fires and amnesties in the wars affecting Nicaragua, El Salvador and Guatemala.

The plan then calls for a timetable for talks between guerrilla groups and the three Governments, leading to new elections, a lifting of press censorship in the three countries and a cutoff of foreign aid to guerrilla groups, a move that would suspend United States assistance to the contras.

In addition, the Costa Ricans called for a general reduction in weapons and the size of armies in Central America and would ban any nation from permitting its territory to be used for attacks against any other nation (i.e., at present Honduras and Costa Rica).

The provisions would be supervised by a commission to be made up of the United Nations, the Organization of American States and the Contadora group of negotiating nations. (Le Moyne, 1987)

The Costa Rican initiative is an effort to have Central American nations formulate their own negotiating position rather than trust the United States or even the Contadora group of eight Latin American nations.

Assistant Secretary of State Elliot Abrams initially supported the Costa Rican proposal, but later retracted his support saying, "the plan did not make sufficient demands on the Sandinista Government." (Sciolino, 1987)

Some White House officials contend that the introduction of new top advisers into the Administration, notably Mr. Carlucci, the national security adviser, and Howard Baker, the president's new chief of staff, was unlikely to push the United States further along the negotiating track, because of President Reagan's continued strong commitment to the contras. "You may have new people, but you still have the same doctrinal rigidity," one official said. "This is not a negotiating Administration." (Sciolino, 1987)

The United States Senate barely voted to endorse the Panama Canal Treaty during the Carter presidency. Acceptance came reluctantly, and would not have come at all without the "De Concini Condition." This condition states that "if the Panama Canal is closed, or its operations are interfered with, [the U.S. and Panama should each] have the right to take such steps as each deems necessary... including the use of military force in the Republic of Panama..." (Sklar, 1987) The treaty thus preserved the United States' perpetual authority to intervene unilaterally in the Americas. In the now famous words of a confidential 1927 State Department memorandum: "We do control the destinies of Central

America and we do so for the simple reason that the national interest absolutely dictates such a course."

All versions of the Contadora Treaty have addressed security concerns with detailed provisions for withdrawal of foreign military advisers, prohibition of foreign military bases and aid to insurgent forces, restriction of military maneuvers and limits on troops and armaments. In the current draft, treaty compliance would be verified by an International Corps of Inspectors and Verification and Control Commission.

Aiming to sabotage the Contadora process and the current Costa Rican proposal at the least cost to itself and the greatest cost to Nicaragua, the Reagan administration has embarked on a three-part strategy:

1. paying public tribute to the Contradora process in order to co-opt Congress and paint Nicaragua as the intransigent party.
2. pressure Contadora nations to realign their policies with U.S. objectives; and,
3. pressuring Central American allies to oppose restrictions on U.S. actions and to isolate Nicaragua--that is, vetoing treaty drafts when Nicaragua approves and professing support of drafts Nicaragua wants changed. (Sklar, 1987)

Nicaragua, which had initially opposed the Costa Rica initiative, due to the fact it was not invited to participate, now supports the principle of Central American dialogue.

In a speech, February 21, 1987, President Daniel Ortega stated that Nicaragua was willing to consider a regional peace plan. Ortega said:

Understanding and coexistence among brothers is possible
when national and regional interests prevail, not the
interests of hegemonic power." (Kinzer, 1987)

REAGAN PLAN VS. ARIAS PLAN

During the first week of August, 1987, the presidents and
foreign ministers of Costa Rica, El Salvador, Guatemala, Honduras,
and Nicaragua, met in Guatemala for the most concerted effort to
date to negotiate a settlement to the conflicts in the region.
Their discussions were based on the peace plan put forward
originally by President Oscar Arias Sanchez of Costa Rica.

On the eve of this meeting the Reagan administration put forth
a new peace proposal for Central America. The "new" Reagan Plan
was presented as a bipartisan effort as the President's newly
appointed special assistant for lobbying Congress to continue aid
to the contras, Tom Loeffler (former Republican Congressman from
Texas) worked closely with Jim Wright (Speaker of the U.S. House
and longtime Democratic Congressman from Texas) in drafting the
proposal. President Reagan stated "I applaud this bipartisan
effort in Congress and I express the hope that it will produce a
peaceful resolution to the conflict in Nicaragua."

The Reagan administration and the House Democratic leadership
pulled off a public relations coup with the new Reagan Plan,
designed to win increased popular support for the upcoming vote on
continuing aid to the contras. However the Reagan administration's
past record on Central America peace initiatives led some

Congressional Democrats to doubt the sincereness of the Administration.

In September, 1984, when the Nicaraguan Government surprised everyone by agreeing to sign a draft of the original Contadora peace proposal, the Reagan administration quickly denounced the plan. The State Department announced that it had several substantive objections, although the Administration had never criticized the Contadora proposal previously. A secret National Security Council briefing paper leaked to the press a few weeks later stated the Administration had "effectively blocked" a Contadora treaty, adding, "We have trumped" the Nicaraguans.

In May 1986, according to a formerly secret White House document made public during the Iran-contra hearings, a National Security Planning Group meeting of Cabinet-level officials and others was convened because Washington expected that "the Sandinistas will likely proclaim that they are prepared to sign another version of" the Contadora treaty.

Reagan's strategy, the document said, was to portray the treaty the Nicaraguans wanted to sign as unacceptable to other nations in the region "while denouncing the Sandinistas for refusing to negotiate." One official who attended the planning group meeting recalled that it had been convened in part because "there was a peace scare." (Brinkley, 1987)

The peace scare theme is also a part of the timing of the latest Reagan peace plan. The Administration is truly frightened by the possibility of the five Central American nations agreeing to a peace plan not initiated by or having the prior approval of Washington. In short, a Central American initiative leading to a negotiated settlement of the conflict in the region is unacceptable to the Reagan administration.

The heads of the Central American states meeting in Guatemala at the time the new Reagan Plan was announced, were caught unaware. They were scheduled to discuss the Arias Plan along with a modified version of that plan put forth by Honduras on August 5 and 6, 1987. Although the initial public statements of all the five nations was positive toward Reagan's new initiative, the press reported that privately officials from the five Central American nations were "upset that the Reagan administration announcement on the eve of their summit meeting seemed to undermine their work." (Brinkley, 1987)

On U.S. official directly involved in Central American affairs reinforced the private fears of Central American leaders by stating, "If the White House had thought the (new) plan was acceptable (to the Sandinistas) they would have changed it." (Brinkely, 1987)

The fundamental point remains: What right does the United States have to dictate a peace in Central America, when it has been, for over a century, the force behind the institutionalization of repression and oppression in Central America. If the Reagan administration was truly interested in peace in Central America it would state its full support for the Arias process, that is, the nations of the region negotiating a Central American solution, free from pressure of the U.S. government. Until this happens the outlook for a successful negotiated end to the Central American crisis remains bleak. Bipartisan U.S. proposals for peace in Central America, including the new Reagan Plan, are still grounded in the Monroe Doctrine, that is, continued U.S. dominance in the region.

On August 7, 1987, to counter Reagan's plan for peace in Central America, the Presidents of Costa Rica, El Salvador, Guatemala, Honduras and Nicaragua, agreed to sign the Arias Plan. Thus, the Central American nations, faced with a Reagan proposal designed to continue the fighting in the region, agreed to a plan for a regional, negotiated settlement. A general outline of the Arias Plan would include the following points:

1. **Amnesty and Dialogue.** After 60 days, in countries where there are armed struggles, a general amnesty for political crimes, to be verified by commissions made up of government, opposition, Roman Catholic Church and Inter-American Human Rights Commission representatives. Immediately, a broad dialogue with unarmed opposition groups.
2. **Cease-Fire.** An immediate cease-fire, beginning simultaneously with the dialogue.
3. **Democratization.** Immediately, the start of a democratic and participatory process, promoting social justice without foreign intervention and including press freedom and political pluralism.
4. **Elections.** After the creation of conditions for democracy, simultaneous elections in the five countries, under supervision of the Organization of American States, to form a Central American parliament. Supervised elections for municipal, legislative and presidential offices.
5. **Suspension of Military Aid.** Immediately, a request by the five countries for suspension of aid to insurgents and irregulars.

6.   **Use of Territory.**   A commitment by the five countries to prevent use of their territories to destabilize the region's governments.

7.   **Arms Reduction.**   Within 60 days, the beginning of negotiations on controlling and reducing arms inventories and troop strength, along with measures to disarm irregulars.

8.   **Supervision and Follow-Up.**   Within 30 days, formation of a committee to supervise achievement of the agreement's goals, to be made up of the United Nations Secretary General, the O.A.S. Secretary General and foreign ministers of the countries supporting the Contadora peace initiative.

9.   **Evaluating Progress.**   Within six months, a meeting of the five Presidents from the region.

10.   **Economic Agreements.**   Efforts to achieve economic and cultural agreements to promote development.

On August 8, President Reagan expressed support for the efforts of the five Central American Presidents to enter into a negotiated regional settlement, but added that the Untied States intended to protect "the interests of the Nicaraguan Resistance (i.e. contras) who have already stated their readiness to take part in genuine negotiations for peace and democracy in Nicaragua."

Administration officials quickly reinforced Reagan's support for the contras, by stating the United States "would be active diplomatically in the coming months in trying to address what it views as shortcomings in the pact." (Engelberg, 1987) Also, contra leaders meeting in Guatemala City issued a statement on August 8, that they "would not observe the conditions of a proposal that they are not party to."

Jim Wright, the Speaker of the House of Representatives, who helped draft the Reagan Plan, warmly embraced the five-nation peace agreement. Wright stated it would be unwise for the Reagan administration to seek any further military aid for the contras while the peace negotiations in the region were under way. However, Wright did not rule out the idea of approving nonmilitary aid for the contras. Such a move would allow the contras to remain alive until it answered what one Administration official said is the key question from our perspective--"Where does the resistance fit in?" Senate Minority Leader Robert Dole has suggested that the Congress should approve Reagan's request for funding the contras on the understanding that assistance would be sent to them if the peace plan collapsed. (Gordon, 1987)

The Arias Plan makes it clear that no Central American nation favors the contras--whatever lip service Honduras, El Salvador, and Costa Rica may have paid them out of fear of Washington. To be rid of this latest intervention from the United States was a unifying factor among five usually contentious nations.

The Reagan administration has clearly been placed on the defensive, but there is little reason to believe that the Administration will abide by the provisions of the Arias Plan.

The Arias Plan says that the territory of one country may not be used to attack another and demands a cutoff of all outside aid to guerrilla groups, a condition that would clearly deny the contras their bases in Honduras and their United States aid. This is unacceptable to the Reagan administration. As Secretary of State Shultz insisted, "any cease fire must be worked out with the

involvement of the contras. Their views have to be represented..."
(Engleberg, 1987)

This is precisely why Nicaraguan President Daniel Ortega asked
for immediate bilateral negotiations to be renewed between his
nation and the United States. President Reagan has refused to
agree to bilateral talks with Nicaragua at this time. However, it
is obvious that for the success of any regional peace plan, the
Nicaraguans must be assured that the United States will not engage
in future attempts to overthrow their government.

Other major differences between the Reagan Plan and the Arias
Plan would lead one to assume that peace in Central America is not
going to be achieved quickly. Reagan's proposal calls for an
immediate cease-fire, to be followed by the immediate suspension
of military aid to the contras by the United States and a cutoff
of military aid of Nicaragua by Communist countries. Humanitarian
aid would be allowed.

The Arias plan would curtail aid to the contras, while
recognizing the legitimacy of the Nicaraguan government, allowing
it to maintain its military force and continue to receive aid from
any nation until later when agreement is reached on the size and
type of military each nation will be permitted.

The crucial point here is that the contras are an insurgent
force, created, financed and trained by the U.S. They have never
been able to militarily control any territory inside Nicaragua.

The other side, the Nicaraguan government (with which the U.S.
continues to have diplomatic relations), is quite different. In

international law, no treaty could bind an independent government not to seek or receive aid from any country it might choose. If the contra war was ended, and the U.S. agreed to recognize the legitimacy of the Nicaraguan government, it would have no legitimate need for continued Soviet or Cuban military assistance. Under the regional agreement, Nicaragua would accept limits as to the size and type of military it maintains. All of this would be subject to international verification.

Before addressing the verification issue, it should be noted that the Reagan Plan demands that the Nicaraguan government agree to internal changes as a prior condition to the United States leaving the region militarily and ending combat maneuvers in Honduras. Nicaragua would have to immediately suspend the emergency law, establish a multi-party electoral commission and, within 60 days, establish a timetable and procedures for elections. The Reagan Plan's timetable called for the negotiating process to begin immediately (August 6, 1987) and be completed by September 30, 1987. This is precisely why the Reagan Plan appeared immediately to be yet another sham. September 30, is when current aid to the contras expires. Additional aid needs Congressional approval. Reagan was demanding a negotiated settlement be started and completed within a period of seven weeks.

As for verification, the Arias Plan calls for the establishment of several monitoring groups. A National Reconciliation Commission is to be organized, consisting of government representatives, opposition parties and church officials to monitor the plan's progress.

In addition, the United Nations, the Organization of American States, the foreign ministers of Central America and the Contadora Group, which includes Mexico, Panama, Colombia and Venezuela, will all be asked to take part in an international verification commission to monitor the plan's progress.

The Arias Plan called on the foreign ministers of the five Central American signers to meet as an executive committee fifteen days following the signing of the agreement. Ninety days after that, they are to meet again to judge how well the plan's provisions have progressed on amnesty, a cease-fire in guerrilla wars and internal democratization in each nation.

In 120 days, the international verification commission is to study how well the plan is being carried out. Then in 150 days, the five Central American presidents are to meet again to hear the report of the international commission.

Central American foreign ministers meeting on August 20, 1987, failed to make significant progress toward the creation of commissions to study how to achieve a cutoff of outside aid, amnesty, negotiations and cease-fires to end guerrilla wars in the region. Decisions of the foreign ministers have to be unanimous in order to be binding. The one nation dragging its feet in this area is Honduras.

Honduras is particularly concerned that an international verification commission, called for in the Arias Plan, will demand to visit well-known contra bases on Honduran soil. The official Reagan administration position is that the contras no longer operate in Honduras--only within the boundaries of Nicaragua. Yet, they control no territory! As Manuel Gamero, the respected editor of the Honduran newspaper, EL TIEMPO, stated: "Honduras is the first and last banana republic. Decisions made by the 'democratically elected' government of Honduras, are made according to what is in the best interest of the United States, not what is in the best interest of the Honduran people." (Hufford, 1987)

Although the governments of Central America may sincerely want peace, an end to the armed conflict in the region will depend upon the United States ending all support (military and "humanitarian") to the contras, while simultaneously assuring the El Salvadoran rebels that, if they lay down their arms there will be no reoccurrence of murders, and disappearances against them. In the history of El Salvador, that has been the pattern. An international peace keeping force may well be necessary to assure that the Salvadoran military remains in check and that the death squads do not pose a threat to a negotiated peace.

Interestingly, President Duarte, of El Salvador, meeting with contra leaders in San Salvador on August 21, 1987, convinced the contra leaders to "formally" accept the Arias Plan.

In a brief statement, contra leaders said, "We accept in good faith the peace plan," with no qualifications. They called for a meeting "at the highest level" on September 15, in Managua with the

Nicaraguan government to discuss the cease-fire mandated by the Arias Plan.

By getting contra "support" Duarte was able to then state that only the Salvadoran resistance (FDR-FMLN) had not agreed to the Arias Plan. Duarte's political power base in El Salvador has been seriously eroded over the past year and a half. Because of this the FDR-FMLN, while agreeing with the key points of the Arias Plan, are demanding assurances they will not be committing suicide when they lay down their arms.

Conversely, the contra leaders were hoping for a public relations victory in the U.S. Congress. By stating that they agree with the Arias Plan and are willing to meet the Sandinista government on September 15 to begin negotiations, it would appear that if the Nicaraguan government refuses "they are not really interested in peace."

The position of the Nicaraguan government is clear. They state bluntly, that the contras are the creation of the Reagan administration. Thus, along with the Arias Plan, a bilateral agreement must be negotiated with the United States, ending all support for the contras and assuring the Nicaraguan government that the Reagan administration and future ones, will not engage in any activity designed to overthrow the Nicaraguan government. A bilateral U.S.-Nicaraguan agreement would be an important first step in giving Central American nations a real chance to negotiate a Central American solution. This is not likely to happen in the near future.

At a press conference after the meeting with President Duarte, contra leaders said they "are not for the moment considering laying down their guns or renouncing armed warfare as a means to power." (LeMoyne, 1987). This statement was made immediately following Duarte's announcement that the contra leaders had "formally" accepted the Arias Plan.

Additionally, the rapid series of developments leading to serious efforts to negotiate a settlement in Central America, has infuriated the right wing in the United States. A movement led by U.S. Representative Jack Kemp (Republican presidential candidate) and U.S. Senator Jessie Helms (friend of Robert D'Aubisson) is challenging President Reagan and the Congress to "stand tall" for freedom by approving $310 million in contra aid over an eighteen month period. While this proposal is not likely to pass the Congress, the Reagan administration has been forced (by the right wing of the Republican Party) to make almost daily statements that it will not abandon the contras.

The Central American nations, supported by the Contadora nations, are seriously trying to develop a process which will lead to a negotiated settlement. The major obstacle blocking changes for success remains the Reagan administration.

SUMMARY

Contadora must be seen within the context of growing Latin American unity, reflected in the mid-December, 1986, agreement by the eight Latin American Contadora sponsors to establish a permanent forum. The so-called Group of Rio de Janeiro will meet three times a year to discuss regional issues including Central America, foreign debt and "independent development." A Brazilian diplomat observed, "We're aiming at something like the Group of Seven," the annual Western summit. (Sklar, 1987)

There are two very basic, fundamental reasons why the United States will not soon support the Contadora process or the Arias Plan, a regional approach to negotiations. First, both of these approaches would mean the end of the Monroe Doctrine. Second, these approaches challenge the Cold War, East/West zero-sum game, by rejecting the mutually-recognized superpower right to police their respective spheres of influence. (Sklar, 1987) The Arias Plan would give a boost to demilitarization efforts around the world and establish a precedent for autonomous systems of regional collective security. In short, both the Contadora process and the Arias regional peace proposal would be a building block for non-alignment and a new international economic order. It is difficult to imagine a United States administration, Democrat or Republican giving up the Monroe Doctrine and superpower spheres of influence without an alternative conceptual framework within which to analyze U.S. relations with Central America specifically and the Third World in general.

It is of paramount importance that citizens of the United States remember that peace in Central America is far more than the absence of war. Peace will only become a reality when justice as outlined by Archbishop Camara, is achieved.

CHAPTER 7

THE ALTERNATIVE: EQUALITY OF RESPECT

The United States needs to examine creative alternatives to the liberal-Lockean U.S. model of citizen participation. According to Archbishop Dom Helder Camara if peace is to be achieved in Latin America, injustice (violence number One) must be overcome. As this clearly means altering the structural or institutional system that perpetuates oppression and repression, alternative forms of citizen participation need to be devised. In other words, if the basic need in Central America is to fundamentally alter existing economic, political, social and military structures how can this best be achieved? What would have been accomplished in Nicaragua by holding elections, U.S. style, immediately following the overthrow of Somoza in 1979? Would an election involving competing bourgeoisie political parties establishing a multi-party parliamentary system, necessitating coalition governments, been able to fundamentally alter the system of structural and institutional violence? Or, would this have been a way for the U.S. to create another facade of democracy in supporting an electoral system which gave the oppressed of Nicaragua "Somocism" without Somoza?

One must realize the important point is to empower people on the local level to meaningfully participate in decision making processes which give them control over their own lives. When speaking of empowerment one needs to examine the Greek meaning of the word "democracy." The term "democracy" does not in itself refer to elections--rather, it comes from the Greek words meaning "people" and "power." Thus the critical question for judging Nicaragua is whether ordinary people have power to participate in decisions which affect their lives. The historical fact in Nicaragua is that until 1979, real power was held by combinations of the military and oligarchs. These groups were not voted into power and they could not be voted out, even though so-called "free" elections were periodically held with competing political parties and constituent assemblies. The people remained powerless to alter the fundamental cause of injustice--the structural and institutional forms of violence. This remains the case today in El Salvador, Guatemala and Honduras.

Two organizational structures have emerged in Nicaragua which are designed to alter the basic cause of injustice in that country. One is the communidades de base, Christian grassroots communities (which has been discussed in Chapter Four). The second major organization in Nicaragua designed to empower people locally are the Sandinista Defense Committees (CDS). These are block or neighborhood organizations. By 1984 there were approximately 15,000 CDS block-level committees with a total membership of more than half a million. This represented about one-third of Nicaragua's estimated adult population in 1983. The block-level CDS elects its own leaders and makes decisions by majority rule. They are integrated into larger CDS structures at the zone, regional, and national levels. (LASA Report, 1985) The CDS' have played an important role in consolidating the revolution, that is, working to fundamentally alter unjust economic, political and social structures. According to the Reagan administration the CDS is an organized coercive instrument of state political control, that is, part of the Marxist-Leninist conspiracy. According to the Sandinistas and liberation theologians in Nicaragua, the CDS is an authentic vehicle of mass participation in the distribution of basic goods and social service.

The "logic of the majority" concept, as used by the Sandinistas, has both a political and economic dimension. In the economic arena it implies redistribution of access to wealth and public services. The state will use its power to guarantee the fulfillment of the basic needs of the majority population. In the political arena, mass organizations created during the struggle against Somoza and afterward involve very large numbers of people in the decisions that affect their lives. Private wealth can be accumulated, private profits can be made as long as the economic elites recognize the interests of the majority and collaborate with the state in meeting the majority's needs; and, recognize that economic power will no longer by synonymous with political power. (LASA Report, 1985)

ALTERNATIVE WORLD ORDER MODEL

Both liberation theology and the Nicaraguan CDS are based on the principle of equal respect. This is fully compatible with a neo-Kantian utilitarian approach to the question of why greater equality is desirable, one finds in current Western political theory. The argument starts with the basic idea that human beings as human beings, have certain basic qualities or properties which entitle them to be respected as equals. Then, this is taken to imply that practical policies should be directed toward implementing a substantial degree of economic, social, and political equality. Otherwise, the needs and capacities of humans cannot be met, and to fail to do this, or to do it for some but not others, means that not all are treated with equal respect.

The argument then moves to a consideration of the qualities or properties which entitle persons to be considered as equals. These properties might be identified as NEEDS and CAPACITIES. Arguing from needs helps establish a MINIMUM level of resources below which no person or group shall fall. Recognition of basic human needs prohibits arguments providing unequal access to food and medical care on grounds of race, sex, class, for example, or any other criterion which does not accord all people equal respect.

If the equalitarian argument is to provide for equal treatment beyond the bare minimum of needs, it must go on to consider human capacities. In this respect human beings have three capacities which matter most. First, we have the capacity to act with some degree of autonomy. We can become aware of the forces that mold our behavior, and we can work some changes in those forces, shaping them to our purposes. We can recognize or formulate alternative paths of actions, and choose among them. We can form intentions and purposes, and design lines of activity that promise to bring us success in pursuing our aims. Secondly, we have the capacity for personal development. Partly, this is what is meant by saying we are capable of some degree of autonomy. But also, by saying human beings have the capacity for self-development, one means to say that we are creatures who can grow and change, and that each of us is capable of realizing some human potential that is worthy of admiration. Thirdly, human beings have capacity to form relationships with others, and to engage in various kinds of activities which seem to them to have value, but which require private, free, and uncoerced space for the development, e.g., love or friendship (Schaar, 1978)

It is because people have these capacities that we treat them with respect (rather than, say, charity, affection, or pity). To respect others means to see and to treat them as having the capacity for autonomy and self-development, and as capable of engaging in valued activities or relationships with others.

Taken as standards for the formation of social policy, these principles of equal respect point toward something like a single-status society, and away from social orders of rigid hierarchy, fixed position, and strict role definitions. Similarly, the principles strike against the structural inequalities of a class system, and move toward the fullest possible measure of equality of condition and opportunity. This way of approaching a justification of equal treatment might help to resolve the old argument of "liberty versus equality." It proposes that equal respect implies equal liberty. It also, so far as general principles can, meets the fear that too much equality would require unlimited state intervention into private affairs, for the idea that persons need private space in which to develop their unique activities and relationships plainly implies a large area both for private liberty and for freedom of association.

To illustrate the possible consequences of the equality of respect doctrine one might examine a possible model for a future world order. At present the international economic order is one of vertical interdependence. (See Appendix A.)

This order is obviously preferable to the imperialistic, colonialist model. Under colonialism Third World peoples did not share in the benefits. In vertical interdependence the Third World shares in the benefits, but still receives a far smaller proportion of the benefits than the First World. This model is the equality of opportunity concept on a worldwide scale. The equality of respect doctrine would lead nations to horizontal interdependence, a model in which all nations benefit in a more equitable manner. Horizontal interdependence is non-oppressive and non-exploitive and, thus, supports the equality of respect doctrine. It is my contention that horizontal interdependence coupled with equality of respect would establish a global decentralization of power that would occur within nations as well as among nations.

For example, one might consider direct linkage between a local community or region in a Third World country and their counterparts in a developed nation. (See Appendix B.) Naturally there would be fear that the developed local community or region would simply dominate the Third World counterpart much in the same way multinational corporations and national governments do at the present time.

After all, local communities and regions in developed countries are the home base for very powerful economic institutions. However, would not the self-reliance possibilities for Third World local communities and regions make this option worth considering under certain conditions? In present practice, Third World communities aspiring for self-reliance are sometimes frustrated by collaboration between their own national government and multinational corporations. Might not Third World local communities and regions be a better match for local and regional organizations in developed countries? Could they not develop symmetrical working relationships with (1) small corporations, avoiding the giant conglomerates, (2) relate to subnational, less powerful government institutions, and (3) collaborate with more responsive local nongovernmental groups? (Alger, 1977) Might this approach usefully fragment the powerful nation if it is carried out in the context of very explicit criteria for self-reliance? Four major guidelines would be proposed for selective participation in the international economic system by Third World countries. Such guidelines, requiring much more specificity when applied to individual cases, could equally apply to linkages between local communities or regions:

1. There is a minimum degree of links required to sustain the development process.
2. There is a maximum degree of links beyond which no effective sovereignty can be maintained.

3. There are affirmative links which reinforce
    self-reliance.
4. There are regressive links which weaken self-
    reliance. (Alger, 1977)

Fragmentation in developed countries would at the same time enhance self-reliance in local communities and regions within developed countries. Increasingly local enterprises are being absorbed into multinational giants, with control over international operations moved to a distant corporate office. Foreign investment of local banks is absorbed into consortia operations, obscuring local perception and understanding of the impact of local investment. Most aid programs are handled by national organizations, with local people simply putting money in envelopes. As a result local people have little perception and understanding of the aid programs they support. Persons desiring involvement in these programs must emigrate to the national headquarters of aid organizations in order to become involved. In this way, local communities lose important competence for international involvement.

If local communities and regions in developed nations were more self-reliant in their domestic and international involvements, it might be possible for humanitarian and fairness sentiments to be reflected in their foreign policies. If more self-reliance existed it would become possible for First World and Third World people to develop agreed norms for symmetric relationships.

This framework of a future world order is quite different from most world order thinking. World order proposals tend to build either from the top down (i.e., with global institutions) or from existing "nation-states" up. Neither of these approaches is concerned with how sub-national communities would link to proposed global structures. This may be because these future world orders have been primarily the creations of cosmopolitans--scholars and elites--who do not relate to the world from local communities or regions but as a part of a national governmental and nongovernmental elite and perhaps also as a part of a cosmopolitan transnational or international elite that is selected from national elites. As these cosmopolitans expound on proposals for future global orders, they ironically believe that most people (i.e., those that inhabit local communities around the world) prevent their implementation because they are inadequately educated with respect to the perspectives of cosmopolitans. Future global orders of most cosmopolitans may simply be irrelevant to the needs of people in local communities.

The fundamental problem is that the public is not consciously linked to present global systems though they live in a sea of transnational linkages in the forms of food, clothing, medicine, information, music, films, and a host of manufactured goods. To those few who receive any international education, it tends to be presented as an activity of foreign ministers, heads of state and the governmental foreign service. If the broader transnational approach is taken, it may also include the activities of corporations and even international nongovernmental organizations. But all of these are presented in the context of academic paradigms that do not link people in local communities. This is largely because academics and the media offer agonizing detail on how a handful of national elites endeavors to control the world and/or how these elites control the participation of the people in their country in the world. This attention to the powerful is not surprising and not necessarily bad. However, the fact that we do virtually nothing in helping people in local communities to acquire a deeper understanding of their daily involvements in the world is regrettable. It is reasonable to conclude that it must be done if Third World communities are to experience "another development" that achieves self-reliance and satisfaction of needs. It is likewise reasonable to conclude that local communities in the industrial world will not be willing to make the sacrifices and adjustments that will be required of them unless they have knowledge through which they acquire confidence that their sacrifices and adjustments are achieving desired goals.

If the debate on equality can move towards developing new participatory mechanisms for public involvement in foreign policy making that overcome traditional abdication of responsibility to a small elite in the national capital, the basic needs of people will be better served. As people in many communities and situations gain participatory experience they will be increasingly able to discern the kinds of links to the world that will service their needs. The desirable role of present national governments will no doubt vary with different issues and with size of country. But it would seem inevitable, particularly in larger countries, that people in self-reliant local and regional communities will require increased capacity to formulate and execute their own policies for relationships across present national boundaries. In this way the world would evolve into a system of self-reliant communities linked together in the service of the needs of the inhabitants of these communities. It is unlikely that the aspirations for self-reliance and satisfaction of basic human needs can be achieved any other way.

A more theoretical way of stating the above is to stress the point that the principle of equality as equal respect would trim the idea of equality of opportunity of its rougher, unjust edges. Equality of opportunity largely means equal opportunity to compete for scarce social goods. Understood in this way, it emphasizes competitiveness and grading, and works to perpetuate structures of hierarchy and inequality.

The principle of equal respect invites us to turn away from competition for scarce goods, and toward efforts to develop equal opportunities for growth and expression of diverse individual powers and gifts. It also implies that all should have an equal voice in deciding what kind of society we shall all live in, what social and economic games we shall play. This illustrates, once again, that a serious regard for equality requires us to give attention to political participation and the quality of public life, and not just to passive notions of fair distribution of social goods, as determined by technical criteria, and implemented by programs formulated and administered by experts. A world in

222

which all persons are treated with equal respect will, therefore, require the creation of a new social, economic and political order based upon an equality of respect doctrine.

CHALLENGE TO U.S. CITIZENS

As Noam Chomsky has written: "Those who wish to play a meaningful role in influencing public policy or changing its institutional base must begin with inquiry, in community with others if it is to be effective." (Chomsky, 1985) The first step is education of oneself and others through an honest search for a new understanding. We may, through a process oriented educational experience find that United States foreign policy towards Central America has consisted of answers to the wrong questions. Perhaps what is needed then is the formation of grassroots learning situations in which questions are rewarded more than answers. Hopefully, questions have been raised in your own mind about past and present U.S. foreign policy; specifically, about strategies such as low-intensity warfare, "bipartisan" efforts (such as the Kissinger led Commission Report) to stifle legitimate public dialogue on foreign policy; and, about the need for a new alternative model for conceptualizing a new world order which would enable the United States to end the Monroe Doctrine, export our nation's greatest gift to civilization--the Declaration of Independence, and transcend hierarchial power models in political, economic and cultural relationships with the nations of Central

America (and Third World), in general. This may sound as though it is an insurmountable task. It is not. The major problem in Central America is "US". Low-intensity warfare has not been predestined. Warmed over Alliance for Progress economic packages have not been predestined. The oppressed of Central America are not the only ones needing to be empowered. We, in the United States, also need to be empowered as individuals, as communities and as a nation. This is a challenge--an exciting one. All is possible. As the eminent humanist Norman Cousins once said "No individual human being could possibly know enough to be a pessimist."

CHAPTER 8

CENTRAL AMERICA UPDATE

MAY 1989

PANAMA

Ronald Reagan is no longer president of the United States. Gone is the hard-line ideological rhetoric regarding events in Central America. Enter George Bush and James Baker -- ultimate pragmatists who set out to fashion a bipartisan U.S. foreign policy in Central America.

The headlines (May, 1989) are currently focused on Panama and General Manuel Noriega. Recent elections were declared fraudulent by both an invited observer group headed by former President Jimmy Carter, and an uninvited observer team sent by President Bush.

To understand the U.S. reaction to the Panamanian elections I would invite the reader to return to my analysis of "promoting political democracy" in Chapter 2. However, there is more to U.S. concern over democracy in Panama than first meets the eye. Certainly there is an unfolding story being ignored by the mainstream press. That story has to do with the goal of the Reagan-Bush administrations to create a crisis that would enable the United States to renege on, or force Panama to renegotiate, the Torrijos-Carter Treaty. The Bush-Baker approach appears to be gaining bipartisan support as several leading Congressional Democrats are stating that it would be "inconceivable to return the canal to Panama if Gen. Noriega remains in power," or "unless political democracy is realized by Panama."

HISTORICAL OVERVIEW

12% of all U.S. trade goes through the Panama Canal. Additionally, 12% of the oil the United States consumes travels by the transisthmic pipeline. More importantly, Panama is the site of the U.S. Southern Command, the largest permanent station of U.S. troops and military equipment in Latin America. From the Southern Command, U.S. forces send supplies to the contras, launch spy flights over El Salvador and Nicaragua and coordinate all military activities from the Rio Grande to Tierra del Fuego. Panama has suffered 18 military interventions and continues occupation of the Canal Zone. Sociologist Raul Leis, director of the Panamanian Center for Research and Social Action (CEASPA) argues that U.S. policy in Panama has given rise to "a class of elite politicians who specialize in bowing and scraping before Uncle Sam. For them, nationalism is the opiate of an idealistic people; realism demands obedience to the imperial master."

From 1903 until 1968, Panama suffered a high degree of political instability: 38 governments in 65 years. All this political instability did nothing to disrupt the power of the ruling economic oligarchy. Until 1968, when the National Guard rose up to put an end to oligarchic rule, Panamanian politics was little more than family rivalries within the ruling class. In fact, Panama was referred to as the "cousins' republic," with Uncle Sam playing favorites with whichever nephew claimed to love him the most. In 1944, a U.S. official in Panama summarized the country's politics with candor: "As a matter of fact, there has never been a successful change of government in Panama but that American authorities have been consulted beforehand...." (Weeks, 1988)

With its rule guaranteed by the presence of thousands of U.S. troops, the economic oligarchy had little reason to take steps to co-opt the poor with reforms. From 1936 until 1968 Panama's oligarchy faced political competition from the Authentic Panamanian Party headed by Arnulfo Arias Madrid. Arias, a rancher, coffee grower and member of the oligarchy, was at once a nationalist, pro-United States, pro-fascist and populist. (Leis, 1988) His election to the presidency in 1941 and 1948 resulted in military coups. In 1949 Arias was installed as president by a coup, but was impeached and banned from public life a year later.

In 1968 the legendary Arias triumphed once more. However, eleven days after taking office, a military coup forced him to flee the Canal Zone. (Leis, 1988)

The National Guard emerged, in 1968, as the only force capable of maintaining stability, but it had no base of support in society. After several purges, Omar Torrijos Herrera gained control of the National Guard and government. Torrijos sought to build a new political system in which the poor would participate but the military would rule in their name.

Torrijos focused nationalist attention on the canal treaty negotiations with the United States (which had been ongoing since 1964). Domestically Torrijos instituted a program of labor, agrarian, political and social reforms benefitting the poor. Undercutting the old economic oligarchy's political power (political parties were banned), General Torrijos also built an alliance with a sector of the new elite by developing a center for international banking and related transnational services. (Leis, 1988)

In 1977, Torrijos signed treaties with President Jimmy Carter by which the Canal would be turned over to Panama in the year 2000. The United States conditioned its ratification of the treaties on Panama's adopting political democracy. Thus, Torrijos resigned from the government in October, 1978, allowing political parties to reappear. (As head of the National Guard Torrijos remained the real power in Panama, even with a democratically-elected President).

Gen. Torrijos died in an airplane crash in July, 1981. With the strongman no longer in power, the United States pressured Panama to weaken its agrarian policy, weaken the Labor Code, cut back progressive health, education and housing programs, and restored the pre-1968 Legislative Assembly. (Leis, 1988)

From 1981 to 1983 there were four presidents and three commanders of the National Guard (the name was changed to the Defense Forces in 1983). Finally power was consolidated by Manuel Antonio Noriega in 1983.

During the Torrijos years Noriega was head of intelligence for the Panamanian National Guard. From this position Noriega obediently catered to U.S. interests. He supplied the CIA and U.S. military intelligence with information on developments in Panama, Central America and the Caribbean region.

Noriega approved joint U.S.-Panama military exercises in January 1985, 1986 and 1987. With the exception of Honduras, these exercises represented the largest participation of U.S. troops in Latin America in the 1980s. (Weeks, 1988)

More significantly, Noriega tolerated whatever the U.S. Southern Command cared to do with its forces in the Canal Zone. From the Zone the Southern Command trained and supplied the contras, spied on Nicaragua, coordinated air strikes in El Salvador and contributed logistic support for the invasion of Grenada. All of these activities were in clear violation of the Torrijos-Carter Treaties which explicitly restricts the bases in the zone to the defense of the canal.

In return the U.S. tolerated Noriega's involvement in the drug trade. Noriega's drug activities peaked between the years 1981 and 1984. After 1984, there is no evidence of further cocaine production in Panama and few examples of transhipment. Activity was limited to low-risk, high security money laundering activities. (Dinges, 1988) The Reagan Administration was also "tolerant" of the fraudulent 1984 election in Panama. Thus, the key question is: Why, in 1987, did Noriega suddenly become a major target of U.S. foreign policy?

Latin American nationalists argue that the U.S. decision to move against Noriega was made in June, 1987. The move was part of a larger campaign to prevent the Canal from passing out of U.S. control. The timing of the move was prompted by the Panamanian presidential elections scheduled for 1989. The argument of Latin America nationalists, is that this strategy was intended to clear the way for a Panamanian government which would agree to revisions in the Torrijos-Carter Treaties, allowing U.S. military bases to remain in the country, and U.S. control over the Canal to continue after the year 2000. (Weeks, 1988)

The Latin American nationalists are correct in their assessment of ultimate U.S. goals in Panama. In July, 1988, President Reagan signed a secret order authorizing the CIA to foment a coup against Noriega by dissident military officers. The plan was not approved by the Senate Intelligence Committee, because no assurances could be given that Noriega would not be assassinated in the coup. Hence, a more subtle covert campaign to undermine Noriega's support began. (Robbins, 1988)

In February, 1989, President George Bush in one of his first intelligence initiatives, signed a secret directive launching a new covert operation to unseat Noriega. Bush personally lobbied the plan through the congressional intelligence committees and won approval for the CIA to provide more than $10 million in aid -- including printing, advertising, transportation and communications -- to Noriega's opponents. (Robbins, 1988)

Regarding the goal of renegotiating the Torrijos-Carter Treaties, the Bush administration has launched a major disinformation campaign. While ignoring the blatant U.S. violations of the Canal treaties (mentioned earlier), the Defense Department issued a statement May 18, 1989, saying that Panama had violated the Canal treaties over 1,200 times in the last 15 months. The New York TIMES headlines read "Canal Treaty Violated Often, U.S. Says." (Pear, 5/19/89)

Meanwhile, in Washington, D.C., Republican Senator Dan Coats (Indiana) introduced a bill May 18, 1989, that would defer the next step toward Panamanian control of the Canal until President Bush certifies there is a democratically elected government. (Panama is supposed to replace a U.S. citizen as administrator of the Canal on January 1, 1990). Senate Minority Leader, Bob Dole (R. Kansas), supported the Coats bill. (Pear, 5/19/89)

The United States urged Venezuela to request an emergency meeting of the Organization of American States (O.A.S.). The meeting was held in Washington, D.C. on May 17, 1989. The initial resolution proposed by Peru was opposed by the United States as too weak. It did not mention Noriega by name and did not call for the O.A.S. members to withdraw their ambassadors from Panama. A resolution was finally adopted by the O.A.S. with much tougher language.

The O.A.S. appointed a delegation to travel to Panama on a fact-finding mission and report back to the organization on June 6. The key point is that the delegation was not to report back to the O.A.S. until June 6. Yet on May 22, a day prior to the delegation arriving in Panama to begin its investigation the Los Angeles TIMES Service (wire service) put out a story stating that "U.S. military intervention in Panama is becoming more likely, according to diplomatic and intelligence sources, because a mission from the Organization of American States is expected to fail." The story goes on to state: "The stage is thus set for an armed confrontation sometime after July 1 when all military dependents will either have been removed from Panama or placed in housing at one of the eight U.S. military facilities in Panama."

This wire service story provides one with the opportunity of analyzing the mainstream press. The San Antonio EXPRESS-NEWS (San Antonio, Texas) carried the Los Angeles TIMES Service story as its front page headliner (5/23/89). The headline read "Action on Panama Grows More Likely." The sub-heading read "Diplomats foresee U.S. military intervention." Thus, to read only the headlines or the first few paragraphs leads one to believe U.S. military action is imminent.

However, if one reads the last seven paragraphs of the story buried on page 14 one learns that this is, at present, psychological warfare. More interesting is a passing remark that there is no recent example of danger to U.S. lives that is the pretext used by President Bush to justify sending additional combat ready troops to the Canal Zone (protecting U.S. lives is the standard rationale for resorting to use of the military in Latin America). The last paragraphs read as follows:

"You have to realize the threat of intervention is part of the psy-ops," said a diplomat using the military term for psychological operations intended to undermine an enemy's will. "The U.S. must establish in the minds of the Panamanian Defense Forces that it isn't kidding, that they risk everything if Noriega stays."

The U.S. policy is primarily aimed at promoting a military coup of the "decent officers and men" of the Defense Forces.

President Bush on May 11 reacted to the alleged election abuses by ordering all military and embassy dependents to move to U.S. military facilities.

But according to a senior officer in the Fifth Mechanized Infantry Division, the troops were placed on alert after the May 7 election.

The troop movement was opposed by the U.S. embassy, Ambassador Arthur Davis, who learned about it at the last minute, made a vain attempt to telephone the president directly but couldn't get through.

Many U.S. officers here could cite no recent example of Panamanian harassment against U.S. citizens or military personnel, the reason President Bush gave for sending combat troops.

The Panamanian forces since the troop arrived are all but invisible near U.S. military facilities." (San Antonio EXPRESS-NEWS, 5/23/89)

The message is clear. If one reads beyond the headlines the bankruptcy of U.S. policy becomes evident.

DEMOCRATIC OPPOSITION?

The Bush administration takes the position that Panamanian democracy would become a reality if the opposition presidential candidate Guillermo Endara and vice-presidential running mates Guillermo "Billy" Ford and Arias Calderon were allowed to take

office.   Endara was a long-time aide to the late Arnulfo Arias
Madrid.   A State Department spokesman recently dubbed "President -
elect" Endara as an "ally for now, but he is no staunch friend."
(Hedges and Cary, 1989)

U.S. diplomats generally agree that the opposition won the
election on the anti-Noriega votes.   In other words, the opposition
candidates won an election, but have no strong base of support to
mobilize the people against Noriega, or to govern, if permitted to
take office.   The U.S. supported opposition leaders represent the
old economic oligarchy.   The real struggle for power in Panama is
between a civilian elite based on old wealth, and a military elite
based on power and new wealth accumulated over the last twenty
years.   This power struggle illustrates why the Reagan and Bush
administrations simply want change at the top, i.e., Noriega out.
Preoccupied with the security of the Canal and region, the U.S.
considers the Defense Forces an indispensable ally.   The ideal
negotiated solution from the perspective of the Bush administration
would be for Noriega to leave Panama, replaced by a staunchly pro-
U.S. commander of the Defense Forces who would agree to sharing
power with a pro-U.S. "democratically" elected economic oligarchy.
The problem is that this "solution" is unacceptable to the bulk of
the Panamanian citizenry.

FAILURE OF ECONOMIC SANCTIONS

In Panama the top 5% of the population receives 17.8% of the national income, while the bottom 20% receives only 2.1%. (Elton, 1988) Hence, more demonstration elections that bring little or no structural changes in the economy are unlikely to have mass support.

More specifically, thirty percent of the economically active population works in agriculture. Another 28 percent are employed in the area of social and personal services. Only 9% of Panama's gross national product comes from industry. 10 percent comes from agriculture.

In 1987, 140 million long tons of cargo passed through the Panama Canal, 5% by volume of all world trade. The Canal accounts for 8% of Panama's gross domestic product (GDP).

The Colon Free Zone is the second largest in the world after Hong Kong, accounting for $4 billion of business in import and re-export of predominantly high value, low volume luxury items and electronic goods from the Far East, the U.S. and Europe, for sale throughout Central and South America. The Colon Free Zone accounts for 3 percent of the GDP.

Panama's ship registry covers 10% of the world merchant fleet, but neither the management or real ownership of the fleet is Panamanian. The major owners are Japan, the U.S., West Germany and the United Kingdom.

Panama's international banking center benefits from tax-free, unrestricted, anonymous accounts. In 1984, total assets were $39 billion, with 24 percent in 11 U.S. banks and 16 percent in eight Japanese banks. This network of anonymous banking and paper companies employ over 8,000 people, all of whom reacted negatively to the 1986 Reagan effort to change Panama's bank secrecy laws to curtail the laundering of illicit drug money. The move was viewed by Panama's financial sector as "the thin end of a wedge...to penetrate Panamanian sovereignty." (Elton, 1988)

In 1986, U.S. direct investment in Panama totalled $4.5 billion, the third largest in Latin America. Japanese direct investment, however, was over $8 billion, the largest in the world after its investment in the United States. Japan does not have one single manufacturing subsidiary in Panama. Japanese investment in Panama is -- registered ships, financial services and corporations using Panama as a marketing and service center for their business activities throughout Latin America. (Elton, 1988)

The economic strength of Japan makes that country a major financial player in Latin America. The United States is losing its monopoly dominance of Latin American economies. It is obvious that Japanese economic interests may run counter to U.S. economic and/or perceived national security interests.

The economic sanctions, if maintained, will have a long term devastating effect on Panama, but it is unlikely to cause the collapse of the economy due to the use of the dollar for its currency, the anonymous banking system, non U.S. foreign investment, and the option of, if needed, encouraging the Latin American drug cartel to launder money in Panama. Add to this the fact that the more Panamanians suffer because of U.S. economic sanctions, and the more Bush administration officials and Congressional leaders speak of reneging on the Canal treaties, the more nationalism will play into the hands of Noriega (or another Panamanian leader).

The United States has not designed a foreign policy for U.S. - Panamanian relations rooted in an understanding of the historical reality of our relationship with that nation. Until the U.S. succeeds in doing this, following a conceptual design such as that outlined in Chapter 7, Washington's relationship with Panama will continue to resemble the story of Br'er Rabbit and Tar Baby.

EL SALVADOR

ARENA ASSUMES POWER

With President Jose Napoleon Duarte terminally ill and his Christian Democratic party in disarray, accused of widespread corruption and inefficiency, the recent presidential election was won by the right-wing ARENA party.

On March 19, 1989 Alfredo "Fredy" Cristiani became El Salvador's president-elect. Cristiani is forty-one years old, comes from a rich coffee family whose members have branched out into pharmaceutical and other industrial enterprises. Educated at

Georgetown University, Cristiani formerly headed the coffee processors' association and was a national squash champion.

Cristiani was the choice of Washington -- a man who speaks fluent English, is a modern media politician, and the person who gives ARENA a "new" image. The new image is necessary as the founder of ARENA is Roberto d'Aubuisson, the man Robert White (Carter's ambassador to El Salvador) called a "pathological killer" in refusing d'Aubuisson a visa to enter the United States. His past link to the notorious death squads in El Salvador made d'Aubuisson a political liability. Realizing this, d'Aubuisson agreed to allow Cristiani to head the party's ticket, but only if he would accept as his running mate Francisco "Chico" Merino, a close associate of d'Aubuisson. (Massing, 1989)

Roberto d'Aubuisson, the honorary lifetime president of ARENA, remains in control of the party apparatus, while his close friend Col. Sigifrido Ochoa, the current vice-president of the National Assembly will continue to manage that body.

In the March, 1989 presidential election ARENA got approximately the same support it won in 1984. It did not do better; the Christian Democrats simply did worse. Out of a population of about 5 million, 2.3 are eligible to vote. About 1.9 million registered and received voting cards. About 900,000 actually participated. Less than 50 percent went to the polls. Of those who voted ARENA received 54 percent of the vote (10% of the population or about 20% of the eligible voters). ARENA spent over 5$ million dollars on the campaign, including high chunks of

TV time to show the "seductive made-in-America commercials." (Cockburn, 1989)

ARENA and Cristiani received tremendous assistance in creating a "new" image for the party within the United States. In June, 1988 former U.N. Ambassador Jeane Kirkpatrick wrote an op-ed piece for the Washington POST, calling ARENA a "legitimate political party that espouses market approaches, private ownership, personal initiative and deregulation."

Two months later the Heritage Foundation, a right-wing think tank, prepared a "backgrounder" for circulation at the Republican convention. It claimed that "since 1985 ARENA has reformed itself fundamentally. It is now governed by a 14 member executive committee and has appointed a new president, Alfredo Cristiani, a well-respected businessman and civic leader." (Silverstein, 1989)

Just prior to his election Cristiani embarked on a public relations tour of Capitol Hill with the help of the Washington, D.C. law firm of O'Connor and Hannan. According to one congressional aide, State Department officers also helped Cristiani by setting up briefings and meetings with the liberal "troublemakers" in Congress. At a Carnegie Endowment breakfast Cristiani said that since he joined the party in 1984 "there have been no appearances of dark forces in this enterprise. However, in the Fall, 1988, candidate Cristiani told PROCESSO of Mexico that the Salvadoran military is moving too slowly and that "political and military pacification is essential." Cristiani then went on to explain that "Major Roberto d'Aubuisson has not enjoyed a good image. This is due to what has been unjustly said about him, though nothing has been proven about him up to now." (Silverstein, 1989)

A NEW EL SALVADOR?

Is El Salvador changing? In a New York TIMES story, April 20, 1989, reporter Lindsey Gruson wrote that "The 57,000 - man Salvadoran military forcibly enlists 12,000 youths a year, often snatching teenagers as young as 14 from poor and rural families." There is no draft, so the sons of the wealthy do not have to serve. Auxiliary Bishop Gregorio Rosa Chavez of San Salvador took up the issue in a recent homily. Fr. Chavez stated: "I am sure the wealthy people, who defend a military solution with such vehemence, would think differently if their own sons, who now peacefully study or work or simply waste their youth in a frivolous and superficial life, had to go to the battlefields." (Gruson, 4/21/89)

In January, 1989, ARENA members of the National Assembly successfully blocked the trial of the case involving the assassination of Archbishop Oscar Romero. On April 1, 1989, a Salvadoran judge dismissed all charges against "politically well-connected" former military officers and civilians accused of running a right-wing kidnapping ring. The judge, Juan Hector Larios ruled that there was insufficient evidence to prosecute the eight suspects. All are close associates of Roberto d'Aubuisson. (Hufford, 1989)

One of the men, former army lieutenant Rodolfo Lopez Sibrian, had been charged in the 1981 murder of two U.S. labor experts who were in El Salvador to work as advisers on land reform programs the government was considering.

Another officer, accused of heading a kidnapping-for-profit ring, is Col. Mauricio Staben, a member of the "tandona" or the "big class" which consists of colonels who graduated from El Salvador's military academy in 1966. The tandona now holds five of the six prestigious brigade commands; five of the seven military detachments; the three security forces (National Guard, National Police and Treasury Police); and, the intelligence, operations and personnel posts in the high command. Chief of staff Col. Rene Emilio Ponce is also a key leader of the tandona.

From 1969 to the present, the size of its officer corps has tripled. Its goal is not a negotiated political settlement, but a clear military victory. The tandona fully understands, according to Jesuit priest, Fr. Martin Baro, vice rector of Catholic University in San Salvador, that the appearance of democracy is crucial if U.S. military aid is to continue. Elections will be tolerated as long as the military officers and economic oligarchs retain real power. (Hufford, 1989)

During the week of April 10, 1989, a report released by Tutela Legal, the human rights office of the San Salvador archdiocese, stated that the three journalists murdered while covering the Salvadoran presidential election March 18-19, were killed "by abusive actions by members of the military." Salvadoran journalists Robert Navas and Mauricio Pineda were shot dead at army checkpoints. Dutch journalist Cornelio Lagrouw was shot and wounded by the army as it tried to retake a town that had been captured by the FMLN. When fellow journalists tried to evacuate Lagrouw in a car clearly marked with "TV" signs and a white flag, an air force helicopter pinned them down with machine gun fire so heavy that they twice had to abandon the car and take cover. Lagrouw was pronounced dead on arrival when the journalists finally reached a hospital. The surviving journalists noted that the army and air force knew their car having cleared them at a nearby checkpoint just prior to their being attacked. (Palumbo, 4/14/89)

On April 28, 1989 the Jesuit-run Central American University (UCA) was bombed (the fourteenth such attack). University officials blamed the attack on a "campaign of defamation and aggression" by the armed forces and the right-wing political party ARENA. (Palumbo, 5/12/89)

The attack followed recent accusations against the UCA. The campaign began when ARENA, in what San Salvador Auxiliary Bishop Gregorio Rosa Chavez described as a "frenzied" declaration called Jesuit Father Segundo Montes "immoral" and "inhuman," charging that in a television interview, he had "justified terrorist acts" by guerrilla forces.

Montes, who heads the UCA's human rights institute, replied that terrorism had never come up in the interview. What Montes actually said in the interview was that "as long as the two parties in war cannot come to an agreement, violent actions will continue and may increase, as both sides seek a position of strength to bargain from." (Palumbo, 5/12/89)

A week after ARENA's attack on Montes, a high-ranking army official charged that the UCA "serves as the refuge for leaders who arrive there to plan the terrorist strategy which the guerrillas are carrying out."

Referring to the bombing and other recent events, UCA president Jesuit Father Ignacio Ellacuria said, "What's being created (in El Salvador) is an atmosphere that's very dangerous, and that could destroy any possibilities for a negotiated end to the civil war." (Palumbo, 5/12/89)

There is a little doubt that Roberto d'Aubuisson is the power in ARENA or that he represents the traditional oligarchy and military. There is little doubt that the military is the major power in El Salvador today. A former U.S. military adviser with many year's experience in El Salvador was originally a strong booster of the Salvadoran military. However, early on he had an experience that changed his attitude. It came when he was training the Atlacatl Battalion, one of several "rapid-reaction" units that the United States set up in the early 1980s to improve the army's search-and-destroy abilities. One day, the adviser learned to his horror that members of the battalion had gone on a rampage and killed one hundred peasants. Today, he says, the army continues to kill civilians. "The commanders still have their eyes and ears, their right-wing anti-communist squads. Anybody who's vocal, they go out and kill them." He adds: "Upgrading the life of the rural

peasant is not something high on their list of priorities."
(Massing, 1989)

The adviser's experience illustrates an important paradox
concerning relations between the United States and the Salvadoran
armed forces. Over the last eight years, Washington has invested
more than $800 million in the Salvadoran army, helping to transform
it from a ragged band of 17,000 into a much more efficient army of
57,000. In the process, though, it has greatly increased the power
and autonomy of the army, turning it into a swollen, uncontrollable
organization accountable to no one but itself. In some cases, the
very elite units that have received the most attention from the US
have been those most guilty of committing human right abuses.

The Salvadoran air force is a good example. At the start of
the war, the air force was a flying scrapheap of some twenty
aircraft, most of them obsolete. Today, it has 135 aircraft,
including 72 helicopters, all supplied by the United States. The
US has helped modernize the air force's base at Ilopango, just east
of San Salvador, turning it into one of the best-equipped
facilities this side of the Panama Canal. This has immeasurably
increased the power of the air force and of its chief, the hard-
line General Juan Rafael Bustillo, who runs Ilopango as his own
republic, wholly independent of the government. Not surprisingly,
the air force has been implicated in many human rights violations.
(Massing, 1988)

Today, the Salvadoran military is by far the most powerful
institution in the country. It's not as blatant in exercising its

power as it once was -- generals no longer sit in the Presidential Palace -- but on matters that really count, the military always gets its way. Thus, when the recent talks in Mexico between the government and the FMLN threatened to gain momentum, the military, using the constitution as a cover, intervened to stop them. Later, during the election campaign, Defense Minister Vides Casanova let it be known that the army would not tolerate a strong showing by the Convergence. (The Democratic Convergence is the political party of the left, associated with the FMLN, headed by Ruben Zamora). Indeed, it is assumed in El Salvador that the military would never allow the Convergence to take power, no matter how clearly it were elected." (Massing, 1989)

The future of El Salvador appears to be one of continued violence and suffering. Unemployment (officially) stands at 50 percent and is rising. Inflation is soaring and corruption rampant. El Salvador is experiencing a full-fledged civil war. The cycle of violence continues, and will worsen if ARENA attempts to win a total military victory rather than negotiate an end to the conflict.

GUATEMALA

TECHNICAL COUPS

On May 9, 1989, troops loyal to President Vinicio Cerezo put down a coup attempt by air force officers and soldiers. This was the second abortive coup attempt in the past year. General Hector Gramajo, the Defense Minister supported the Cerezo government, but Guatemala has never sustained a modern democratic government and civilian authority exists only with military consent and supervision.

There have been three military-led coup attempts since Cerezo assumed the presidency in 1986 after 32 years of military dictatorship. In the face of economic collapse and a tarnished human rights image, the generals had little choice but to allow his election. Knowing the importance of having a "democratically" elected president for U.S. economic and military aid to continue, why would the military attempt to regain political control through a coup d'etat?

The fact is that the three coup attempts have been "technical" coups. A technical coup is one that is not successful by design. The intent is to make a strong statement to the President. Success is thus defined, not by actually overthrowing the President, but by forcing him to adopt the policies favored by the military and traditional oligarchy. One can illustrate this point by examining the first two coup attempts.

On October 11, 1987, after 18 months of coup rumors, more than 1,000 troops from two military battalions headed for Guatemala City to overthrow the civilian government. Seven of 19 army zone commanders either actively participated or were "fence-sitters." (Epstein, 1988)

The rebellious troops never reached the capital, ending their attempt after President Cerezo accepted a series of conditions. The "new" political agenda of Cerezo included ending direct talks with the guerrilla coalition; closing the Soviet Union Tass and Cuba's Prensa Latina news agencies; ending government purchase of lands for peasant families; and, replacing a cabinet minister who headed the Spanish peace talks and advocated bolstering police forces at the expense of the army (Epstein, 1988). According to Roland Castillo, a government critic exiled in Mexico, "Guatemala is now a controlled democracy and Cerezo can't go beyond the limits set by the military." Mario Solorzano, a 1986 presidential candidate for the Popular Socialist Party stated that a coup actually overthrowing Cerezo was no longer necessary: "There have been so many concessions, what else could they (the army/business alliance) want?" (Epstein, 1988)

Nevertheless, the Cerezo government passed what was for Guatemala, a bold tax reform at the end of 1987 - the first in over three decades, followed by a historical accord in March, 1988 with unions and grassroots organizations. A few exiles returned to Guatemala and the first Social Democrat oriented news weekly since the 1970s, LA EPOCA, began circulating on a mass scale. More importantly, at the end of 1987 the Cerezo government held the first conversations with guerrilla organizations since the rebel war began in the 1960s. (Robinson, 1989)

The military and economic oligarchy began to criticize these "socialist tendencies." Then, on May 11, 1988, hundreds of troops marched on Guatemala City from two rural army bases in a second "attempted" coup. The coup was easily put down. In June, 1988 the Government reneged on all the agreements contained in its March accord with the unions and mass organizations (grouped in the Labor and Popular Action Unit, USAP) and passed new conservative economic measures. An 8 percent devaluation of national currency, combined with the authorization of huge price increases for most fuels and basic food items led to rampant inflation. This led USAP to organize a general strike in August.

After the May coup attempt, political freedoms also began to disappear. Independent counts tallied 95 political murders and abductions in May alone, a fourfold jump over the 21 cases reported in April. GAM (human rights organization) says "at least 492 people were assassinated and 186 kidnapped from January to November, 1988." The Washington based Council on Hemispheric Affairs, labeled Guatemala the worst civil rights violator in the Western Hemisphere in 1988, claiming President Cerezo is "essentially incapable of impeding continuous human rights violations by extremist civilians and the military." (Robinson, 1989)

Shortly after the May coup attempt the offices of LA EPOCA were destroyed by bombs. From October through December death squads assassinated at least two union activists, a member of GAM, and leaders of various peasant and grassroots organizations. Bomb attacks against two directors of the Political Studies Center

(CEDEP) which drew up an elaborate cease fire proposal, convinced CEDEP to drop the project. (Robinson, 1989)

The conclusion is a straightforward one. In Guatemala, one can expect periodic "technical" coups designed to warn "democratically" elected presidents not to proceed with policies unacceptable to the military and traditional economic oligarchy.

Finally, the National Reconciliation Commission was appointed in mid-September, 1987, in accordance with the Arias peace plan. Its members were Vice-President Roberto Carpio Nicolle; representing the political opposition is a right-wing evangelical politician; representing the Catholic Church is a conservative bishop who is opposed to liberation theology; and, the prominent civilian is co-owner of a right-wing newspaper. The Government avoided dealing with the provision in the peace plan that requires a cease-fire by saying that "there is no internal state of war in Guatemala." (Cockburn, 1988)

Also, in October and November, 1987 the army increased its efforts in northern Quiche. The Catholic Church reported that the purpose was not to go after the guerrillas, but to control the civilian population. This is accomplished by forcing the population out of the mountains via aerial bombings or army sweeps. After being driven out, all civilians are interrogated for a day and then relocated in "model villages." This operation was the largest since 1984. Little wonder fewer than 200 of the more than 200,000 refugees who fled the intense repression of 1979-83 have returned. (Cockburn, 1988) A 1987 Americas Watch report stated that since the 1960s Guatemala has experienced over 200,000 (political) deaths, 40,000 disappearances, 80,000 orphans and 1 million displaced (Epstein, 1988).

ECONOMIC REALITIES UNCHANGED

Guatemala still has the most skewed distribution of wealth in all of Latin America. One percent of landowners still own 35 percent of the nation's farmlands. Two percent own well over half of all arable land. The Cerezo Government says production not redistribution is the key. (Cockburn, 1988)

The wealthiest 20 percent receives 57 percent of the income, while the poorest 20 percent receive 5 percent. 79 percent of all Guatemalans live in poverty. 40% live in extreme poverty, with this figure reaching 83 percent in rural areas. The average life span in rural areas is 49 years, more than half the population earns less than $150 annually and the nation's infant mortality rate trails only Haiti's in the hemisphere with 79 deaths per 1000 (according to the Latin American Economic Planning Council). Half of all children die before reaching the age of nine and 81 percent die from malnutrition. 70 percent of all deaths in Guatemala result from readily curable diseases, such as tuberculosis and pneumonia. Most of the poor in Guatemala are indigenous Indians who are descended from the Mayas, speak one of twenty-three languages, and comprise over half the country's population. (Epstein, 1988 and Cockburn, 1988)

In Guatemala one clearly recognizes a facade of democracy. The military and economic oligarchy remain firmly in control.

HONDURAS

MILITARIZING HONDURAS

Commensurate with the strategic role Reagan (and now Bush) assigned Honduras, U.S. military aid has mushroomed. In the last five years of the 1980s, military aid amounted to $16.3 million. In the first five years of the 1980s, the figure hit $169 million. Between 1980 and 1987, Honduras received over $1 billion in U.S. aid with 27.8 percent of it in military subsidies. (Meza, 1988)

Honduras law stipulates that each commander-in-chief of the armed forces must serve a fixed term of office; yet, from 1980-87 there were four commanders-in-chief, precisely the number of U.S. ambassadors during this period. Relations were often so chummy that some top embassy officials became godparents for officers' children. (Meza, 1988)

Under General Gustavo Alvarez Martinez (whose command lasted from January 1982 until March 1984) Battalion 3/16, a special counterinsurgency force which many considered a death squad was strengthened. Battalion 3/16 had been formed in 1980. General Humberto Regalado current chief of the armed forces defined it in May 1987 as "a technical and professional squadron that processes information and whose strategic conception is to support each of the brigades comprising the National Army." (Meza, 1988)

However, Florencio Caballero, a former battalion commander and presently a political refugee in Canada, described Battalion 3/16 as "a clandestine paramilitary structure for repressing leftists." Caballero, who studied interrogation techniques in Houston in 1980, said the CIA was extensively involved in training squad members. (Meza, 1988)

Young officers who participated in the March 1984 overthrow of General Gustavo Alvarez now control the main channels of power in the Army, exercising the day-to-day command of the most important battalions. They are Lieutenant Colonels of the 6th Promotion, including Alvaro Romero, Mario Amaya, Rene Fonseca, Ramon Rosa and Reynaldo Andino. Almost all were junior officers during the 1969 Soccer War and directly confronted the Salvadoran Army on the battlefield. This group controls almost half of the current members of the Superior Council of the Armed Forces (COSUFFA). COSUFFA, dubbed the "parliament of the Honduran military" is a general assembly which meets periodically to discuss basic problems of the country in general and of the armed forces in particular. Its decisions become official military policy. (Meza, 1988) COSUFFAA is the real power in Honduras, not the "democratically-elected" civilian government. COSUFFAA meetings are the stage on which political struggles are played out, influence and control won, and alliances formed amidst constant political maneuvering.

In Honduras, few have doubts about the permanence of the U.S. military presence. At Palmerola, 1,200 soldiers of Joint Task Force Bravo are permanently stationed. Constant joint military maneuvers allow for an endless and sizeable flow of U.S. troops through Honduras. Between October 1981 and August 1987, 58 joint military operations were conducted.

The U.S. militarization of Honduras is having an interesting side effect. Many colonels and lieutenant colonels are now part of the landed class. Some illicitly cut off a slice of state land; others received a farm from grateful landowners. (Benjamin, 1988) For example, the former head of the military in San Pedro Sula, Col. Miguel Angel Garcia, was a reliable buddy of local cattlemen. Thus, when he retired they set him up with his own ranch. Today he heads the conservative landowners' association, FENAGH. The list of ex-generals-turned-landowners includes Melger Castro, Policarpo Paz Garcia and Lopez Arellano. The trend is definitely toward greater links between the military and landed class. (Benjamin, 1988)

The U.S. effort to militarize Honduras has had considerable repercussions. The U.S. policy will inevitably lead to a nationalistic fervor in many different sectors of society. Occasionally, even military officers, including commander-in-chief Gen. Humberto Regalado, state their opposition to war with Nicaragua, reject the permanent contra presence in Honduras, and speak of a new Honduran foreign policy based on effective neutrality and non-interference in the domestic affairs of neighboring countries. These tendencies are not yet strong enough to succeed, but it is increasing clear that their numbers are growing.

U.S. ECONOMIC AID

The Reagan administration radically transformed U.S. aid to Honduras. Twice as much military support was granted by Reagan in 1982 and 1983 as had been allocated to Honduras in the preceding 35 years. However, the most extraordinary changes occurred in "economic" aid. Economic Support Funds (ESF) - which serve to close the balance of payments gap and fiscal deficit, thus "bailing" out the economy, subsidizing military spending and propping up elite consumption - became dominant. ESF had been less than .5% of all aid to Honduras from 1946-1981. From 1982-1987 ESF accounted for 41 percent of the whole aid program and around 55 percent of all economic aid. ESF and military aid are defined by U.S. law as "security aid," for use "where the U.S. has special security or foreign policy objectives." (Shepherd, 1988)

Economic aid to Honduras between 1982-1987 has been three times the total amount provided between 1946-1981. Honduras now hosts more Peace Corps volunteers than any nation in the world. Several kinds of food aid projects have grown considerably. One grants low-interest credits to the Honduran government to buy U.S. food, which it then sells for local currency. (Shepherd, 1988)

Despite the $1.2 billion assistance during the Reagan years, the Honduran economy is worsening. The gross domestic product (GDP) has been falling for seven years (1981-1987) and is now the lowest in a decade. Underemployment affects twice that number. Only one in ten Hondurans has a secure job. Real GDP per capita has fallen over 15 percent since 1980. Private investment declined 67 percent from 1980 to 1985. Gross investment has fallen from 25 percent of GDP in 1980 to an average of 18 percent in 1985. External debt has been growing at a relatively high rate of 10 percent a year and debt service absorbed 39 percent of all export earnings in 1985. Stated more dramatically, 79 percent of all new loans is automatically returned to lenders to service previous debt. In 1980 almost two-thirds of government monies went to social and economic programs such as public health, education and agriculture. Only one-third went to defense and debt service. By 1984 the reverse was true: debt service and defense were absorbing nearly two-thirds of spending, while other programs received only 35 percent. (Shepherd, 1988) Such is the Reagan legacy in Honduras.

AID: THE SHADOW GOVERNMENT

The U.S. Agency for International Development (AID) now functions in Honduras as a "shadow government" with parallel bureaus matching Honduran ministries and agencies. AID constantly monitors "progress," cutting off funds when U.S. - imposed targets are not met, threatening prodding and generally harassing the

are not met, threatening prodding and generally harassing the
Hondurans, a process known as "policy dialogue" in AID jargon.
(Shepherd, 1988)

The conditions are tough: monies are released in portions as
targets are met. For example, twenty-nine conditions were placed
on disbursement of $61.2 million in ESF in June 1986. The
conditions covered four general areas: streamlining the public
sector; increasing export competitiveness; promoting private
investment; and others, such as renegotiating the foreign debt.
(Shepherd, 1988)

Reagan's economic policies in Honduras are beset with two
major contradictions. First, any attempt to revitalize the economy
through private investment will not work in a climate of declining
investor confidence. Honduras was ranked as a "high-risk" for
investors in 1986, by Frost and Sullivan. (Shepherd, 1988) Second,
AID's private sector approach clashes head on with huge government
deficits caused by U.S.-fostered militarization. Honduras is
increasingly a war economy. Under Reagan, Honduras became an
international welfare case. When AID steps in and runs things,
becoming a shadow government, it does little to foster independence
and/or democracy. It is a policy predestined to failure. Yet, the
early signs are that the Bush administration will follow Reagan's
policy approach. Honduras, the second poorest country in the
hemisphere, has little hope of escaping its desperate economic
situation under current U.S. policy.

NICARAGUA

A SHATTERED ECONOMY

By the end of 1987 and throughout 1988 the economy was the principal issue facing the Nicaraguan government. Devastated by eight years of a U.S. policy of low intensity warfare and a hurricane that swept over the country, Nicaragua's economy is in ruins.

By the end of 1987, hyperinflation raged at 1,300% per year, shortages of food and other basic commodities were commonplace, and a lack of foreign currency and mounting foreign debt threatened to shut Nicaragua out of the international economy.

Without doubt, the economic cost of U.S. sponsored military, trade and financial aggression has been severe. Estimates range up to $4 billion, equivalent to the destruction of nearly three years of Nicaragua's gross domestic product (GDP). The contra war devours 62 percent of Nicaragua's state spending, forcing drastic reductions in social programs. The 1985 trade embargo has cost Nicaragua an additional $50 million in lost exports, as well as production losses associated with shortages of spare parts and mismatched technology. Additionally, the United States has "blocked" Nicaragua's loan application to the IMF and the World Bank. (Miller and Ricciardi, 1989)

There are, however, other reasons for problems found in Nicaragua's economy. A second principal reason for the economic crisis is the financial cost of maintaining a political alliance with wealthy producers (who would gladly throw the Sandinistas out of power).

In 1987 financing the war consumed 25 percent of Nicaragua's GDP. Subsidies aimed at inducing private investment produced deficits amounting to 11.7% of GDP. Most of these deficits (9.8% of GDP) arose from exchange rate losses caused by government subsidies to exporters. Those in export agriculture were able to purchase dollars at 70 cordobas from the government and then sell them back to government for 20,000 cordobas. Large producers, who control the majority of private lands farmed for export crops, were the beneficiaries of these subsidies. (Miller and Ricciardi, 1989)

The other private-sector subsidy contributing to the deficit is the free credit granted to producers. The Nicaraguan government financed 100% of working capital and new investments at interest rates far below the rate of inflation, while much of private capital was in flight to Miami. In addition, Sandinista price guarantees meant that the state, not private producers, shouldered the losses from declining world prices for exports. Although more than 60 percent of production has remained in private hands since the revolution, the private sector has accounted for only 20 percent of investment. (Miller and Ricciardi, 1989)

The Sandinistas, like the IMF in other third world countries, are administering an austerity program: credit concentration, price liberalization, currency devaluation and exchange rate unification. The Sandinista program differs from those of the IMF in two important ways, however. They have raised wages and preserved in-kind subsidies to the poor. (Miller and Ricciardi, 1989)

The economic devastation caused by the war and the hurricane will have long-term lasting effects. The battle may well prove more difficult for the Sandinistas to win than the war itself.

THE MELTON PLAN

On July 11, 1988 the government of Nicaragua ordered the closing for 15 days of LA PRENSA, the country's leading opposition newspaper; the closing for an indefinite period of Radio Catolico, the leading opposition radio station; and, the expulsion of U.S. Ambassador Richard Melton and seven other U.S. embassy officials. The outcry from Washington was almost unanimous in condemning the Sandinista government.

However, according to eyewitness reports by the Associated Press, Reuters, NBC-TV and other media, U.S. officials at the Nicaraguan demonstration at Nandaime were seen waving their arms and shouting among the protestors, i.e., actually participating in the demonstration. (Lernoux, 1988)

The Economical Committee of U.S. Church Personnel in Nicaragua reported that U.S. Embassy officials had been physically and financially supporting groups whose known goal was the overthrow of the Nicaraguan government; embassy activities had violated the Vienna Accords regulating diplomatic conduct.

On May 23, the Mexican newspaper EL DIA reported that Melton (who previously worked under Elliot Abrams) was devising a strategy to destabilize the government through financing and manipulating opposition groups. The intent was to provoke a repressive response by the government. Melton had served as the liaison between Elliot Abrams and the clandestine network headed by Gen. John Singlaub. The Council on Hemispheric Affairs, a Washington based human rights group, claimed the U.S. embassy provided $180,000 to finance the protest. Under Congressional testimony, Abrams had earlier admitted that Washington has funded $1.9 million to opposition groups in Nicaragua through the National Endowment for Democracy. (Lernoux, 1988)

REAGAN, BUSH AND PEACE PLANS

Nearly a year after the Arias peace plan was signed by the Presidents of the five Central American nations, Nicaragua seemed on the verge of a national peace accord between the government and the contras. Suddenly, on June 9, 1988 the talks broke down. As the smoke clears, the picture of the negotiations breakdown becomes more complete. What was portrayed to the public by the Reagan Administration as Sandinista intransigence appears to have been more of an internal disagreement among the contra leadership - most notably between contra negotiator Alfredo Cesar and the hard-line ex-Somoza national guardsman and new chief of the contras, Enrique Bermudez.

The Sapoa Accords, signed by the contra negotiating team and the Sandinista government on March 23, 1988, instituted a temporary cease fire, national dialogue, and other provisions cited in the Arias plan of August 1987. In subsequent meetings, the government largely agreed to the democratization measures proposed by the contras. On June 9, the contras proposed a sweeping new set of demands, stating that they would break off the talks if the government refused to accept the demands in total. They gave the government two hours. According to the two verification commission members, Cardinal Obando y Bravo and Organization of American States Secretary-General Suarez, the Nicaraguan government agreed to negotiate the new proposals, but not to accept them. The contras balked and refused to negotiate. Following the breakdown a top contra leader stated that the contras had deliberately broken off the talks in order to seek new U.S. military aid. He said that, "so long as we are talking we have no chance of a revival of military aid, now we may." (Policy Education Project, Sept. 1988)

The Bush administration, on April 13, 1989 persuaded Congress to approve a "bipartisan" aid package for the contras. The total package was $66.6 million. $49.7 in aid, plus $7.7 million to transport the aid, $4.2 million for medical assistance for civilian victims of the war, and $5 million for administrative expenses of the U.S. AID. The Bush administration promised Congress that no aid would be sent to the contras after November 30, unless Bush receives approval from four Congressional committees, from the Speaker and minority leader of the House, and from the majority and minority leaders of the Senate. This would appear to be a check and balance of presidential power, but one ought to remember the ease with which the Reagan administration created periodic crises as votes on contra aid came before the Congress. Also, James Baker, the current Secretary of State, was chief of staff for Reagan's first term. In this position, Baker helped create and build the contras.

The Bush administration was caught off guard when the presidents of five Central American countries announced on February 14, 1989, that they had signed an agreement under which contra bases in Honduras would be closed in return for open elections in Nicaragua in February, 1990. (Pear, 2/16/89)

The plan called for a proposal to be submitted within 90 days for dismantling the contra bases in Honduras and for relocating the thousands of contras and their families back into Nicaragua or to a third country.

The plan was quickly endorsed by the chief of the Honduran armed forces, General Humberto Regalado. The General stated that "the problem of the contras is no longer a problem of Honduras alone. It is a problem of all the countries of Central America." (Uhlig, 2/28/89)

As part of the accord, Nicaragua agreed to release approximately 1,700 former National Guardsman held in prison. On March 17, the Nicaraguan government kept its promise by releasing 1,894 members of Somoza's National Guard. (Cockburn, 4/12-18/89)

On February 15, having been caught off guard, Administration officials issued a statement saying that the "U.S. had not yet decided whether to acquiesce in the plan, resist it or seek changes." (Pear, 2/16/89) A month later, Honduras agreed to let the contras remain on Honduran soil for another year. Secretary Baker said the United States needed "carrots and sticks incentives and disincentives..." (Pear, 3/14/89) Another Administration official was quoted as saying, "Short of the 82d Airborne, the contras are our stick." (Pear, 3/14/89)

The reality remains that the United States will not, in the foreseeable future adopt a policy based on the equality of respect doctrine and horizontal interdependence discussed in Chapter 7 (Specific proposals which fit this model can be found in Appendices H,I,J). The United States is not ready to transcend the Monroe Doctrine and allow the Central Americans to negotiate an end to the conflicts without Uncle Sam having full veto power over all proposals.

The challenge remains for citizens of the United States. To change U.S. foreign policy citizens need to be empowered - the collective social consciousness raised - to enable grassroots organizations/individuals to engage in effective action to change the course of U.S. foreign policy as stated in the first edition of this book, to a great extent the suffering, oppression and violence in Central America is the result of 'US.' This fact leaves all U.S. citizens with a responsibility to assist in creating a foreign policy that will provide an environment in which

Central Americans can negotiate a peaceful end to the violence, engage in fundamental structural reform and demilitarize the region.   It begins with equality of respect.   It begins in the United States.

APPENDICES

APPENDIX A
Vertical and Horizontal
Model of Independence

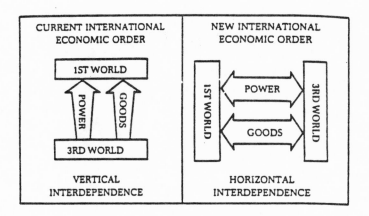

Vertical and Horizontal Model of Interdependence.

Source: Diagram 3, James B. Mcginnis, BREAD
           AND   JUSTICE: TOWARD   A   NEW
           INTERNATIONAL   ECONOMIC   ORDER,
           Paulist Press, 1979.

APPENDIX B
Regional and Local Linkage
Between Third World and Developed World

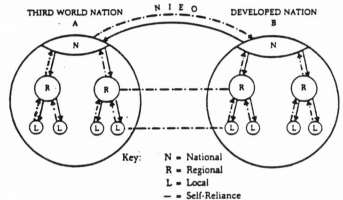

Key: N = National
       R = Regional
       L = Local
       — = Self-Reliance
NIEO = New International Economic Order
       Implications of Within-Nation Self-Reliance for
       Regional and Local Linkage Between Third World and
       Developed World (dotted lines)

Source: Chadwick F. Alger, "People in the
          Future Global Order," paper
          presented at the Seventh General
          Conference of the International
          Peace Research Association,
          Oaxtepec, Mexico, 1977.

APPENDIX C
Military Maneuvers in Central America
From Summer 1983 to May 1985

Big Pine II--August 6, 1983 to February 5, 1984
The longest military exercise held in Honduras. Big Pine II
brought a total of 10,000 U.S. troops--as many as 5,000 U.S.
troops at one time--to Honduras. the exercise included military
training in interdiction and counterinsurgency techniques,
airlifts, an amphibious landing similar to the invasion of
Grenada, and vast construction projects.

Small Scale Emergency Readiness Exercises--late-March, 1984
These "no notice" exercises involved U.S. and Honduran troops.
U.S. special forces from Panama trained with Honduran soldiers.
The exercise involved troops picking up weapons and moving to the
field to test their ability to respond in a crisis.

Kilo Punch--March 24, 1984
Starting with a paratroop drop from C-130s by a unit from the
82nd Airborne Divsion near Palmerola Air Base, Honduras, 350 U.S.
and 130 Honduran troops proceeded to San Lorenzo Air Base for
combined airborne and air assault practice.

Fuerzas Unidas--April, 1984
National Guard Units from Louisiana, Florida, and Puerto Rico,
along with the personnel from the 193rd Infantry Brigade and the
Panama Defense Force, joined in Panama for a road-buliding
exercise.

Grenadero I--April 1-June 30, 1984
This exercise took place in Honduras, mostly at Cucuyagua near
the Salvadoran border and Jamastran near the Nicaraguan border.
In the first phase U.S. Army engineers constructed C-130-capable
airstrips at Cucugayua and Jamastran; the second phase involved
joint practice of airborne and helicopter assault operations.
Panamanian, Guatemalan and Salvadoran armed forces were invited
to join U.S. and Honduran troops; only the Salvadorans accepted.

Lightning II--April 13, 1984
This paratroop drop near Aquacate, Honduras, involved 170
Honduran special forces and 120 U.S. Army troops; its purpose was
"to secure an operations base from which to stage an assault on
an airfield."

King's Guard--April 26-May 7, 1989
This coastal surveillance exercise in the Gulf of Fonseca
involved 500 U.S., seventy-five Honduran, and a hundred
Salvadoran personnel, two U.S. Navy destroyers, and patrol boats,
officially for practice in interdiction techniques.

Operation Lempira--Phase 1, July 23-August 6, 1984

This counterinsurgency exercise based in west-central Honduras involved a small team of U.S. Army Green berets and troops from the Honduran Army's 10th infantry battalion. the official purpose of this exercise was to "improve the skills of U.S. and Honduran personnel to deploy and operate in realistic conditions, usually on very short notice." It included a parachute jump near Palmerola Air Base and a mock helicopter attack at Marcala.

Operation Lempira--Phase 2, August 20-31, 1984
The counterinsurgency exercise based in the mountainous areas west and southwest of Comayagua, Honduras, battalions of the Honduran army, and included a parachute drop near Palmerola Air Base. Its official purpose was to give counterinsurgency forces experience in rapid deployment tactics "under combined operating conditions."

Crown Dragonfly--September 22-27, 1984
Four U.S. A-37 planes and eight from the Honduran Air Force practiced bombing runs using dummy noise bombs near San Pedro Sula and Palmerola Air Base.

Army Preventive Medicine Exercise--September 1984-end of 1984
Army medical teams of about two dozen soldiers each were deployed for two week tours to the hospital at Palmerola Air Base, Honduras.

Air Force Exercise--October 28-November 17, 1984
A-37 attack planes from the Pennsylvania Air National Guard and observation planes from the Howard Air Force Base, Panama, participated in exercises in Honduras at Palmerola Air Base, La Mesa, near the Guatemalan border, and San Lorenzo, near the Nicaraguan border.

High Altitude Training--November 1-15, 1984
Four U.S. helicopters and crew from Howard Air Force Base, Panama, trained in Costa Rica, the helicopters were used to assist the Costa Rican National Park Service and in a joint "nation-building" activity with the Costa Rica Civil Guard.

Medical Exercise--November 7-20, 1984
A medical clearing company from Fort Stewart, Georgia, which would conduct triage in wartime, trained at Palmerola Air Base, Honduras.

Engineering Exercise--November 7-20, 1984
About 120 engineers from Fort Bragg, North Carolina, built roads at Palmerola Air Base, Honduras, and built and resurfaced dirt airstrips.

Patrolling exercises--November 7-20, 1984
A company of 150 to 180 infantry troops from Fort Hood, Texas, conducted patrolling exercises near Palmerola.

King's Guard--November 8-19, 1984

This exercise in the Gulf of Fonseca involved a U.S. ship and several hundred U.S., Honduran and Salvadoran troops. According to the Pentagon, a small contingent of U.S. military personnel were to be deployed to El Salvador for "command and control" purposes. The exercise was officially designed to practice interdiction techniques.

Minute Man II–January–May 1985
Members of the Panama Defense Forces, 193rd Infantry Brigade and units of the U.S. National Guard from Puerto Rico, Louisiana, Missouri, Alabama, Florida, Texas, New Jersey and other states joined to construct about twenty-seven kilometers of roadway on the Azuero Peninsula, Panama. Up to 1600 National Guard personnel were involved at any one time. Special units provided command. logistical military police, communications and medical support. U.S. participation was funded from money for U.S. Army National Guard training exercises, while the Panama Defense Forces paid for fuel and materials.

Kindle Liberty '85--February 4-13, 1985
An annually held, joint SOUTHCOM-Panama Defense Forces exercise series. Kindle Liberty '85 was conducted outside the immediate Panama Canal area in order to add "realism to the guerilla insurgency scenario." There was ground, air and sea activity; U.S. troops from SOUTHCOMN were augmented by units of the U.S. Readiness Command and Atlantic Command. A total of 4000 U.S. and Panamanian military personnel took part.

Universal Trek '85--April 12-27, 1985
On the northeastern coast of Honduras 3000 U.S. troops practiced an amphibious landing with support from attack helicopters and a guided missle ship, destroyer and frigate. A total of 7000 troops participated in the exercise.

Big Pine III--Februaury 11-May 3, 1985
Eleven weeks of joint U.S.-Honduran military maneuvers involving 2200 U.S. troops, including units of the U.S. National Guard. The exercises included construction and improvement of runways and aprons at Cucuyagua, near the Salvadoran border, and at San Lorenzo, near the Nicaragua border, extending tank obstcales in the border region between Honduras and Nicaragua, countersinsurgency training in Yoro province and antitank maneuvers near san Lorenzo. M60A3 tanks and M113 armored personnel carriers were flown to Honduras for the anti-tank maneuvers.

Postscript:

Two members of the Pennsylvania National Guard were killed when their plane crashed while on a training flight during Big Pine III.

During one week in April, Universal Trek '85 and Big Pine III overlapped, bringing a total of 5300 U.S. troops to Honduras at one time.

U.S. military maneuvers in Honduras have continued nonstop up to the present. Such maneuvers are a crucial component of low intensity warfare.

APPENDIX D
Contadora 21-Point Peace Plan

* Reduce tension and end situations of conflict in the area abstaining from any action which may endanger political confidence or jeopardize peace, security and stability in the region.

* Ensure strict compliance with the principles of international law previously outlined and hold countries responsible for non-compliance.

* Respect and guarantee observance of human, political, civil, economic, social, religious and cultural rights.

* Adopt measures conducive to the establishment and, in some cases, to the improvement of democratic, representative and pluralistic systems, which guarantee effective popular participation in decision making and ensure free access of the different currents of opinion to honest and periodical electoral processes, which should be based on a total respect for citizens' rights.

* Promote national actions towards reconciliation in cases of deep social divisions, allowing participation in democratic political procedures according to the law.

* Create political conditions directed to guarantee international security and the integrity and sovereignty of states of the region.

* Halt the arms race in all its manifestations and initiate negotiations on the subject of control and reduction of the current arms inventory and actual number of arms.

* Forbid the establishment in the region of foreign military bases or any other form of foreign military interference.

* Concert agreements to reduce, and eventually eliminate, the presence of foreign military advisers and other forms of foreign military and security actions.

* Establish internal mechanisms of control for the prevention of the traffic of arms from the territory of one country to the region of another.

* Eliminate the traffic of arms, within the region or from abroad, forwarded to persons, organizations or groups attempting to undermine Central American governments.

* Prevent the use of their own territory for, and neither to lend nor allow, military or logistic support of persons, organizations or groups attempting to destabilize Central American governments.

* Abstain from promoting or supporting acts of terrorism, subversion or sabotage in the countries of the area.

* Create mechanisms and coordinate systems of direct communication aimed to prevent or, if necessary to resolve incidents among states of the region.

* Continue with humanitarian aid directed to help Central American refugees who have been displaced from their country of origin, providing also conditions suitable for their voluntary repatriation, in consultation or cooperation with the high commissioner of the United Nations--UNHCR-- and other interested international organizations.

* Undertake economic and social development programs with the purpose of achieving a higher standard of living and a more equitable distribution of wealth.

* Revitalize and normalize the mechanisms of economic integration in order to achieve a continuous economic development based on solidarity and mutual benefit.

* Negotiate and acquisition of external monetary resources which will guarantee additional means to finance the reactivation of intraregional commerce, overcome the severe difficulties in the balance of payments, secure working capital funds, support programs for the expansion and restructuring of the systems of production and promote short and long term investment projects.

* Search for a greater and wider access to international markets in order to expand the commercial flow between Central American countries and the rest of the world in particular with

industrialized countries, through a revision of commercial practices and elimination of tariffs and non-tariff barriers, while assuring profitable and fair prices for the products exported by countries of the region.

* Promote mechanisms of technical cooperation to plan, program and execute multisectoral projects of investment and promotion of commerce.

The Ministers of Foreign Relations of the Central American countries initiated, with the participation of the Contadora Group countries, consultations with the purpose of preparing the conclusion of agreements and adopting the mechanisms necessary to formalize and develop the objectives contained in this document, and to ensure the establishment of appropriate systems of control and verification. To that effect, the initiatives presented will be taken into account in the meetings summoned by the Contadora Group.

The Nicaraguan government announced its acceptance of this peace proposal in September, 1984.

A proposal from the alliance of the FDR/FMLN to the President of the Republic and the High Command of the Armed Forces for an immediate negotiation toward a political solution to the conflict.

The FDR and the FMLN formally present the following two-part proposal:

1. A far-reaching agreement for the humanization and reduction of the economic, social and political impact of the war.
2. An offer and a proposal to reopen dialogue for a comprehensive political solution.

I. PROPOSAL for a far-reaching agreement for the humanization and reduction of the economic, social and political impact of the war: this proposal consists of achieving an immediate negotiation that encompasses the following points:

1. Suspension of the air war (bombings, use of rockets, strafing from aircraft), keeping in mind that a small and densely populated country such as ours, the air war seriously affects the civilian population and is used to force depopulation and impede repopulation.
2. Suspension of the use of long-range artillery (81 and 120 mm mortars, 105 and 155 mm rockets, etc.) since the firing of these weapons is indiscriminate and causes tremendous physical and psychological suffering to the civilian population.
3. Suspension by both sides of the use of all types of land mines and booby traps.
4. Suspension of FMLN economic sabotage, including transportation boycotts, sabotage against the electrical infrastructure, export crops, mills and other economic infrastructure owned by the upper classes and the government.
5. An end to the destruction of homes, peasant villages, social infrastructure, crops and livestock of the entire population living in the zones of conflict; also, abstain from obstructing in any way the efforts of the civilian population in the reconstruction of their homes and in the general economic, social and physical rehabilitation of the affected areas.

6. Full respect for the right of the population to live in the areas they freely choose; permit unrestricted repopulation; stop forced removal and all actions that uproot the population, creating displaced persons and refugees, a practice which has affected one-fifth of the Salvadoran population.

7. Freedom of movement of the population, including food and supplies; free development of trade in the zones of conflict and an end to all obstacles and control over these activities.

8. No military interference in the work of mayors, justices of the peace and other political officials of the government.

9. Release of all imprisoned leaders and members of the popular movement and professional organizations; an end to all persecution, arrest, kidnapping, disappearance and assassination of those demanding economic, social and political reform. Within the context of the war, only the arrest of military personnel would be allowed and not the arrest of those dedicated to political activities.

10. An end to the persecution and arrest of civilians living in the zones of conflict.

11. Respect for the lives of prisoners; the elimination of all physical and psychological torture; an end to the practice of systematic disappearances.

12. End the execution of spies and members of the intelligence networks of both sides.

13. Respect for the right of medical and paramedical personnel on both sides as well as the rights of religious personnel accompanying them, to fully carry out their duties, exercise their right to freedom of movement and respect their physical integrity and freedom; clinics, hospital facilities, instruments and all medical equipment of both sides should also be respected.

14. Respect for wounded combatants on both sides, permitting their removal from, and medical attention in, any part of the country without being subjected to capture, interrogation or any form of pressure.

15. Measures must be taken in order to effectively eliminate the practice of disappearances and to exercise respect for the family members of combatants, commanders, militants and leaders of the FMLN and FDR as well as the relatives of soldiers and officers of the Salvadoran Armed Forces and government officials.

16. Suspension of any form of forced recruitment by both sides, accepting only voluntary integration based on a free decision by each person to join either of the two armies, as corresponds to a

conflict of an internal nature; the Supreme Court has recognized the internal nature of the conflict by declaring the War Tax unconstitutional.

17. In order to reduce the impact of the conflict on the economy of the people, taxes enacted in the last two years, allegedly due to the war, must be repealed; for the same reason the rationing of electricity and the announced increase in tariffs for this service should be abandoned.

18. An end to psychological warfare operations which instill terror, anxiety and deceive and misinform the population.

The above eighteen points constitute a comprehensive offer to humanize the conditions of war and reduce its economic, social and political impact, by means of a truly serious and profound effort. Taking into consideration that this offer implies mutual concessions, our Fronts propose that any agreement must embrace the eighteen points in their entirety. In order for these negotiations to achieve a greater coherence and depth, as well as progress in the important national effort to recover our sovereignty, we propose that both sides include in the negotiations a discussion on measures to resolve the problem of the presence of U.S. advisors. This discussion should be aimed at their removal from our country. This becomes necessary because the advisors directly promote bombings, depopulation and the scorched earth practices which have meant the loss of thousands of lives and an ever greater impoverishment of the population.

The partial agreements reached previously have been subject to violations and delays by the Salvadoran Government and Armed Forces. The agreements made in the two negotiation sessions in Panama concerning the evacuation of those wounded in action have been the object of obstructions and delays, including the abduction of wounded combatants in San Salvador. The Christmas truces and the agreements not to target relatives and to end disappearances have also been violated by the Government and the Armed Forces. This demonstrates the need to reach an agreement which encompasses all eighteen points proposed by the FDR/FMLN and the necessity to include clear criteria and mechanisms for their effective observation and verification.

For this immediate negotiation the FDR/FMLN proposes:

a. Negotiations must be carried out directly between delegates from the FDR and FMLN on one side and delegates from the Armed Forces High Command the

Government on the other; both delegations must
arrive with clearly invested powers.

b. The participation of designated representatives
of the Armed Forces High Command is absolutely
indispensible; negotiations would not be possible if
only delegates of the Duarte government participate.

c. We propose that immediate negotiations begin on
July 15. The location and the procedural terms
should be agreed upon through the intermediary,
Archbishop Arturo Rivera y Damas in a meeting to
take place in the second half of June in
Chalatenango or Morazan provinces, between the
intermediary and our delegates. At this meeting,
the intermediary would bring the response and
proposals from the other party. In proposing these
dates, we have taken into account the breadth and
importance of the agreements to be made which will
require multiple consultations. Cur Fronts, the
FDR/FMLN are prepared and ready to achieve a far-
reaching agreement based on the aforementioned.

II. Offer and Proposal to Reopen the Dialogue Toward a
Comprehensive Political Solution

We, the FDR and the FMLN, are aware of the desirability
and necessity of reaching the aforementioned accord in
order to humanize the armed conflict and reduce other
negative effects on the population. Yet we do not lose
sight of the fact that our central objective is to
supercede the state of war and achieve a peace with
justice and dignity for our people. In order to truly
achieve a humanization of the conflict, it is necessary
for the advances in this area to be linked with the
process of dialogue and negotiation for a comprehensive,
political solution which assures a just and lasting
peace. We therefore make the following offer and
proposal:

OFFER:

1. At this stage in the development of events, the
dialogue-negotiation for a comprehensive solution cannot
be limited only to the FDR and FMLN on one side and the
government and the Armed Forces on the other. The depth
of the national crisis reveals the state of economic and
military dependence of the Salvadoran government on the
United States government. This situation demands an
effort by all patriotic sectors in the search for, and
construction of, a national solution among Salvadorans.
The participation of all the social and political forces
in the country in a broad and sincere dialogue is
indispensable in the search for and implementation of a

solution to the crisis. Only this can defeat the resistance from the United States government which, in accordance with its regional and global policy, persists in escalating the war in El Salvador and rejecting a real and just negotiaticn of the conflict.

2. Therefore, only by joining together all the efforts and national factors of power will it be possible to overcome these obstacles, retake the destiny of the country and build a just peace. A direct dialogue between our Fronts and the Government must be sustained by a broad national dialogue, as agreed upon by both sides at the meeting in La Palma. This would allow all sectors to express their opinion and contribute to the formation of a patriotic platform for a national solution.

3. In July 1986 we presented an offer for a national solution to all sectors in El Salvador as a contribution by our Fronts to achieve a national dialogue. In brief, six points of our offer are:

- a solution between Salvadorans
- amplitude and pluralism in the government
- a cease-fire after the recomposition of the government
- the initiation of an economically just regime
- democracy and establishment of human rights
- a peaceful foreign policy

PROPOSAL: Finally, we propose that in the meeting to negotiate the eighteen points listed above, the issue of the organization and promotion of a national dialogue between all political and social sectors of the country be included. We propose that there also be a discussion on the solution between both parties to the conflict.

Ruben Zamora Rivas
For the Executive Committee
of the FDR

Shafik Jorge Handal
For the General Command
of the FMLN

Excerpts from Contragate Calender

by Jim Naureckas, In These Times, June 10-23, 1982

July 1979   Sadinistas take power in Nicaragua.

Fall 1980   President Carter authorizes a CIA program to
                 funnel $1 million to Nicaraguan political
                 opposition, while continuing overt aid to the
                 private sector in Nicaragua.

Mar 9, 1981   President Reagan authorizes the CIA to undertake
                 covert activities against Nicaragua.

Nov 23, 1981   Reagan allocates $19 million to the CIA to
                 establish a paramilitary opposition to the
                 Sadinistas.

Dec 22, 1981   Congress passes its first version of the Boland
                 Amendment, barring CIA and Pentagon from
                 spending money for the purpose of "overthrowing
                 the government of Nicaragua or provoking a
                 military exchange between Nicaragua and
                 Honduras."

June 1983   Reagan approves "Operation Elephant Herd" to
                 bypass potential congressional restrictions on
                 contra aid, according to CBS news.

Oct 1983   The Reagan-appointed Kissinger Commission tours
                 Central America in preparation for a report on
                 U.S. regional policy; Oliver North serves as
                 escort.

Oct 10, 1983   CIA operatives attack fuel-storage tanks at
                 Corinto, Nicaragua.

Dec 8, 1983   Congress says that no more than $24 million can
                 be spent by the CIA, the Pentagon, or any agency
                 "involved in intelligence activities" for the
                 purpose of "supporting, directly or indirectly,
                 military of paramilitary operations in
                 Nicaragua by any nation, group, organization,
                 movement or individual."

Dec 9, 1983   "Operation Elephant Herd" is carried out:
                 $12 million in military eqipment is declared to
                 be worthless and given to the contras. The
                 administration does not count the material as
                 part of the $24 million spending limit.

June 1984	Congress rejects administration request for $21 million for the contras.
Sep 1984	Reagan authorizes North to establish "private aid network" for the contras, according to the WALL STREET JOURNAL.
Oct 12, 1984	Congress passes its second version of the Boland Amendment, which says that "no funds available" to "any agency or entity of the United States involved in intelligence activities" may be spent "for the purpose or would have the effect of supporting, directly or indirectly, military or paramilitary operations in Nicaragua."
Apr 24, 1985	Congress rejects request for $14 million in covert aid to contras.
May 1, 1985	Reagan declares an embargo against Nicaragua.
Aug 15, 1985	Congress approves $27 million in non-lethal aid to contras. All other prohibitions remain in effect.
Dec 4, 1985	Congress amends the Boland Amendment to allow communications and advice for contras. Other prohibitions remain in effect.
Jan 1986	North and Secord begin paying contra leader Arturo Cruz $7,000 a month.
Jan 1986	North sets up secret communications network and Swiss bank accounts for contras.
Feb 27, 1986	Proceeds from an arms shipment to Iran are diverted to the contras
Mar 20, 1986	Congress rejects $100 million in military aid for contras.
Apr 4, 1986	North writes a memo for the president saying profits from Iran arms sales will go to the contras.
Jun 27, 1986	The International Court of Justice rules U.S. support for contras violates international law.
Aug 6, 1986	North lies to Congress about relationship with contras, Singlaub and Robert Owen. Poindexter tells him "well done."
Sep 9, 1986	North threatens the president of Costa Rica with a cut-off of U.S. funds if Costa Rica publicizes

the secret air strip.

Oct 1, 1986   Boland Amendment expires.

Oct 5, 1986   Eugene Hasenfus' plane shot down while carrying arms to contras, leading to exposure of North's network.

APPENDIX G
The Domestic Contra Aid Network
A Pictoral View

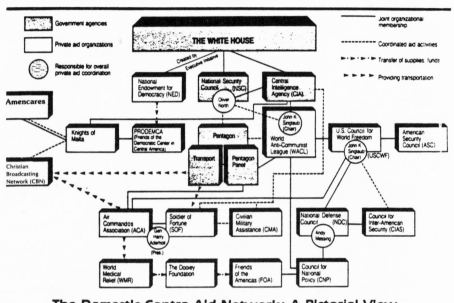

The Domestic Contra Aid Network: A Pictorial View

Source: Robert Matthews, ''Sowing Dragon's Teeth: The U.S.
War Against Nicaragua,'' NACLA REPORT ON THE
AMERICAS, Vol. XX, No. 4, July/August, 1986.

THE CARABELLEDA DECLARATION
January 1986

Any permanent solution to the Central American conflict must be based on fair balanced principles, which express traditional values and the desire of the Latin American peoples for civilized coexistence. It is for this reason that the Ministers of the Contadora Group and of the Group of Support have determined the following permanent principles for peace in Central America:

1. A LATIN AMERICAN SOLUTION: meaning that the solution to Latin America problems must come from, and receive the support of, the region itself, so that it will not be included in the East-West strategic conflict.

2. SELF-DETERMINATION: meaning the independence of each of the Latin American countries to determine its own form of social and political organization, establishing at a domestic level the type of government which is freely chosen by the entire population.

3. NON-INTERVENTION IN THE AFFAIRS OF OTHER STATES: which means that no country will be able to influence, directly or by acting indirectly through a third party, the political situation of the Latin American states, or in any way that affects their sovereignty.

4. TERRITORIAL INTEGRITY: meaning the recognition of limits of action for each of the countries, within which each country can exercise its sovereignty and outside which each country must observe a strict compliance with the norms of international law.

5. PLURALISTIC DEMOCRACY: meaning the right to universal suffrage by free and regular elections, supervised by independent national organizations: a multiparty system that will allow the legal and organized representation of all kinds of political action and thought. A government of the majority, ensuring the basic liberties and rights of all citizens and the respect of political minorities according to the society's constitutional order.

6. NO PRESENCE OF ARMS OR MILITARY BASES which threaten peace and security in the region.

7. NO UNDERTAKING OF MILITARY ACTIONS by countries in the region or with ties to the region, which may present a threat to the region or its peace.

8. NO PRESENCE OF FOREIGN TROOPS OR ADVISERS.

9. NO POLITICAL, LOGISTICAL, OR MILITARY SUPPORT to any group
   intending to subvert or destabilize the consitutional order of
   any Latin American state through force or terrorist act of any
   kind.

10. OBSERVANCE OF HUMAN RIGHTS: meaning the unrestricted defense
    of civil, political and religious liberties, thus ensuring
    the complete material and spiritual fulfillment of all
    citizens.

APPENDIX I

EQUITABLE DEVELOPMENT

With a diplomatic solution, the economic deterioration that Central
America has suffered as a result of war can be halted. But a truly
lasting peace requires not simply economic growth, but equitable
development, to enhance the economic and social well-being of the
majority of Central Americans.

To begin, Central America will need substantial relief help to
repair war damage. El Salvador and Nicaragua have suffered
billions of dollars of war damage. Millions more will be needed
to resettle refugees and finance essential reconstruction
throughout the region.

Beyond reconstruction and resettlement, however, loom fundamental
issues of political and economic change. Agrarian reform, programs
to meet basic needs, and mechanisms to encourage democratic
participation are among the key problems that must be faced if new
patterns of development are going to be sustained. Even this short
list suggests how potentially divisive the development process will
inevitably be - particularly in El Salvador and Guatemala where
military and oligarchical power have traditionally blocked just
such reform, basic human needs, and democratic participation -
forcefully articulated by peasants, workers, the Church, and
sectors of the middle class, that have been so ruthlessly repressed
over the past decades.

In other words, real development implies a new and different social
pact in which the majority of Central Americans are given voice and
eventually opportunities and benefits that they have not
traditionally enjoyed. This new social pact will not be forged
with the stroke of a pen. A long, difficult, and conflict-ridden
road lies ahead.

- From Chapter 6 of FORGING PEACE

     The following are the principal issues that postwar
development in Central America will have to tackle:

* AGRARIAN REFORM: Redistribution of agricultural land to
  alleviate poverty and inequality, and to increase production of
  basic food crops for domestic consumption, instead of
  concentrating on exports.

* INDUSTRIAL REFORM: Encouragement of local manufacture of
  consumer goods, as well as export-oriented industry.

* FISCAL REFORM: Progressive tax structures, so the wealthy pay a
  higher percentage of their income to finance development.

* BASIC NEEDS: An emphasis on providing food, health, housing, employment, and education to the entire population.

* EDUCATION: Needed to lay the groundwork for broadly-based progress, rather than development based on a small educated elite.

* DEMOCRACY: Broad citizen participation in national economic policy making - a crucial ingredient in the reform process.

* REGIONAL TRADE AND COOPERATION: Measures to encourage regional trade, such as improving transportation and reviving the Central American Common Market.

* DEBT RELIEF AND FOREIGN ASSISTANCE: Central America will need foreign aid and relief from its crippling debt burden. The United States should play a major role in providing aid. The initial costs, including reconstruction, will be substantial, but in the long run even a generous aid program will cost less than continued militarization.

Source: Policy Alternatives for the Caribbean and Central America, FORGING PEACE: THE CHALLENGE OF CENTRAL AMERICA, 1987.

APPENDIX J

A POLICY OF RESPECT

An alternative policy combines demilitarization in the short term
with equitable development in the long term. Such a policy must
be built on a new respect for Central America and an understanding
of the importance of popular participation.

The United States must also come to terms with Central American
nationalism. Because the United States has so long dominated
Central America, intervening at will, Central American nationalists
want to reduce U.S. influence in the region. U.S. policy makers
must understand that this nationalism is not the same as anti-
Americanism, and is ultimately a constructive force in the region,
often uniting contending groups.

The United States should also be keenly interested in international
law. We cannot expect other countries to abide by principles such
as non-intervention if we flagrantly violate those principles, nor
can we expect domestic support for interventionist policies.

New Economic Relations

In addition to its political aspects, a policy of respect for
Central America should yield several important shifts in U.S.
economic ties with the region:

* Diversified economic relations between Central America and the
  rest of the world.

* Regional planning and stronger economic integration among those
  countries, emphasizing complementary policies rather than
  competition.

* Policies that strengthen regional markets rather than relying
  solely on exports to fuel growth.

* Long-term planning aimed at solving fundamental problems,
  rather than quick fixes that reinforce flawed policies.

* A new U.S. economic policy should not try to impose economic
  orthodoxy on the countries of Central America. Instead,
  Washington should allow these countries to experiment with a
  mix of policies to combat the problems of underdevelopment.

Source: Policy Alternatives for the Caribbean and Central America,
FORGING PEACE: THE CHALLENGE OF CENTRAL AMERICA, 1987.

APPENDIX K

THE PUBLIC RECORD ON CIA ACTIVITY IN NICARAGUA

1) The CIA created the contras in 1981 out of a band of former National Guardsmen who served under the Somoza regime before the Sandinistas took over in 1979. According to a chronology provided in the Iran-Contra Report, President Reagan signed a Finding authorizing covert operations against Nicaragua on December 1, 1981 and put the CIA in charge. (Chronology of Events, Iran-Contra Report, p.1)

2) On April 6, 1984 Congress learned that the CIA had mined Nicaraguan harbors. The revelation infuriated former Senator Barry Goldwater, then chair of the Intelligence Committee, who upbraided CIA Director William Casey for not informing Congress.

The mining of the harbors violated the Boland amendment that had been adopted in the fiscal year 1984 Continuing Resolution on November 18, 1983. It stated "no funds available to the CIA, the DOD or any other agency or entity of the United States involved in intelligence activities may be obligated or expended for the purpose of supporting, directly or indirectly, military or paramilitary operations in Nicaragua by any nation, group, organization, movement or individual."

3) In September 1984 the public also learned about an "Assassination Manual" written by the CIA for the contras which advised "selective use of violence" to "neutralize carefully selected and planned targets such as court judges, police and state security officials, etc." (VEIL: The Secret Wars of the CIA 1981-1987, by Bob Woodward, p. 388)

4) When Congress cut off funds for the contras, the Iran-Contra Affair was perpetrated and a secret resupply operation was set up to fund the contras. The CIA knew about, and some of its agents participated in, this effort. CIA agent Joseph Fernandez now faces five-count indictment by Iran-Contra special prosecutor Lawrence Walsh for organizing and directing a resupply airlift that dropped weapons to the contras while he was CIA station chief in Costa Rica from July 1985 to December 1986. He is also accused of making false statements to conceal his role in testimony before the Tower Commission. (Washington, POST, September 21, 1988)

5) Colonel Enrique Bermudez, one of the most senior officers to have served Somoza, was anointed by the CIA in 1981 to be the contra's military commander. Now a member of the contra

political directorate Bermudez has served as the administrative link to the CIA through his tenure. (Washington POST, July 20, 1988) As recently as May, 1988 the CIA intervened directly in a contra meeting of the political directors on behalf of Bermudez who faced opposition from the contras internally. The CIA agent delivered a 20-minute harangue through a remote telephone hookup, calling a director who proposed removal of Bermudez "stupid" and "an imbecile". (Miami HERALD, May 18, 1988)

6) Under oath in testimony before the World Court on September 16, 1985, former CIA official David MacMichael revealed the outlines of a CIA plan to destabilize the Nicaraguan Government internally. A better script for what has happened within Nicaragua in the last few months could not be written. According to MacMichael, who had participated in discussion of the plan: "the principal actions to be undertaken were paramilitary which hopefully would provoke cross-border attacks by Nicaraguan forces and thus serve to demonstrate Nicaragua's aggressive nature and possibly call into play the Organization of American States' provisions. It was hoped that the Nicaraguan Government would clamp down on civil liberties within Nicaragua itself, arresting its opposition, demonstrating its allegedly inherent totalitarian nature and thus increase domestic dissent within the country, and further that there would be reaction against United States citizens, particularly against United States diplomatic personnel within Nicaragua and thus serve to demonstrate the hostility of Nicaragua towards the United States." (Philadelphia ENQUIRER, April 26, 1988)

7) According to an August 7, 1988 UPI report, "several million dollars have poured into the coffers of internal Nicaraguan opposition groups in the past year from private conservative groups and CIA accounts, according to U.S. officials and participants in the efforts." According to the article, the CIA has spent money from a $10 to $20 million dollar "political" account earmarked for Nicaragua's internal opposition. The report was attributed to CIA and State Department officials. The officials said they had encouraged internal opposition members to take "a bolder approach to test the limits of pluralism."

Reprinted from the office of Chief Deputy Majority Whip David Bonior (Democrat-Maine)

APPENDIX L

TEXT OF AGREEMENT BY CENTRAL AMERICAN PRESIDENTS ISSUED IN
EL SALVADOR
FEBRUARY 14, 1989

The Presidents of El Salvador, Guatemala, Honduras, Nicaragua and
Costa Rica, meeting in the province of La Paz in the Republic of
El Salvador on Feb. 13 and 14, 1989, analyzed the current situation
in the Central American peace process and adopted the measures
necessary to enforce this process based on the understanding that
commitments assumed under Esquipulas 2 and the Alajuela Declaration
are harmonious and indivisible wholes.

The Presidents of Costa Rica, El Salvador, Guatemala and Honduras
were informed of the position of the constitutional President of
Nicaragua, Daniel Ortega Saavedra, developed a process of
democratization and national reconciliation in his country, within
the framework of the Esquipulas 2 Accord and in keeping with the
following actions, among others:

Once reforms have been made in electoral legislation and laws
regulating expression, information and public opinion in such a
way as to guarantee political organization and action in the
broadest sense for political parties. Then an initial four-month
period for preparation, organization, mobilization of the parties
will be opened. Immediately following the expiration of the said
period, a new six-month period for legal activity will begin. At
the end of this six-month period, elections for President, Vice
President and representatives to the National Assembly,
municipalities, and Central American Parliament will be held.
Elections should take place no later than Feb. 25, 1990, and unless
the Government and opposition political parties mutually agree that
they should be held on another date.

The Government of Nicaragua will form a Supreme Electoral Council
with balanced participation of representatives from opposition
political parties. In this spirit, the Presidents call on all
Nicaraguan political parties to participate in the electoral
process.

FREEDOM FOR NEWS AGENCIES

International observes will be invited to participate in all the
election districts during the two aforementioned stages for the
purpose of certifying the integrity of the process. A special
invitation will be extended to delegates of Secretaries General of
United Nations and the Organization of American States.

The Government of Nicaragua will guarantee the free functioning of
communication media by means of a review and modification of the
law on media. Furthermore, it will guarantee equal access to

transmission schedules and broadcast time on television and state radio stations for all political parties. The Government of Nicaragua will authorize all communications media to supply themselves from within the country or abroad, at their convenience, with all materials, instruments and equipment necessary for the full completion of their work.

In accord with the proposal by the President of Nicaragua, and at the initiative of the President of Honduras, the Central American Presidents commit themselves to formulate, within a period of no more than 90 days, a joint plan for the voluntary demobilization, repatriation or relocation in Nicaragua and in third countries of Nicaraguan resistance members and their families. For that purpose, the Presidents will request technical assistance from specialized organizations of the United Nations.

In order to contribute to the creation of conditions for the voluntary demobilization, relocation or repatriation of Nicaraguans who may have been involved in direct or indirect armed activities and who are in Honduran territory, the Government of Nicaragua has decided to proceed with the release of prisoners, in keeping with the classification made by the Inter-American Commission on Human Rights.

VERIFYING RECONCILIATION

This joint plan also contemplates assistance for demobilization of all those persons who were or are involved in armed actions in countries of the region, when they voluntarily request it.

In order to comply with the commitments on verification of security, the Executive committee is hereby charged with the task of immediately organizing technical meetings to establish the most appropriate and efficient mechanism for verification, in accord with talks held in New York with the Secretary General of the United Nations.

The Presidents reaffirmed the authority of the National Reconciliation Commission to continue verification in the areas outlined by the Guatemala procedure and the Alajuela Declaration. These commissions should periodically inform the Executive Committee of the result of their work.

The Central American Presidents firmly repeated the request contained in Numeral 5 of the Esquipulas 2 Accord that regional and extra-regional Governments which either openly or secretly supply aid to irregular forces or insurrectional movements in the area immediately halt such aid, with the exception of the humanitarian aid that contributes to the goals of this document.

ECONOMIC INTEGRATION PLAN

The Presidents urge all sectors, especially in the insurrectional movements and irregular forces in the region, to join the consitutional political process in each country. In this spirit, the Presidents appeal to all sectors in El Salvador to participate in the next election.

The Presidents reiterated the importance of the Central American Parliament as a forum where all peoples of the region, by means of free and direct elections of representatives, will discuss and draft appropriate recommendations regarding the political, economic, social and cultural problems of Central America.

The Presidents made an urgent appeal to the international community to support the process of social economic recovery in the Central American nations, both in the short and long term, given the seriousness of the foreign debt problems and the necessity for recovery of the levels of intra-regional trade as the fundamental factor for strengthening the process of integration. In particular, the Presidents request the support of the European Community in the implementation of a program of restructuring, reactivating and strengthening of the process of economic integration on the Central American isthmus, which was officially represented in Guatemala this past January. Similarly, they conceived with great approval the report by the International Commission from Central American Recovery and Development, which is a significant contribution to the consolidation of democracy and the creation of a system of social and economic welfare and justice in the region.

NATURAL RESOURCES PANEL

The Presidents remain committed to primarily research for directly negotiated solutions to overcoming the conflicts that have arisen due to the Central American crisis.

The Presidents agree to create a Central American Commission on the Environment and Development as a regional mechanism of cooperation to achieve the optimal and rational use of natural resources in the area, control against contamination and re-establish an ecological balance. The Executive Committee, at this next meeting, will appoint and immediately convene the aforementioned commission so that it may draft a treaty to regulate its character and functions.

Moreover, the Presidents granted their first support to the International Conference on Central American Refugees to be held in Guatemala in May of this year. This conference will contribute positively to the research for solutions to the flow of refugees and displaced affected by the crisis in the region.

The Presidents agreed to foster a Regional Cooperation Accord for the elimination of illegal drug trafficking. To that end, the Executive Committee will draft an accord to be delivered to the affected Governments.

Similarly, the Presidents expressed the intention of their

Governments to support the initiative favoring the formulation of a convention on rights of children in the United Nations.

The Presidents agreed to meet in the Republic of Honduras, on a date to be determined subsequently.

The Presidents of Guatemala, Honduras, Nicaragua and Costa Rica thank the people and Government of El Salvador, and most especially the President, Jose Napoleon Duarte, for the hospitality which provided the appropriate conditions for this meeting to be held.

NOTES

CHAPTER 1

The National Bipartisan Commission on Central America was chaired by former Secretary of State Henry A. Kissinger, and included both Republicans and Democrats (key Democrats were Lane Kirkland, the head of the AFL-CIO and a harsh critic of President Reagan's domestic economic program, and, former Ambassador and chairman of the Democratic National Committee, Robert Strauss). Among the Senior Counselors were U.S. Ambassador to the United Nations Jean Kirkpatrick. According to President Reagan and Ambassador Kirkpatrick, the Report issued by the Commission accurately reflects the Reagan administration's view of the crisis in Central America and accurately portrays the Administration's security concerns in the region. Therefore, the findings of the Report of the National Bipartisan Commission on Central America are taken as synonymous with the views of the Reagan administration in the writing of this paper. The Report was issued January 10, 1984.

The passages from the Report, quoted at length in this essay, are representative of the document as a whole. Emphasis in the quotes has been added by the author.

Members of the Commission

Dr. Henry A. Kissinger, Chairman
Nicholas F. Brady
Mayor Henry G. Cisneros
Gov. William P. Clements Jr.
Dr. Carlos F. Diaz-Alejandro
Wilson S. Johnson
Lane Kirkland
Richard M. Scammon
Dr. John Silber
Justice Potter Stewart
Amb. Robert S. Strauss
Dr. William B. Walsh
Amb. Harry W. Shlaudeman, Executive Dir.

Senior Counselors
Rep. Michael D. Barnes
Sen. Lloyd Bentsen
Rep. William S. Broomfield
Sen. Pete V. Domenici
Sen. Daniel K. Inouye
Rep. Jack F. Kemp
Amb. Jean Kirkpatrick
Winston Lord
Sen. Charles McC. Mathias
William D. Rogers
Rep. James C. Wright

SOURCES

CHAPTER 1

Aguilar, Alonso, PAN-AMERICANISM: FROM MONROE TO THE PRESENT, Monthly Review Press, 1968.

Anderson, Thomas P., "El salvador's Grim Prospects," CURRENT HISTORY, Jan. 1986

"A Plan For Fully Funding the Recommendations of the National Bipartisan Commission on Central america," U.S. Department of State, March, 1987.

Arnson, Cynthia, EL SALVADOR: A REVOLUTION CONFRONTS THE UNITED STATE, Institute of Policy Studies, Washington, D.C.

Ash, T.G., "Back Yards," NEW YORK REVIEW, Nov. 22, 1984.

Barry T., & Preusch, D., THE CENTRAL AMERICA FACT BOOK, Grove Press, 1986.

Chamorro, Edgar, Excerpts from his affadavit presented to the World Court in FIRST PRINCIPLES, Center for National Security Studies, Washington, D.C., Vol. II, No.1, Sept. -Oct., 1985.

"Changing Course," SOJOURNERS, March, 1984.

DEMOCRACY AND DICTATORSHIP IN LATIN AMERICA; VOICES AND OPINIONS OF WRITERS FROM LATIN AMERICA, Foundation for the Independent Study of Social Ideas, New York, N.y., 1982.

Drinan, Robert F., "Reagan Embargo Flouts U.S. Treaties and Values by Obsession with Force, "NATIONAL CATHOLIC REPORTER, May 24, 1985.

Dugger, Ronnie, ON REAGAN: THE MAN AND HIS PRESIDENCY, McGraw-Hill Book Co., 1983.

Fuentes, Carlos, "High Noon in Latin America," VANITY FAIR, Sept., 1983

Gillganon, Michael, "Grenada Invasion Part Long History of Interventionism," NATIONAL CATHOLIC REPORTER, nOV. 25, 1983.

Guillermoprieto, Alma & Hoffman, David, "U.S. Blocked Latin American Peace Pact," INTERNATIONAL HERALD-TRIBUNE, Nov. 7, 1984.

Haig, Jr., Alexander, CAVEAT; REALISM, REAGAN AND FOREIGN POLICY, MacMillan Publishing, New York, 1984.

298

IN THESE TIMES, May 4-10, 1983.

IN THESE TIMES, March 26-April 1, 1986

Jones, Arthur, "Reagan vs. Nicaragua", NATIONAL CATHOLIC
REPORTER, May 27, 1983.

Jones, Arthur, "Three-Pronged Nicaraguan Attack, NATIONAL
CATHOLIC REPORTER, Jan. 3, 1983.

Kizner, Stephen, "Nicaragua and Costa Rica Hope for Pact," NEW
YORK TIMES, February 1986.

Kirkpatrick, Jeane J., "Doctrine of Moral Equivalence," U.S.
Department of State, Current Policy No. 580, April 9, 1984

Kornbluh, P., and Hackel, J., "Is it Live or is It Memorex?",
NACLA REPORT ON THE AMERICAS, Vol. XX, No. 3, June, 1986.

La Feber, Walter,"The Burdens of the Past," CENTRAL AMERICA;
ANATOMY OF A CONFLICT,Robert Leiken, ed., Pergamon Press.
See also La Feber's book INEVITABLE REVOLUTIONS: THE U.S. IN
CENTRAL AMERICA, nORTON pUB., 1983

La Feber, Walter, "How We Make Revolution Inevitable," THE
NATION, January 28, 1984.

Leiken, Robert, ed., CENTRAL AMERICA; ANATOMY OF A CONFLICT,
Pergamon Press, New York, 1984.

Lernoux, Penny, CRY OF THE PEOPLE, Doubleday & Co., Inc., Garden
City, N.J., 1980.

Lernoux, Penny and Finn, James, "Kissinger Report May Be
Divisive," NATIONAL CATHOLIC REPORTER, January 20, 1984.

Los Angeles TIMES, March 3, 1985.

Matthews, Robert, "The CIA's War," NACLA, REPORT ON THHE
AMERICAS, Vol. XX, No. 4, July/August, 1986.

Miles, Sara, "Preparing the Battlefield," NACLA, REPORT ON THE
AMERICAS, Vol. XX, No. 2, April/May, 1986.

Millman, Joel, "False Connection," THE NATION, November 22, 1986.

Morelli, Maj. Gen. D.R., and Ferguson, Maj. M.P., "Low Intensity
Conflict: An Operational Perspective," MILITARY REVIEW,
November, 1984.

Nairn, Allan, 1984, "Behind the Death Squads," THE PROGRESSIVE,
May, 1984.

Omang, Joanne, "4 Latin American Nations Accept U.S.-Promoted Contadora Pact Revision," INTERNATIONAL HERALD-TRIBUNE, November 10-11, 1984.

Pastor, Robert, "The Reagan Administration and Latin America: Eagle Insurgent," from EAGLE RESURGENT/; THE REAGAN ERA IN AMERICAN FOREIGN POLICY, Pye, Lieber and Rothchild, Little, Brown & Co., 1987.

Reagan, Ronald, "U.S. Intersets in central America," U.S. Department of State, Current Policy No. 576, May 9, 1984.

REPORT OF THE NATIONAL BIPARTISAN COMMISSION ON CENTRAL AMERICA, Washington, D.C., January 10, 1984.

Shipler, David K., "Reagan Asks $100 million for Contras," New York TIMES, February 26, 1986.

The Committee of Santa Fe, "A New Inter-American Policy for the Eighties," Council for Inter-American Security, Washington, D.C., 1980.

"3000 U.S. Troops Begin Am Exercise in South Honduras," New York TIMES, December 31, 1986.

CHAPTER 2

Bell, Peter D., "Democracy for Latin America is Scarcely a Reagan Concern," INTERNATIONAL HERALD TRIBUNE, March 22, 1985.

Bonner, Raymond, "A One-Sided Press," THE NATION, December 8, 1984

Bonner, Raymond, "WEAKNESS AND DECEIT; U.S POLICY AND EL SALVADOR," Times Books, New York, 1984.

Charles, Daniel, "U.S. Will Fund Anti-Sadinista Newspaper," NATIONAL CATHOLIC REPORTER, May 24, 1985.

Coffin, William Sloane, "Nicaragua is Not an Enemy," New York TIMES, July 31, 1983.

Fuentes, Carlos, "High Noon in Latin America," VANITY FAIR, September, 1983.

Geyelin, Philip, "Nicaragua: Congress is Warned," INTERNATIONAL HERALD TRIBUNE, Febrauary 27, 1985.

Gwertzman, Bernard, "Schultz, Seeing Tyranny: Asks Aid to guerillas in Nicaragua," INTERNATIONAL HERALD TRIBUNE, February 25, 1985.

Herman, E.S., and Brodhead, F., DEMONSTRATION ELECTIONS IN THE DOMINICAN REPUBLIC, VIETNAM AND EL SALVADOR, South End Press, Boston, Massachusetts, 1984.

Hufford, Larry, interview with Father I. Martin Baro, Central American University, San Salvador, January, 1986

"Into the Fray: Facts on the U.S. Military in Central America," THE DEFENSE MONITOR, Washington, D.C., 1984.

La Feber, Walter, INEVITABLE REVOLUTIONS: THE U.S. IN CENTRAL AMERICA, W.W. Norton and Co., New York, 1983.

LaMoyne, James, "Progress is Seen in El Salvador," INTERNATIONAL HERALD TRIBUNE, May 17, 1985.

Lernoux, Penny, CRY OF THE PEOPLE,Doubleday and Co., Garden City, New York, 1980.

Leiken, Robert S., ed., CENTRAL AMERICA; ANATOMY OF CONFLICT, Pergamon Press, New York, 1984.

"Nicaragua Baiting," THE NATION, November 24, 1984.

Norton, Chris, "Guatemalans Blase about Getting Civilian Ruler," CHRISTIAN SCIENCE MONITOR, October 31, 1985.

Oberdorfer, Don, "Sadinistas Are Puppets of Russians, Reagan Says," INTERNATIONAL HERALD TRIBUNE, March 27, 1985.

"Reagan Claims Nicaragua Poses a New Danger," INTERNATIONAL HERALD TRIBUNE, January 25, 1985.

Report of the Latin American Studies Association Delegation to Observe the Nicaraguan General Election of November 4, 1984, LASA Forum, January 1985.

REPORT OF THE NATIONAL BIPARTISAN COMMISSION ON CENTRAL AMERICA, Washington, D.C., January 10, 1984.

Riding, Alan, "Uruguay is Returned to Civilian Rule: Problems of Prisoners Remains Divisive," INTERNATIONAL HERALD TRIBUNE, March 2-3, 1985.

Robinson, William, "Contras Overstay Welcome in Honduran countryside," IN THESE TIMES, March 18-24, 1987.

Smith, Hendrick, "Reagan Says He Wants Removal of Sadinistas," INTERNATIONAL HERALD TRIBUNE, February 23-24, 1985.

Steele, Jonathan, "A Revolution that Proved itself at the Poll," THE GUARDIAN, November 18, 1984.

"Uruguay Struggles Back," INTERNATIONAL HERALD TRIBUNE, December 3, 1984.

Volman, Dennis, "Guatemala, Pushed by U.S. Plans to Try Democracy," CHRISTIAN SCIENCE MONITOR, October 31, 1985.

Wicker, Tom, "Unintended Eloquence from Reagan," INTERNATIONAL HERALD TRIBUNE, March 27, 1985.

CHAPTER 3

Barry, T. and Preusch, D., THE CENTRAL AMERICAN FACT BOOK, Grove Press, Inc., 1986.

Cody, Edward, "Honduras: Cooperation Doesn't Come Cheap," WASHINGTON POST NATIONAL WEEKLY, November 19, 9184.

Jones, Arthur, "U.S. Pressures for Remilitarization if Costa Rica," NATIONAL CATHOLIC REPORTER, November 1, 1985.

La Feber, Walter, "The Burdens of the Past," CENTRAL AMERICA; ANATOMY OF CONFLICT, Leiken, ed., Pergamon Press, New York, 1984.

La Feber, Walter, INEVITABLE REVOLUTIONS; THE UNITED STATES IN CENTRAL AMERICA, W.W. Norton, New York, 1983.

"Laying Down Machetes," THE ECONOMIST, February 2, 1985

Leiken, Robert S., ed., CENTRAL AMERICA; ANATOMY OF CONFLICT, Pergamon Press, New York, 1980.

Lernoux, Pemnny, CRY OF THE PEOPLE, Doubleday & Co., Inc., Garden City, New York, 1980.

McGinnis, James B., BREAD AND JUSTICE; TOWARD A NEW INTERNATIONAL ECONOMIC ORDER, Paulist Press, New York, 1979.

Millett, Richard, "Praetorians or Patriots? The Central American Military," Leiken, op. cit., 1984.

"Nicaragua is the Issue," THE ECONOMIST, February 2, 1985.

Perea, Victor, "Chaos in the Scorched Earth," THE NATION, January 28, 1984.

REPORT OF THE NATIONAL BIPARTISAN COMMISSION ON CENTRAL AMERICA, Washington, D.C., January 10, 1984.

Rosenthal, Mario, "Is El Salvador on a U.S. Subsidized Road to Serfdom?", WALL STREET JOURNAL, January 31, 1986.

Rubin, Jerry, "Reagan Administration Policymaking and Central Amercia,: Leiken, op. cit., 1984.

Wiarda, Howard J., "at the Root of the Problem: Conceptual Failures in U.S.-Central American Relations," Leiken, op. cit., 1984.

CHAPTER 4

Barry, T. and Preusch, D., THE CENTRAL AMERICAN FACT BOOK, Grove Press, Inc., 1986.

Berryman, Philip, THE RELIGIOUS ROOTS OF REBELLION; CHRISTIANS IN CENTRAL AMERICAN REVOLUTIONS, Orbis Books, Maryknoll, New York, 1984.

Brown, R.M., MAKING PEACE IN THE GLOBAL VILLAGE, The Westminster Press, Philadelphia, 1981.

Cardenal, Fernando, "Why I was Forced to Leave the Jesuit Order," NATIONAL CATHOLIC REPORTER, January, 1985.

Donahue, John, "Choose Life, Not Death," San Antonio EXPRESS -NEWS, August 7, 1983

Edmonds, Patty, "Obando Talk with U.S. Executive Told in Memo, " NATIONAL CATHOLIC REPORTER, July 20, 1984.

Fox, Thomas C., U.S. Money for Murder and Rape," NATIONAL CATHOLIC REPORTER, November 9, 1984.

Hebblethwaite, Peter, "Cardenal Must Choose Post or Priesthood," NATIONAL CATHOLIC REPORTER, August 3, 1984.

Hedges, Chris, "Sadinistas Say Church Gets Aid: Archbishop Denies Claim," NATIONAL CATHOLIC REPORTER, August 31, 1984.

Kelly, David C., "An Examination of Liberal Theology, spiritual Animator of Latin America's Church," NATIONAL CATHOLIC REPORTER, August 17, 1984.

Koo, Samuel, "From Operating Room to the Capital, Red Hat of Cardinal Signals Power," INTERNATIONAL HERALD TRIBUNE, May 23, 1985.

Lernoux, Penny, CRY OF THE PEOPLE, Doubleday & Co., Inc., Garden City, New York, 1980.

Lernoux, Penny, "Debate's Less on Theology than on Who Runs Church," NATIONAL CATHOLIC REPORTER, September 14, 1984.

MacEoin, Gary, "Jesuits Take on Nicaraguan Bishops," NATIONAL CATHOLIC REPORTER, June 8, 1984.

MacEoin, Gary, "Relion Focus of Conflict Between Sympathy Torn Nicaraguans," NATIONAL CATHOLIC REPORTER, August 12, 1983.

304

"Managua Official Suspended as Priest," NATIONAL CATHOLIC REPORTER, February 6, 1985.

REPORT OF THE NATIONAL BIPARTISAN COMMISSION ON CENTRAL AMERICA, Washington, D.C., January 10, 1984.

Whitman, Alden, "Nicaragua: While Sadinistas Plan Health Care Network...", NATIONAL CATHOLIC REPORTER, August 17, 1984.

Wright, Tennant C., "Mixing Church, Politics in Nicaragua," NATIONAL CATHOLIC REPORTER, October 30, 1981.

CHAPTER 5

AMNESTY INTERNATIONAL REPORT 1984, Amnesty International
Publications, London, 1984.

Barry, T., and Preusch, D., THE CENTRAL AMERICAN FACT BOOK, Grove
Pres, Inc., 1986.

Collins, Ginger, "Media Polish Belies Guatemalan Tarnish,"
NATIONAL CATHOLIC REPORTER, May 13, 1983.

Day, Mark R., "Next Cardinal Critical Issue," NATIONAL CATHOLIC
REPORTER, July 15, 1983.

Golphin, Vincent, "U.S. Army Trains Costa Ricans," NATIONAL
CATHOLIC REPORTER, May 31, 1985.

Jones, Arthur, "U.S. Pressures for Remilitirization of Costa
Rica," NATIONAL CATHOLIC REPORTER, November 1, 1985.

Kemper, Vicki, "In the Name of Relief: A Look at Private U.S. Aid
in Contra Territory," SOJOURNERS, October, 1985.

Klare, M.T., and Arnsin C., SUPPLYING REPRESSION; U.S. SUPPORT
FOR AUTHORITARIAN REGIMES ABROAD, Institute for Policy
Studies, Washington, D.C., 1981.

La Feber, Walter, INEVITABLE REVOLUTIONS: THE U.S. IN CENTRAL
AMERICA, W.W. Norton, New York, 1983.

Leiken, Robert S., ed., CENTRAL AMERICA: ANATOMY OF CONFLICT,
Pergamon Press, New York, 1984.

Le Moyne, James, "U.S. Trains Police in El Salvador as Congress
Ban is Lifted," New York TIMES, February 25, 1986.

Lernoux, Penny, CRY OF THE PEOPLE, Doubleday & Co., Inc., Garden
City, N.Y., 1980.

Long, William, R., "U.S. to Help Salvadorans Set Up Urban Police
Unit," INTERNATIONAL HERALD TRIBUNE, March 29, 1985.

Nairn, Allan, "Behind the Death Squads," THE PROGRESSIVE, May 20,
1984.

Ottaway, David B., "Congress Balks at Counterterrorism Aid,"
WASHINGTON POST NATIONAL WEEKLY, December 2, 1985.

Pichirallo, J. and Codey, E., "U.S. Training Anti-Terror Units
for Other Nations," INTERNATIONAL HERALD TRIBUNE, March 25,
1985.

306

Reagan, Ronald, "Central America: Defending Our Vital Interests," Address to Joint Session of Congress, April 27, 1983.

"Reagan Seeks Escalation in aid to Guatemala," INTERNATIONAL HERALD TRIBUNE, February 6, 1985.

REPORT OF THE NATIONAL BIPARTISAN COMMISSION ON CENTRAL AMERICA, Washington, D.C., January 10, 1984.

CHAPTER 6

Brinkley, Joel, "Crews Flying Arms to the Contras Are Said to Have Smuggled Drugs," New York TIMES, January 20, 1987.

Brinkley, Joel, "Plan for Peace, or Arms?", New York TIMES, August 6, 1987.

Conason, J., and Ridgeway, J., "Anatomy of a Coup: What the Tower Report Left Out," VOICE, March 10, 1987.

"Contra Leader Quits U.S. Backed Group," Dallas MORNING NEWS, March 10, 1987.

Engelberg, Stephen, "Reagan Supports Peace Agreement by 5 Latin Leaders," New York TIMES, August 9, 1987.

Hufford, Larry, interview with Manuel Gamero, Tegucigalpa, Honduras, June 1987.

Janeway, M.C., "The Tower Commission's Oversight," New York TIMES, March 4, 1987.

Johnstone, Diana, "A U.S. Ambassador's Crusade to Aid the Contras," IN THESE TIMES, April 8-14, 1987.

Kinzer, Stephen, "Mangua Calls Latin Pact a Historic 'First Step'", New York TIMES, August 9, 1987.

Kinzer, Stephen, "Nicaragua and Costa Rica Hope for Pact," New York TIMES, March 19, 1987.

LeMoyne, James, "CIA Plan Said to Have Been Slowed By Contras View", The Mexico City NEWS, August 21, 1987.

LeMoyne, James, "Central America Backs Peace Plan," New York TIMES, August 6, 1987.

LeMoyne, James, "Envoys at Latin Peace Talks Say Peace Fades," New York TIMES, February 11, 1987.

LeMoyne, James, "Five Central American Presidents Agree On a Tentative Peace Plan," New York TIMES, August 8, 1987.

LeMoyne, James, "4 Latin Leaders Meet on Ending Nicaraguan War," New York TIMES, February 16, 1987.

LeMoyne, James, "Latin, Hope, and Evasion," New York TIMES, August 10, 1987.

LeMoyne, James, "Major Power Struggle Reported to Split Nicaraguan Rebel Leaders," New York TIMES, January 23, 1987.

LeMoyne, James, "Nicaraguan Rebel Leader Withdraws Threat to Resign," New York TIMES, February 20, 1987.

LeMoyne, James, "Sadinista and Contra Leaders Differ Sharply on Peace Proposal," New York TIMES, August 7, 1987.

LeMoyne, James, "Top Contra Quits Citing Disillusionment," New York TIMES, March 10, 1987.

Lewis, Anthony, "The Avalanche Starts," New York TIMES, May 1, 1987.

Matthews, Robert, "Franchising Aggression," NACLA, REPORT ON THE AMERICAS, Vol. XX, No. 4, July/August, 1986.
New York TIMES, May 1, 1987.

"Nicaragua Transition," WASHINGTON POST NATIONAL WEEKLY, March 23., 1987.

Pichviallo, Joe, " As Aid Resumes U.S. Hopes Contras Can Be Viable Alternative," WASHINGTON POST, November 19, 1986.

Riding, Alan, "8 Latin Countries Push Peace Talks," New York TIMES, December 22, 1986.

Roberts, Steve, "Reagan Reports 'General' Accord on Latin Proposal," New York TIMES, August 6, 1987.

Roberts, Steve, "U.S. and Mangua Openly Disagree on a Peace Plan," New York TIMES, August 7, 1987.

Robinson, Keven, "Europe Buttresses Contadoa Peace Plan, IN THESE TIMES, February 25-March 10, 1987.

Ryan, Richard, "An Independent Report Sheds More Light than the Tower Commission," IN THESE TIMES, March 11-17, 1987.

Sciolino, Elaine, "Key Contra Leader said to have Plan to Quit in Dispute with Rival," New York TIMES, January 29, 1987.

Sciolino, Elaine, "Latin Peace Plan Divides U.S. Aides," New York TIMES, March 19, 1987.

Shenon, Philip, "Contras Are Focus of Seven Investigations," New York TIMES, January 30, 1987.

Sklar, Holly, "Still Alive, Contadora Challenges Cold War," IN THESE TIMES, April 8-14, 1987.

TIME, May 27, 1985.

THE TOWER COMMISSION REPORT, Bantam Books, Times Books, February, 1987.

Trainor, Bernard, "Main Contra Faction Unveils Strategy for War," New York TIMES, January 22, 1987.

Tunnermann, Carlos, "Nicaragua's Peace Aims," New York TIMES, March 19, 1987.

"Worse than a Blunder: A Crime," New York TIMES, February 19, 1987.

Wicker, Tom, "Testing Both Sides," New York TIMES, August 10, 1987.

CHAPTER 7

Alger, Chadwick, "People in the Future Global Order," paper
presented at the Seventh General Conference of the
International Peace research Association, Oaxtepec, Mexico,
1977.

Chomsky, Noam, TURNING THE TIDE; U.S. INTERVENTION IN CENTRAL
AMERICA AND THE STRUGGLE FOR PEACE, South End Press, 1985.

Hufford, Larry, "Defining Political Equality: Modernizing
Isonomia," IN WORDS COMMEMORATED, Sr. Alacoque Power, ed.,
Incarnate Word College, San Antonio, 1982.

Report of the Latin American Studies Association Delegation to
Observe the Nicaraguan Genearal Election of November 4,
1984, LASA FORUM, 1984.

Schaar, John, EQUALITY; ITS BEARING ON JUSTICE AND LIBERTY, APSA,
Washington, D.C., 1978.

CHAPTER 8

"Action on Panama grows more likely," San Antonio EXPRESS-NEWS
May 23, 1989.

Benjamin, Medea, "Campesino: Between Carrot and Stick," NACLA:
REPORT ON THE AMERICAS, Vol. 22, No. 1, January/February,
1988.

Cockburn, Alexander, "After the Press Bus Left: The Case of
Guatemala," IN THESE TIMES, June 8-21, 1988.

Cockburn, Alexander, "The Vote and the Accord: Old Piss in New
Bottles," IN THESE TIMES, April 12-18, 1989.

Dinges, John, "General Coke?", NACLA: REPORT ON THE AMERICAS,
Vol. XXII, No. 4, July/August, 1988.

Elton, Charlotte, "Serving Foreigners," NACLA: REPORT ON THE
AMERICAS, Vol. XXII, No. 4, July/August, 1988.

Epstein, Jack, "Guatemala's Civil War Winds Down for Now," IN
THESE TIMES, November 9-15, 1988.

Goshko, John, "A Rock and a Hard Place," WASHINGTON POST
NATIONAL WEEKLY, May 15-21, 1989.

Gruson, Lindsey, "Judge Frees Ex-Officers in Salvadoran
Abductions," New York TIMES, April 3, 1989.

Gruson, Lindsey, "Latin Presidents Announce Accord on Contra
Bases," New York TIMES, February 15, 1989.

Gruson, Lindsey, "Opposition Tells Noriega to Face the Facts and
Urges Washington to Hold its Fire," New York TIMES, May 10,
1989.

Gruson, Lindsey, "Salvador Army Fills Ranks by Force," New York
TIMES, April 21, 1989.

"Guatemala Soldiers Repel Coup," Dallas MORNING NEWS, May 10,
1989.

"Guatemala's Civilian Chief Foils a 2d Coup Attempt," New York
TIMES, May 10, 1989.

Halloran, Richard, "U.S. Troops to go Slowly into Panama," New
York TIMES, May 12, 1989.

Hedges, Stephen, and Cary Peter, "Standoff in Panama," U.S. NEWS
& WORLD REPORT, May 22, 1989.

312

Hufford, Larry, "Illusion of Democracy Masks a Brutal Regime," San Antonio LIGHT, April 16, 1989.

Leis, Raul, "The Cousins' Republic," NACLA: REPORT ON THE AMERICAS, Vol. XXII, No. 4, July/August, 1988.

Lernoux, Penny, "Sandinistas Unveil Evidence of 'Melton Plan'," NATIONAL CATHOLIC REPORTER, July 29, 1988.

Lewis, Flora, "The New Contra Issue," New York TIMES, February 29, 1989.

Massing, Michael, "Sad New El Salvador," THE NEW YORK REVIEW, May 18, 1989.

Meza, Victor, "The Military: Willing to Deal," NACLA: REPORT ON THE AMERICAS, Vol.XXII, No. 1, January/February, 1988.

Miller, John and Joe Ricciardi, "Nicaragua's Other War," DOLLARS AND SENSE, January/February, 1989.

Palumbo, Gene, "Church: Salvador Army Killed Reporters," NATIONAL CATHOLIC REPORTER, April 14, 1989.

Palumbo, Gene, "Salvador's UCA Bombed Again," NATIONAL CATHOLIC REPORTER, May 12, 1989.

"Panama: Reagan's Last Stand," NACLA: REPORT ON THE AMERICAS, Vol. XXII, No. 4, July/August, 1988.

Pear, Robert, "Bush Aid To Contras is Seen in Conflict with Peace Plan," New York TIMES, March 15, 1989.

Pear, Robert, "Canal Treaty Violated Often," U.S. Says," New York TIMES, May 19, 1989.

Pear, Robert, "Latin Agreement Raises Eyebrows At White House," New York TIMES, February 16, 1989.

Pear, Robert, "Latins Debate the Future of Noriega," New York TIMES, May 18, 1989.

Pear, Robert, "U.S. Envoy Urges Hondurans to Let the Contras Stay," New York TIMES, March 14, 1989.

"Policy Education Project," Center for Global Education, September, 1988.

Reed, Jon, "Despite Terror Guatemalan Students Protest Openly," IN THESE TIMES, January 25-31, 1989.

Robbins, Carla, "Taking Aim at Noriega," U.S. NEWS & WORLD REPORT, May 22, 1989.

Robinson, Kevin, "Slamming the Door Shut on a 'Democratic Opening'", IN THESE TIMES, January 25-31, 1989.

Shepherd, Philip, "The CAse of the Invisible Aid," NACLA: REPORT ON THE AMERICAS, Vol. XXII, No. 1, January/February, 1988.

Silverstein, Ken, "From Death Mask to Happy Face," IN THESE TIMES, April 5-11, 1989.

Uhlig, Mark, "Honduran Army Backs Dismantling of Contras," New York TIMES, February 28, 1989.

Weeks, John, "Of Puppets and Heros," NACLA: REPORT ON THE AMERICAS, Vol. XXII, No. 4, July/August, 1988.

Zindar, John, "Opposition Outflanked," NACLA: REPORT ON THE AMERICAS, Vol. XXII, No.4, July/August, 1988.

INDEX